Descendants of
Hayburn Jackson, Sr.
and
Wiley Calvin Jackson,
Sampson County, North Carolina

by

Nancy Jackson Pleitt Fenner

authorHOUSE®

AuthorHouse™
1663 Liberty Drive, Suite 200
Bloomington, IN 47403
www.authorhouse.com
Phone: 1-800-839-8640

First published by AuthorHouse 4/2/2008

ISBN: 978-1-4343-6965-9 (sc)

Printed in the United States of America
Bloomington, Indiana

This book is printed on acid-free paper.

Contents

Dedication

To my children, their spouses and my grandchildren for their patience, understanding and encouragement during my busy years of research.

Acknowledgments

In addition to my immediate family, I thank all those relatives and friends named below who have contributed in various ways to make this book, and others a reality. I will always be grateful for your assistance.

My sister, Jackie and her husband, Phillip Smith, my Aunt Idell (nee Tyndall) Holland and my cousin, Woodrow Smith. On several occasions, they walked cemeteries with me and transcribed inscriptions or they graciously sat with me in libraries or courthouses and copied data. Aunt Mattie Ruth (nee Jackson) Parker Holland, deceased, Aunt Idell (nee Tyndall) Holland, Aunt Freda (nee Holland) Strickland, and Woodrow Smith provided data and shared their family memories, often giving me clues that made it easier to track down an elusive ancestor.

Priscilla Jackson Fields for providing data and thanks to her for her patience and encouragement during all those long telephone calls when I questioned her about Jackson ancestors and living relatives. I remember visiting Priscilla's family when we were children. She and I started to visit by telephone after I called her about eight years ago.

Wanda Royal has published a history of the Royal Family in eastern North Carolina. She is another one who has patiently provided encouragement through e-mails and during long telephone calls. She recently visited me and graciously made some great suggestions about the format of this, my first book..

Sue (nee Cannady) Barefoot has published two family histories: one for the Cannady Family and one for the Barefoot family of Sampson County, North Carolina. She has shared data, knowledge and encouragement through many e-mails. James Jackson for his data and input on the Jacksons and the Hudsons and to Daniel Jackson for confirming my link for Hayburn Jackson to his children and for other data.

Phyllis Hall Kelly, a new friend. She has shared data and ideas. We've had a few telephone conversations, and I welcome her e-mails in which she candidly shares her genealogical research experiences.

Becky Owens, researcher who has published a history of the Smith Family in eastern North Carolina and more recently a history of the Lee Family.

Jerome Tew shared his research on the Jacksons, Tews, Hollands and others in Sampson County. All others who work so diligently to record and share the history of the early settlers of Sampson County, North Carolina, through their books and newsletters.

Thanks to all those other relatives who have shared their family data.

Introduction

As a child, I especially enjoyed listening to the adults relate stories about family. Over the years, I often wished I knew more about the history of my family lines. Eventually, I realized that perhaps I could learn more, but I didn't actually accomplish much when I started in 1994. I was working full-time Monday through Friday and part-time on the weekends until my retirement in 1998 when I finally had the opportunity to actively pursue genealogical research.

When you live over a thousand miles away from the state and county where the records you need are located, your research proceeds slowly. Several long visits to Sampson County, North Carolina, gave me time to visit libraries where I, and sometimes others with me, found records that included county and family histories, indexes for various state and county records, and transcribed cemetery inscriptions. In county offices I reviewed and copied vital statistics, deeds and wills. I purchased county and family history books, histories and data on CDs, transcribed census records and deed and will abstracts, and historical family newsletters. On each visit, interviews and visits with relatives yielded precious data and memories or presented clues for further research.

In the records noted above, I found poor, faded writing, errors on birth and death certificates and marriage records which included strange spellings of names, erroneous dates, and errors in given and maiden names and place names. I found incorrect names and dates on tombstones! Many death certificates provide an incorrect burial place. Of course, it wouldn't be unusual when an informant who was a grandchild or a neighbor would not know the full name of parents or a birth year for a 90 year old deceased individual.

Computers and the internet have allowed me to find much data on-line and fill in many blanks. Familysearch.org and Ancestry.com and a few other sites paved the way for on-line genelogical research. Ancestry.com has extraordinary records and it continues to add records everyday, but early naming patterns present a challenge for those importing data from those sites directly into their trees; the John Doe found there with about the same year of birth as your John Doe, may not be the correct one.

Almost everytime I try to confirm a record, I find a clue that leads to another search. When this happens my desire to leave the best family histories that I can possibly write makes me want to continue searching for that other link, but then reality hits me right in the face and elsewhere. The face in the mirror and my slow moving legs remind me of my age.

This history for my Hayburn (Haburn) Jackson line is my first book and may be the shortest one. My database contains information for paternal lines: Naylor, Cannady, Hair, Honeycutt, Royal and a few collateral lines including Lockamy. On my maternal side: Holland, Howell, Carter, Hair, Hudson, Peterson, Tatum, Sessoms and a few collaternal lines, including Tyndall.

My intent when I started my research was to first search only two lines: Jackson and Holland. Then I found that the other direct and collateral lines intersected like a huge spider web and within that web was a network of small dense webs. It made sense at the time, to enter all the information and this became more true as time went on and the web became denser.

I have not proven that Hayburn, Sr., was related to any other Jackson in Sampson County. However, records show that he settled in the same northern area of the county where the other early Jacksons settled. They sold land to each other and worked together clearing the roads and rivers.

I've enjoyed almost every minute of my research. My heart beats faster and I want to shout everytime I find data that clearly bridges a gap and connects two individuals or families. After almost a year of health problems in 2003, I prayed for time to continue my research and complete a few histories to leave for my family. I thank the Lord for willing me that time.

Since 1998, I have read and studied thousands of records; some I have read several times and I've cross-checked, compared and confirmed much of the information in my database. The responsibility for some of the errors you will find are mine and I apologize only for those. I have found a lot of conflicting names, dates and other information and most of our ancestors and others who recorded events, wrote and spelled poorly. A few census enumerators in southern states entered initials for every person they recorded!

Folks, my love of family and research can be found on the following pages. I hope that this book is the flare that will light the way for at least one of its readers from the Hayburn (Haburn) Jackine line to continue to research the family.

Descendants of
Hayburn Jackson, Sr.
and
Wiley Calvin Jackson
Sampson County, North Carolina

Generation No. 1

1. Hayburn[3] **Jackson, Sr.** (Unidentified[2], Unknown[1])[1,2,3] was born before 1767; his date of death is unknown[4]. He married **Unknown Female Bullard**[5], daughter of Thomas Bullard and Mary (maiden name unknown). His wife was born about 1771 and date of her death is unknown[6].

Jackson name meaning and origin: English, Scottish, and northern Irish: patronymic from Jack 1. As an American surname this has absorbed other patronymics beginning with "J" in various European languages.

Also see notes for Hayburn Jackson, Jr.

Land Grant Number 185 to Haborn (Habon) Jackson is recorded in Sampson County, North Carolina, Letter Book B, page 40 Grant No 185:
"Haborn Jackson. 100 Acres.
"This grant to Haborn (Habon) Jackson for one hundred acres of land is in the same form as the aforesaid registered grant in this Book Pages 27 and 28 all to the difference of the person and the various courses of the same, viz. lying on Williamsons Swamp Beginning at two pines on the side of said Swamp near John Sessoms' corner and runs north thirteen west one hundred and twenty seven poles to a pine near Sessoms other corner thence South seventy seven west

1

one hundred and twenty seven poles to a pine thence south thirteen east one hundred and twenty seven poles to a juniper in Williamsons Swamp thence up the swamp to the Beginning, including Lowdon Jacksons improvements.

"This grant is dated the 10th of July in the thirteenth year of our Independence and in the year of our Lord 1788.

"Signed   Samuel Johnston.

"by his Excellency's Command   W. Williams, D. Sec.y.

"Sampson County. Registered in Book Letter B. Page 33 this 6th day of February 1790.

"Owen Holmes, Registrar."

It is interesting that the above grant to Habon (Hayburn) Jackson included Lowdon (Lowden?) Jackson's improvements. Did Lowden settle and live on the land and die without going through the grant process and was he the father of Hayburn?

The first step in the land grant process was to find some vacant land. The man could choose land on which he had been living, an adjoining tract, or a tract far from his current residence. the second step was to have the claim recorded in the land office in the county where the land was and was called "making a land entry". In 1778, entry fees, surveying fees and grant fees were required at the time of recording, but this soon changed and only the small entry fee was required when the claim was recorded.

In an effort to keep tories from claiming land, between 1778 and 1781, the individual making an entry was required to pledge allegiance to the state. Next came a waiting period to allow time for others to become aware that the tract of land had been claimed and decide whether the claim included land that was already owned by someone else. "If there were no disputes, the entry taker would issue a land warrant. The warrant was a form letter addressed to the county surveyor instructing him to survey the claim without delay". The surveyor was paid based on the number of acres. When the survey was finished, the land warrant and two copies of the survey were sent to the North Carolina Secretary of State and some would include the name of the surveyor and names of chain carriers. Chain carriers may have been neighbors or the person whose land was being surveyed, depending on who was present on that day.

The Secretary was required to make sure that the State Treasurer had received the state's share of the fees before he proceeded with a grant. The state charged 50 shillings per hundred acres between 1778 - 1781. In 1781 the county entry offices were closed possibly because the state wanted to change the fee structure. The grant process continued and grants were still issued provided the required fees were paid. When the county entry offices re-opened in 1783, the state fee was raised to 10 pounds per hundred acres. Afterward the fee varied; lower fees were charged if the land included a swamp or was mountainous. The Secretary (or one of his clerks) filled out a land grant, the Governor signed the grant and the state seal was attached. One copy of the survey was attached to the grant. The land description was recorded in the land grant books kept by the Secretary of State and the Secretary kept the second copy of the survey and the land warrant. Prior to the Governor signing a grant, a 'last minute' protest could be made. Paperwork survives for petitions dated between 1778 and 1835; these were settled by a jury trial in the county where the land was located.

The grant was either returned to the grantee or to the county courthouse where an advertisement was placed in the local newspaper announcing the arrival of grants. The grantee had one year in which to have the grant recorded in books kept by the county Register of Deeds. He paid a small fee for the recording. For at least 50 years, no one was actually in charge to make sure each grant was recorded and some of the grants were never recorded.

Many men never followed through on their land entry; some stayed on the land for a few years and moved on, leaving the land for others to claim.

"Haybuim" Jackson's line is mentioned in a deed of 5 November 1796 when John Watson sold 100 acres to John MCCORQUODALE.

"Deed: John Dickson (of Cumberland County) Attorney for Robert Charles Johnson ("of the City and State of Newyork') to Haburn Jackson. Dated: 26 January 1802. Transferred: ....for 100 acres "in the fork of the land Hill branch and Jumping run the north side of Starling swamp Beginning at... the fourth Corner of the land Whereon he lives." Deed mentions the marsh of Jumping Run, a slash, Solomon Godwin and said Jackson's line. Land was "part of the Contents of a patent granted to Roger Alden for 30,000 acres in the year of 1796 and by said deed conveyed to Robert Charles Johnson by deed.' Witnesses: Joseph Dawson and Benjamon Dorman."

On 20 August 1802, "Habon Jackson" sold 100 acres for 25 pounds to John McCorquadille (McCorquadill, McCorquodile). Land was "On the side of Williamson's Swamp Near John Segress' Corner. The land included 'Lowden Jackson's improvements.' Witnesses: Sherrod Holly and John Keen."

On the 3 of November 1802, a deed from John Dickson to "Halburn" Jackson for 100 acres was proved by Joseph Dawson.

I have not found Hayburn with any spelling variations of his name in either the 1790 or the 1800 census records. We know that deeds from Sampson County, North Carolina, mention a Hayburn, Sr. and Hayburn, Jr. (born about 1790.) Hayburn Sr. must have been born by 1767 in order to have received a land grant in 1790.

In the 1810 Federal Census for Sampson County, the name is spelled either "Habran" or "Habrun." He was 26-44 years of age and a female in the household was 26-44; Listed with him were two males under ten and four females under ten, one female 26-44 and one female 45 or older. If the oldest male was Hayburn, Sr., where was Hayburn, Jr.? It's well known that some Census enumerators made errors of their own, entered erroneous information provided by parents, children or others and they did not visit some homes. It has also been said that for some families not visited, the enumerator entered data by guessing names and ages and in some cases, he did not wish to include the family. This 1810 Census record could have been Haburn (Hayburn?) Jackson, Jr., with his age listed incorrectly.

Hayburn Jackson is listed in the 1820 Federal Census in Capt. Godwins District in Sampson County, North Carolina. (Roll: M33_85, Page 304, Image # 223). He is aged 26-45 and living in his household are two males under 10, one male 10-16, one male 16-18, two females under 10, two females 10-16, one female 16-26 and one female over 45 for a total of five males and 6 females. This appears to be Hayburn, Jr., who is head of household; but I believe he was living in the household of his mother and siblings. Apparently, it was the custom at the time to list a male child, aged 21 or older, as head of household when his mother was widowed. Age errors in Census records and other factors make it difficult to determine whether it was Hayburn Jackson, Sr. or Hayburn, Jr. who was listed "head of household" in 1820, but the fact that I have only found one Hayburn (Habran, Haburn?) listed in 1810, 1820 and 1830 certainly creates a puzzle. Who was the female listed as forty and under 50 (40-49) in 1830. It wasn't Hayburn, Jr.'s mother and it wasn't Mary, unless the enumerator listed ages incorrectly!

Mary may have been the female who was listed as aged 15-19, but this would indicate that she was born before 1811 or Hayburn, Jr. married twice; the older female could have been some other relative of Hayburn. Of course, researchers are well aware that the census enumerators often listed incorrect ages, dates and names.

In 1830 Federal Census for Sampson County, North Carolina, "Habon Jackson" was listed next to "Dickson Jackson" which may indicate they were related in some way. Dickson Jackson was born about 1792 and was the son of Nathan Jackson. Habon was head of household aged 50-60 with one female 40-50. Others in the household were :

One male under 5, one male 10-15, one male 15-20 and two females under 5 and one female aged 15-20. In the event the ages are correct, this would have been Habon, Sr. and his spouse. Dickson Jackson was between 30-40 years with one female aged 40-50. His children were one male and one female under 5, one male and one female 5-10 and one male, one female 10-15.

I have been unable to find any various spellings of Hayburn in the 1840 census. "Dikson" (Dickson" Jackson was living next door to Nathan Jackson in 1840.

In some instances, it is not possible to say whether the event was for Hayburn, Sr. or Hayburn, Jr., and, therefore, some of the notes for Hayburn Jackson, Jr., may list records for Hayburn, Sr. or vice versa. There may also have been more than two men named Hayburn (Haborn, etc.), but deeds clearly indicate that there was a Senior and Junior named Hayburn. Of course, a minor could inherit land and it would be managed by his guardian until the minor reached the age of 21 when he could sign a legal document. We also need to remember that today, Hayburn, Jr., would be the son of Hayburn, Sr, but at that time, Hayburn, Jr., could mean Hayburn, Sr. was a grandfather, uncle or an older cousin.

The fact that it was "Thomas Bullard and his wife, Sarah Bullard" who willed a plantation to Haburn (Habon) Jackson in 1802 may also indicate that either another Thomas Bullard was in the area or Thomas Bullard had a second wife. The Sampson County, North Carolina, deed dated 16 February 1802 reads: "Thomas Bullard to Haburn Jackson ... for and in consideration of the love and natural affection I have and do bear unto and toward my grandson Haburn Jackson .. I have given and granted and by this presents do fully give and grant unto the said Haburn Jackson his heirs ... the land and plantation whereon Thomas Bullard and Sarah Bullard (sic) his wife containing eighty acres and 100 acres of land whereon said Haburn Jackson is now living for him to be possesed ... after the death of aforesaid Thomas Bullard and Sarah Bullard his wife the whole stock remaining of cattle hogs and sheep to belong to said Haburn Jackson and I the said Thomas Bullard of which before the signing of these presents I have delivered him the said Haburn Jackson an inventory signed with my own hand and bearing date (blank) to have and to hold all the said goods and chattel in the said premises ...

Wits: Nathan Godwin and Zelpha Williams."

Hayburn Jackson, Sr. could have been the grandchild of Thomas Bullard.

On 13 August 1799, the Sampson County, North Carolina court ordered Richard Jackson, Duskin Blue, Lewis Jackson, Lewis Tew and others to work on the new road from Readick (sic) Holley's to the pine log...Micajah Williford be overseer.

On 2 May 1803 "Hardy Draughon came into court and presented a petition ...a new road ... across upper end of the county, beginning at a new road lately open through Johnston County direct from Fayetteville, then the nearest and best way to Starling's bridge. Ordered that Macajah Williford, HABORN JACKSON, William Godwin, Nathan Godwin, Jonathan Godwin...Lewis Tew III, William Knowles, Seth Starling ...or any 12 of them be a jury to lay off the road aforesaid as the law directs...."
11 May 1807: "Ordered Habon Jackson be overseer of the road in the room of LEWIS JACKSON..."
15 August 1809: "Ordered that Henry Godwin be overseer of the road in the room of HABORN JACKSON."

The later placement of orphaned children of "Hayburn Jackson" indicates that the following could have possibly been related to Hayburn, Sr. or Jr.:
Nancy Jackson, born about 1801, married Isaac Strickland, born about 1788.
Rachel Jackson, born about 1805, married William Strickland, born about 1801.
Delitha Jackson, born about 1810, married Sherwood Holly, born about 1807.

Rachel and Delitha were mentioned as children of Thomas B. Jackson.

In 1810, the Federal Census records of Sampson County, North Carolina listed the number of looms and the quantity of cloth for each family. One loom was listed for Habran(?) and his family and 50 was listed for the quantity of cloth. This was 50 yards? One loom was listed for almost every family. The quantity usually ranged from 50-200 with an occasional 300 or 500. The highest number of yards I came across was 1600 yards for a Marley family which may have been an error, but may show that one or more of his daughters or others worked often at the loom(s).

Some of the earliest known Jacksons in what later became Sampson County, North Carolina: Allen, Archibald (who was murdered after 7 May 1794---see deed below), Asa, Donalson, Edward, George, Hayburn, Sr. and Hayburn (Habon, Habern, Habron, Haburn), Jr., Irwin (Irvin), James, Joel, John, Josiah, Lewis, Lowden, Middleton, Nathan, Needham, Richard, Thomas, and William, Sr. and Jr. Many of these names are represented in deeds in the late 1700s and early 1800s for land descriptions that mention Williamson Swamp, Jumping Run, Starling Swamp, Williams Lake (then known as Joel Jackson Pond), Pussel's Branch (today known as Opossum Swamp) and Caesar Swamp.

Archibald Jackson mentioned above may be the man who on 27 January 1777 purchased 100 acres for 20 pounds from John Jackson. Land was "on the west side of Little Cohara Including the Pretty place" and was granted to John Jackson by patent dated 27 April 1767. Witnesses: William Odom, Anne Ryal and Dinah Odom." I found the "Pretty Place" mentioned several times in Jackson land transactions. On 7 May 1794, Archabald (sic) sold this property to William (Will) Bass for "25 pounds specia." The "Pretty Place" was again mentioned.

Archibald (Archabald?) Jackson is mentioned in census records and deeds transactions before 1790. There may have been more than one Archibald Jackson, but one is said to have been murdered.

Caesar Swamp in Mingo Township in Sampson County, North Carolina is an area about 2-3 three miles southeast of Williamsons Swamp, Jumping Run and Starling Swamp, the places mentioned in the deeds for Hayburn Jackson Sr. and Hayburn, Jr. Tradition says that "Caesar" was an Indian who lived east of present-day Caesar swamp, about one mile north of Williams' Lake. He is said to have stolen what he wanted from white settlers who lived over a large area. They became so frustrated they finally formed a group to track him to his home where he was killed and buried. The name "Caesar" does not match any word in the Iroquoian languages and Caesar probably adopted it for his name.

Thomas Jackson, Jr. is another early Jackson who is listed in the 1769 Bladen County, North Carolina, Tax Lists as a white taxable. Two taxables named Thomas Jackson are listed in 1774. Thomas Jackson and John Jackson are listed together in 1770 and English Thomas Jackson is listed separately. English Thomas Jackson is also listed in 1771. Thomas Jackson and brother, John are listed in 1771 and listed in 1774 in separately households. Two taxables named James Jackson are listed separately in 1774; one listed with one (1) bonded man.

John Bullard is listed in 1769, 1771 and 1772 as a white taxable in Bladen County. In 1772, John Bullard, Senior, and another John Bullard are listed in separate households . In 1770, James Jackson is listed. Thomas Chance is listed in Bladen County as a white taxable in 1770. Thomas Bullard and Ambrous Bullard are listed in separate households as white taxables in 1771 and 1772; "Ambrouse" is listed in 1774. One "Thomas Bullard" a few years later paid taxes in Cumberland County and Sampson County. It appears he lived near the border of Sampson and Cumberland.

Hayburn's "Unknown Spouse" may have been "Elizabeth Bullard," daughter of Thomas and Mary.

Children of Hayburn Jackson and Unknown Bullard are:

+   2   i.   Hayburn Jackson, Jr., born 1790 in Sampson County , North Carolina; died About 1842.

3   ii. One Male Jackson[6], born Bet. 1802 - 1804 in Sampson County , North Carolina[6].

4   iii. Two Daughters Jackson[6], born Bet. 1804 - 1810 in Sampson County , North Carolina[6].

5   iv. Two Daughters Jackson[6], born Bet. 1810 - 1820 in Sampson County , North Carolina[6].

6   v. One Male Jackson[6], born Bet. 1805 - 1810 in Sampson County , North Carolina[6].

7   vi. One Male Jackson[6], born Bet. 1810 - 1819 in Sampson County , North Carolina[6].

8   vii. One Son Jackson[6], born Bet. 1810 - 1819 in Sampson County , North Carolina[6].

Generation No. 2

2. Hayburn[4] Jackson, Jr. (Hayburn[3], Unidentified[2], Unknown[1])[7,8] was born 1790 in Sampson County , North Carolina[9], and died About 1842[10]. He married **Mary M. Chance**[11], daughter of John Chance and Amy (maiden name unknown). She was born about 1812 in Sampson County , North Carolina[11], and died after 1880.

The year 1778 is also listed for Hayburn, Jr.'s year of birth and 'after 1870' has been reported for his death by one researcher. Where was he and why can't census or other records be found for him after 1842? Specific lineage for Haburn Jackson, Sr.'s family may never be found. I have attempted to include records and data I have found in the hope that it could help others in their research. Please understand that the lineage here may be incorrect. My age and health may preclude my ability to do further research and I believe that it is highly unlikely further research will reveal more information about the Hayburn (Haburn), Sr. and Hayburn, Jr. At the time "Junior" may have only designated that a younger living man had the same name and he could have been named after a grandfather, uncle or an older cousin.

Hayburn may have been spelled "Habon, Haburn, Habern, Haborn, Habron, Hebron, Halburn and possibly other ways." Sources noted below indicate a Hayburn, Sr. and Jr. Of course there may have been more than two men named Hayburn Jackson.

Williams Lake in Caesar Swamp was known earlier as "Joel Jackson Pond." Much of the land around this area was owned by several Jackson families.

From Sampson County, North Carolina deed records:
"27 January 1802. "...Richard Godwins Corner On the North side of the said Hill a little Below said Godwins Mill Dam. Deed mentions HABON JACKSON, 'one of the patent corners in Bullards line.'..." Deed Book 12, Page 100.
"16 February 1802. Deed of Gift: Thomas Bullard to HABURN JACKSON (his grandson). ' Haburn Jackson was given the land and plantation Whereon Thomas Bullard and Sarah Bullard his wife live... Containing eighty acres and 100 acres of land whereon said Haburn Jackson is now living ...." Hayburn Jackson, Sr., was possibly the grandson mentioned here.

On 29 November 1806, Haburn was granted 100 acres between Sand Hill Branch and Jumping Run including his own plantation. Registered September 1808. This would have been Haburn (Hayburn), Sr.

Jesse Strickland on 5 July 1821 sold 25 acres to Haborn for $25.00. Land was on both sides of Jumping Run beginning on the north side of Jumping Run at the mouth of Bullards branch. Wits: Isaac and Jacob Strickland. Proved in February Term 1823, in open court and registered 15 April 1825.

On 7 November 1823 (or 1829) Reddick Holley sold 100 acres to Haborn Jackson for $93.17. Witnesses: Edward Holley and Larry Holley. Deed was proven in May 1831 term and was registered 11 August 1831. Hayburn named a son "Reddick" which could mean that the families were related in some way. The given name Reddick is found several times in the early Holley (Hawley) families.

A deed from H. Jackson to Raiford Jackson for 50 acres was proved by Burrell Dawson on 19 August 1825.

Deed dated 30 January 1828 from Larry Holly to Habon Jackson for 136 acres was witnessed by Ollen Jackson and Reddick Holly and was proved by Reddick Holly on 10 August 1829. Registered 20 October 1829.

On the 5 January 1835, Haborn sold 100 acres to John J. King for $50.00. Sand Hill Branch and Jumping Run mentioned in deed. Witnesses. Edward Holley and Thomas B. Jackson. Proved in February Term 1836. Registered 13 April 1836.

Haborn sold 227 acres to Mirick Tew on 8 August 1835. Land lay "on both sides of Jumping Run to the mouth of Jumping run. ... Starling Swamp ... to the mouth of jumping Run to the road then with said road to the beginning... Wits: Martin Tew and William Godwin. Proved in open court in August 1848. Registered 23 October 1848." Apparently, Haburn died about 1842; see court order below, appointing guardians for orphans of Haburn Jackson. This deed probably wasn't registered until it became necessary to prove that the sale was made.

It appears that Haburn, Jr., sold most of his land before he died about 1842. Why wasn't the land willed to his children?

On 18 August 1836, Haborn Jackson sold 236 acres to Sherwood Holley for $200. One tract was on west side of Little Coharie, east of Johnson Swamp joining Wright Warren's land. Another tract begin at a cypress in Cypress pond on Samuel Peter's line. Witnesses: Edward Holley and John Holly, Sr. Proved by Edward Holley in August Court 1840. Registered 30 September 1840.

The data in the court order mentioned below imply that this Hayburn, Jr. may have been married twice and some of the children could be from the earlier marriage. Of course, Hayburn, Sr., who is mentioned in at least one deed as owning land in 1796 would have been born before 1775; you had to be 21 to sign a legal document. Hayburn Jackson Sr, could have had a second wife young enough to give birth to the older children mentioned in the court order below, but it seems more likely that they are children of Hayburn, Jr. The placement of these children in the 1850 census suggests that there was a close relationship with the Stricklands living in the area. The wife of Sherwood Holley was "Delitha Jackson," aged 40. Rachel Jackson, aged 45, was the wife of William Strickland. Nancy Jackson, aged 49, was listed as the wife of Isaac Strickland, aged 62. Elvy, aged 24, was listed as a daughter of Isaac and Nancy (Jackson) Strickland in 1850. This may indicate that Nancy was a sister of Hayburn Jackson, Jr. who named a daughter "Elvy." Haburn Rice Jackson born in 1878 named a son, "Elvin Sykes Jackson." William Strickland and Rachel Jackson named a son, William Habron Strickland.

Rachel and Delitha Jackson have been mentioned as daughters of Thomas B. Jackson. Rachel has also been mentioned as the daughter of John Jackson.

"Ailey," aged 24, is listed as the spouse of Joseph Godwin in the 1850 census for Sampson County, North Carolina. Living with them are "Susan Jackson," aged 50, Amy Jackson, aged 12, and Elizabeth Jackson, aged 9. The name "Amy" was passed down in these Jackson families. There was an "Enoch Godwin," aged 24 in the 1850 census. Records suggest that not only do we find Bullards, Jacksons, Godwins and Stricklands living near each other at the time, but it appears that at least a few were related by marriage. There may also be a relationship between the family of Haburn Jackson and the early Holley (Holly, Hawley) families.

Mr. D. Jackson from Western North Carolina was kind enough to share the following with me; on February 20, 2004:
"Nancy, I found a note I made when I was reading the Sampson County Court Minutes at North Carolina Archives for the 1840s. This should be your Wiley Calvin Jackson.
"From CR087.301.9 - August Term 1842 Sampson County Court of Pleas and Quarter Sessions.
"Ordered that William Strickland be appointed guardian to Aley Jackson, Elizabeth Jackson, Enoch Jackson, Reddick Jackson, Elvey Jane Jackson, Andrew W. Jackson and Willie Calvin Jackson, minor heirs of Haburn Jackson, deceased.

"Looking at the Sampson County 1850 census you can find most of these children scattered about with their relatives...

"Elvey J. Jackson, age 17, was living with Sherwood Holly.

"Andrew W. Jackson, age 15, was living with Sampson Strickland.

"Reddick Jackson, age 19, was living with William Strickland.

"I can only assume that Aley and Elizabeth were old enough to be married by 1850, so I can't identify them. Enoch Jackson does not appear at all and the only Wiley C. Jackson on the 1850 census that might be yours is living with Mary Jackson age 38, but I can't explain the other children living in her household.

"Wiley C. Jackson age 23 does appear in 1860 living in household with Elbert Strickland.

"...I believe there was an even older Haburn Jackson. There is a 1796 Sampson County deed that mentions land being adjacent to Haburn Jackson. If he already owned land, he was born in 1770s...."

Before I received Mr. Jackson's message, I had already concluded that the Wiley Calvin Jackson noted above had to be a child of Hayburn Jackson, but I had no proof and descendants of Elisha Moore Jackson said there was no way that my Wiley Calvin was related to Elisha. The descendants could have thought I was asking about a younger "Wiley Calvin Jackson," grandson of Wiley Calvin Jackson and Mary Jane Royal and may not have known about the older connection!

Elisha Moore Jackson has been listed as a son of Hayburn Jackson by another researcher but Hayburn appears to have been deceased by August 1842 and Elisha Moore was born after 1850. Elisha's tombstone shows his birth as May 1853. In the 1860 Census for Sampson County, North Carolina, Elisha Moore appears to be listed as "Eliza M., age 2, f (female)." It was not unusual for an enumerator to enter the sex and aged incorrectly, but the "age 2" listed in that census may show us that Mary had a daughter Eliza M. who either died or was married before the 1870 census. If that was the case, where was Elisha Moore?

I question whether Mary was actually the mother of Aley, Elizabeth and Enoch unless she was born before 1815. She is listed as age 38 in 1850, age 45 in 1860 and age 60 in 1870. She is listed in one source as born about 1811 which would have made her old enough to have been the mother of all the children born before 1842.

It appears that Hayburn, Jr. died before Elisha Moore Jackson and two other children were born. Deeds confirm that Hayburn Jackson Sr. and Jr. owned land. Did Hayburn, Jr. have an occupation other than farming and did it often keep him away from home? Where was he when the 1840 and 1850 censuses were taken?

It also appears from the Census records for Sampson County, North Carolina, that Hayburn Jackson, Sr., died before 1820 and Hayburn Jackson, Jr., was head of household, but he was in the household of his mother and at least some siblings. His mother appears to be deceased by 1830 and Mary is listed as the oldest female. Only one Hayburn, (Habran, Habon) is found in each census (Habran in 1810, Hayburn in 1820 and Habon in 1830.)

In the 1850 Federal Census, Amy Jackson was listed as 10 years old under Mary Jackson, age 38. Amy E. was married by 1860.
On April 1, 2004, I was cross-checking to make sure I had entered all the Royal Wills from "Sampson County Wills 1784 -1900," abstracted by Elizabeth E. Ross, Clayton, North Carolina. I read and re-read the following Will Abstract on page 111 that was written on April 4, 1899:
"ROYAL T. P. and wife, Amma E.   4 April. 1899
probate 10 May 1899
"Brother E. M. Jackson - bed and furniture; cow now in his possession.
"Brother Joseph E. Jackson - 1 hog
"Remaining estate to be sold at our decease and money equally divided between E. M. Jackson, Joseph E. Jackson, W. C. Jackson, Mary J. Stricklin and Hanson Lockerman.
"Bill Jackson - 25 cents.

"Exec: A. H. Herring   signed T. P. Royal, Amma (X)
Royal
"Wit: T. L. Owen, A. H. Herring
"North Carolina State Archives."

I also found that I had a transcribed copy of the above last will and testament that I had copied from the Will book in Sampson County courthouse in Clinton, North Carolina. ALSO SEE NOTES FOR AMEY E. JACKSON.

This Will certainly points to the fact that Amy and those mentioned in the will are related and other records clearly support this and also indicate that Hayburn, Sr. and, or Hayburn, Jr., may have been married twice. Was "Bill Jackson" another brother? I can't find a "Bill." I do find a "William B. Jackson," age 14, living with Reany Andrews, age 31, (female) in 1850. Were "Reany" and William B. also children of Hayburn (Sr. or Jr.) and siblings of the above mentioned children. It appears that Wiley Calvin may have been a full-brother of Amy. Why did Amy Jackson and her husband, T. P. (Talbert P.) Royal name Hanson Lockerman (Lockamy) in their will? Why did Amy and Talbert write a joint will?

Mary A (Mary J. above) is listed as a sister of Amy in 1850. In 1870, John Strickland, aged 26, is listed with wife, Mary J., aged 20 and Ollen D. Strickland, aged 22, is listed with wife, Mary B., aged 20. Mary J., wife of John Strickland in 1870 could have been the "Mary J. Stricklin" mentioned above in the will of T. P. Royal and "Amma Royal." However, Reddick Jackson, aged 19, older brother (orphan of Hayburn Jackson) in 1850 was in the household of William Strickland, father of Ollen D., aged 2, and this strongly suggests that Ollen was the husband of Mary J. (B.?)

In 1850 and 1870 and also 1880, Mary Jackson was listed as head of household. In 1860, she was listed as Mary J., aged 45, and she and her children were living with Amy Chance, age 65, widow of John Chance. Is this evidence that Mary J. was the daughter of John Chance and Amy (maiden name unknown)? Mary J. named a daughter Amy and her son, Elisha Moore, named a daughter "Amy". In 1850, this Mary Jackson also had a son, Wiley Jackson, age 13, listed with her. Also see notes under Hayburn

In 1850 Mary was listed in the Northern District of Sampson County; In 1860 and 1870 she was listed in Dismal Township which is in the Northern half of Sampson. A descendant of Elisha Moore Jackson in a profile on page 486 in the first heritage book of Sampson County states: "Elisha was the son of Mary M. Jackson (1815) and Hayburn Jackson (1790)." May 1861 is listed for Elisha'a birth in that profile, but as noted in other sources, Elisha's tombstone shows his birth as May 1853. Elisha M. later used "Moore" for his middle name and one of Elisha's sons was given the name "Morre" for his middle name; this may have led this descendant to believe that Moore was Mary's maiden name.

We do find errors in transcribed records and I cringe when I think of the ones I've made.

Deeds of Sampson County, North Carolina, reveal that Habron (Hayburn) Jackson owned several hundred acres of land. County records of 1835 and 1836 show that he probably sold much of his land during those two years. On 8 August 1835 he sold 220 plus acres to Mirick Tew. This sale was not proven until August Court Term 1848 and on 23 October 1848 the court ordered it to be registered. This deed may lead some people to believe that Hayburn was still living in 1848. Several reasons could explain why it took so long to prove and register the deed.

One researcher mentions that Travis Jackson, born in 1804 is later found living in exactly the same spot that Haburn (Hayburn) Jackson took for his two land grants and believes the 444 acres owned by Travis was possibly the 444 acres of land not accounted for in the public record. This Haburn was, most likely, Haburn, Sr., but Haburn, Jr, must have inherited the land as he seems to be the one who sold it.

The 1830 census of Sampson County, North Carolina, records Mary Jackson as head of household and under 30 with one male under 20 and one female under 5. This Mary Jackson who was head of household would not have been the spouse of Hayburn; Habon (Hayburn) was also listed in the 1830 census. She is listed as living a few doors away from Nathan Jackson

Children of Hayburn Jackson and Mary Chance are:

9   i.   Elizabeth Jackson[12], born Bet. 1825 - 1830.

10   ii.   Enoch Jackson[12], born Bet. 1825 - 1830; died 05 May 1864 in Wilderness, Virginia[13].

       He may be the Enoch Jackson from North Carolina who moved to Troup County, Georgia, and enlisted in the Civil War on 8 July 1861. He served in Company K, 13th Inf. Reg. and was killed on 5 May 1864 in Wilderness, Virginia.

+   11   iii.   Aley Jackson, born about 1826.

12   iv.   Reddick Jackson[14], born About 1831[15].

13   v.   Elvey Jane Jackson[16], born About 1833[17].

       See notes under her sister Amy and her father. Elvy was spelled "Elvey" in court records. In 1850, Elvy Jackson, aged 17, was living in the household Sherwood Holly (Holley, Hawley) and his wife, Delitha (nee Jackson) in Sampson County, North Carolina.

14   vi.   Andrew W. Jackson[18], born About 1835[19].

+   15   vii.   Wiley Calvin Jackson, born June 1836; died 17 November 1908 in Honeycutts Township, Sampson County, North Carolina, USA.

16   viii.   Amy E. Jackson[20,21], born About 1840[22]; died About May 1899 in Sampson County, North Carolina[23]. She married Talbert P. Royal[23,24]; born About 1832[25]; died About May 1899 in Sampson County, North Carolina[26].

       "Sampson County Wills 1784 -1900," abstracted by Elizabeth E. Ross, Clayton, North Carolina on page 111 records the Will Abstract fo T. P. and Amme C. Royal. The will was written on April 4, 1899 and it was presented to probate on 10 May 1899:
       "ROYAL T. P. and wife, Amma E.   4 April. 1899
       probate 10 May 1899
       "Brother E. M. Jackson - bed and furniture; cow now in his possession.
       "Brother Joseph E. Jackson - 1 hog

"Remaining estate to be sold at our decease and money equally divided between E. M. Jackson, Joseph E. Jackson, W. C. Jackson, Mary J. Stricklin and Hanson Lockerman.
"Bill Jackson - 25 cents.
"Exec: A. H. Herring   signed T. P. Royal,
Amma (X) Royal
"Wit: T. L. Owen, A. H. Herring
"North Carolina State Archives."

I, Nancy Eveline Jackson Pleitt Fenner (nee Jackson), found a copy of this will in the deed books of Sampson County in the courthouse in Clinton, North Carolina. Amy and T. P.'s Last Will and Testament, together with the probate record was ordered to be "recorded and filed on the 10 day of May 1899. W. K. Pigford, Clerk Superior Court." A. H. Herring and T. L. Owen were witnesses.

It is strange that Amy and her husband, Talbert P. Royal wrote a joint will and testament and it went to probate so soon after it was written, leading me to question how they died. A. H. Herring and T. L. Owen subscribed by examination and oath that they witnessed the signing of the joint will on 24 day of April 1899. The date of "4 April 1899" stated in the transcribed record indicates either a date difficult to read or a transcription error.

There was a "Hanson Lockamy" born about 1849, but it is not known whether he was the "Hanson Lockerman" mentioned in the above will. Amy's brother, Wiley Calvin Jackson, had a daughter, Flora Lee Jackson, who married John Martin Lockamy, a brother of the Hanson Lockamy born about 1849, but it remains a mystery as to why he would be mentioned in Amy's will.

Nancy Jackson, Aged 70, was living in the household with Amy and T. P. in 1880 in Clinton Township, Sampson County, North Carolina. Relationship has not been determined. Nancy may have been the "Nancy Jackson," aged 37, living in the household of Sherwood Tew in 1850.

No spelling of Talbert P. Royal 's name (Talbert, Tolbot or Tolbert Royal) was listed in the 1850 Census of Sampson County, North Carolina. Data found at Ancestry.com show him as a son of Reason Royal and Elizabeth Sykes. In that data, Talbert's spouse, Amy E., is incorrectly entered as a child of Reason and his second wife, Catherine Williamson In 1860, "Tolbert P. Royal," age 32, laborer and his wife, Amy E., age 20, were living with Catherine Royal (widow and second wife of Reason Royal) in the town of Clinton, North Township and this 1860 census is, most likely, the source of the data posted on Ancestry.com. Reason doesn't mention Talbert in his will, leaving us with a mystery.

In 1870, "Talbert B. Royal," age 37, mechanic, is listed as head of household in Dwelling 116 in Honeycutts Township with "Amey E.," age 25, wife. Amy's age varies widely with each census.

It appears that Talbert and Amy had no children and they left their estate to some of her brothers, sisters and two others.

Civil War records show:
"Royal, Tolbert P., Pvt., Co. K, Regt. 51. Inf. Born 1832. Sampson County. Farm laborer. Enlisted 14 April 1862, Dismal. Sick May-June 1862. Hospitalized November-December in Sampson County. Wounded 17 December 1862 in Battle of Neuse Bridge and hospitalized at Goldsboro. Found 31 December 1863 in hospital at Wilmington. Continued to be sick in Sampson County throughout 1864."

+   17   ix.   Mary A. Jackson, born about 1846.

+   18   x.   Joseph E. Jackson, born about 1849 in Sampson County , North Carolina; died 06 December 1928 in Sampson County , North Carolina.

+   19   xi.   Elisha Moore Jackson, born May 1853 in North Carolina; died 24 November 1913 in Sampson County, North Carolina.

Generation No. 3

11. Aley[5] Jackson (Hayburn[4], Hayburn[3], Unidentified[2], Unknown[1])[27] was born About 1826[28]. She married **Joseph Godwin**[28]. He was born about 1818[28].

Sampson County, North Carolina Census records for 1850, 1860 and 1870 show an "Aley" (Ailey) as the wife of Joseph Godwin. The records do not mention a maiden name for her. The three census years, show she was born about 1826. I first questioned whether I had linked Aley and Joseph Godwin correctly because quite a lot of Jacksons and Godwins lived near each other. However, data posted on 21 July 2005 on Ancestry.com shows that another researcher either has direct line family data or she has concluded that Ailey (Aley) Jackson was the wife of Joseph Godwin. This researcher has her maiden name as "Jackson."

A grandson, Hugh, aged 2, is living with Aley and Joseph in 1880.

In 1850, Susan Jackson, aged 50, Amy, aged 12, and Elizabeth, aged 9 are listed in the household of Joseph and Aley Godwin. I believe, this Susan Jackson, in some way is related to Ailey, but I have found no record to confirm this.

Children of Aley Jackson and Joseph Godwin are:

20	i.	Flora Godwin[29], born about 1850[29].

> The 1870 Federal Census for Sampson County, North Carolina lists her first name as "Phloria."

+	21	ii.	Soloman Godwin, born about 1852.
+	22	iii.	Saul Godwin, born May 1853.
+	23	iv.	Simeon Godwin, born about 1856; died 22 June 1902.
	24	v.	Sarah Godwin[29], born about 1858[29].
	25	vi.	Mary Godwin[30], born about 1860[30].
	26	vii.	Effy Godwin[30], born about 1866[30].

15. Wiley Calvin[5] Jackson (Hayburn[4], Hayburn[3], Unidentified[2], Unknown[1])[31] was born June 1836[32], and died 17 November 1908 in Honeycutts Township, Sampson County, North Carolina, USA[33]. He married **Mary Jane Royal**[34] 12 February 1861 in Sampson County, Clinton, North Carolina[35], daughter of Gabriel Royal and Sarah Crumpler. She was born December 1841 in Sampson County, North Carolina[36,37], and died 12 May 1935 in Honeycutts Township, Sampson County, North Carolina[38].

Wiley Calvin Jackson is the only person who has a tombstone in the Wiley Calvin Jackson Family Cemetery. He served in the Civil War and his stone cannot legally be destroyed. The current owner of the property told me that there were never any other stones in the cemetery. An elderly Aunt and others say they remember seeing several tombstones near a tree on the farm. Apparently, there were others buried on the farm and they had tombstones; the stone for Wiley Calvin is the only one still there. Others say that Wiley Calvin and the others were buried behind the house, which indicates the stones were probably removed by someone as Wiley Calvin's gravestone was the only one in front of the old house in 2001.

.

Tommy, Patience Lee and Millard Cicero are most likely, also buried in the cemetery.

Civil War records show he served as a Cpl., in Co. I, Regt. 46, Infantry and that he was born in Sampson County, North Carolina. Enlisted "16 March 1862 in Clinton. Hospitalized 19 June 1863 at Goldsboro with pneumonia. Sent in September 1863 to Richmond, Virginia to be instructed in band music. Transferred to Regimental Band in March-April, 1864 and on its roll as non-commissioned staff. Reported present in September-October, 1864. Paroled 9 April 1865 at Appomattox Courthouse, Virginia." A descendant tells that both his ears were hit with bullets during the war; a photograph shows where they were hit.

On 2 March 1901, the State of North Carolina ratified the amendment of Chapter 198 of the Laws of 1889 for the relief of certain Confederate Soldiers and Widows. On 7 June 1901, Wiley Calvin applied for his pension. He stated: "...that while in said service at Sharpsburg, Maryland, on or about .... September 1862 he received a wound or wounds, etc. 'I received a wound on the head and my brain was affected to some extent and my lungs were affected by blowing a horn. I am old and need help.'" His application shows his signature: "W. C. Jackson." It was approved. A note on his application indicates that he "was accused of having deserted and flinched from duty"; this note is crossed through and probably means he wasn't a deserter. There were two other local younger men named Wiley C. Jackson who served in the Civil War. Many men who served in the earlier Revolutionary War and the American Civil War would leave their units for awhile and after a visit to their home would return to service. When they left without approval, they were written up as deserters and this wasn't always removed from their record when they returned.

The "horn" he refers to in his pension application most likely, was the bugle which is known as one of the simplest brass instruments and is essentially a small natural horn with no valves. "Bugle" comes from the Latin word "buculus" (young bull). The earliest musical or communication instruments were called "horns" because they were made of animal horns and the first bugles were hunting horns.

On 19 July 1909, his widow, Mary Jane (nee Royal) Jackson applied for a pension based on Wiley Calvin's service in the Civil War. The state approved her application as Class B. In May 1931, she applied for reclassification to Class A and it was approved. The May 1931 application stated that she was 89 years old, had high blood pressure, her heart showed evidence of myocarditis and she had to have help in walking and dressing and was almost entirely helpless.

Wiley Calvin may not have been a son of Hayburn, but records of Sampson County and state archives certainly strongly support it. Records also suggest a possible relationship with "Holly" (Holley, Hawley families.) Perhaps younger researchers who will have more time to followup with the data presented here will find data that will prove "this Wiley Calvin" was a son of Hayburn.

The W. C. who signed the Civil War Pension Application as noted above was Wiley Calvin Jackson, father of Haburn Rice Jackson. Naming a son Haburn strongly suggests that Wiley Calvin was somehow related to Hayburn Jackson Sr. and Jr. The names "Jemima (Jemimma)" and "Flora" are found in the early Thomas Bullard Family of Sampson County, North Carolina.

Wiley Calvin was a cooper and made barrels for the turpentine and pitch industry. The art of cooperage, barrel and caskmaking required skills in woodworking and blacksmithing to ensure that staves and metal bands were set properly to form a barrel. The 1850 Sampson County, North Carolina census lists "cooper" for the occupation of 78 persons; this was second only to farming. Wiley Calvin was listed as a Cooper, living with Elbert Strickland in the 1860 census and as a farmer in the 1870 census. A granddaughter, Mattie Ruth Jackson Parker Holland confirmed that he was a cooper.

The making of many households items, including churns, washtubs, kegs and buckets, required the skill of the cooper. Cedar was the wood of choice, but some people used the less satisfactory, poplar or juniper. A hand-powered froe, a shaving horse, and a croze were the cooper's tools and a straw filled bag was used to hold the barrel shape as the staves were added.

A Lockamy descendant tells that Wiley Calvin and his son-in-law, John Martin Lockamy found a "bee tree" near a "branch near what is now Coharie Day Center and they wanted Tom Owens to cut down the tree. Apparently, Wiley Calvin was nearby when Tom either cut down the tree or climbed it to get the honey and said to Tom, "Soon as you get the honey bring it to me." Tom pulled out a piece of honey as big as his hand and gave it to Wiley Calvin who had a long, red beard." As Wiley Calvin ate the honey, bees got in his beard and most likely, he was stung more than once. This was told by Tom Owens, son of Fred Owens who married a granddaughter of Wiley Calvin.

It is said that during the Civil War, Mary Jane tied hams with wire and stuck them under water in the river to keep the Yankees from getting them. Wiley Calvin got mad and joined the Army because the Yankees were stealing everything they could get their hands on. Descendants also tell that Wiley Calvin died accidentally. He was sitting on a log, pulled his flintlock gun toward him and it fired, killing him..." Apparently, these stories about Wiley Calvin were well known among his Lockamy descendants! His accidental death occurred before North Carolina required registration of births and deaths. Otherwise, I would probably have known, at least, that his death was accidental.

On 15 April 1892, Wiley Calvin bought 100 acres from the J. H. Turlington, his siblings and their spouses for $100. Land was in Honeycutts Township, Sampson County, North Carolina and was on "the run of Bearskin Swamp to Griffith Wise's corner and thence the dividing line .... on the back line of Reynold's corner....to a stake... to the run of Bearskin." This deed was not recorded and registered until 22 September 1908, sixteen years later, apparently one day after he and Mary Jane deeded their land to four of their children as entered below. It probably had to be registered at that time to prove that Wiley Calvin and Mary Jane owned the land.

21 September 1908:

"W. C. Jackson and wife to H. R. Jackson and others. North Carolina, Sampson County.

"Know all men by these presents: That we, W. C. Jackson and wife Mary J. Jackson for and in consideration of the sum of two hundred and fifty dollars in services heretofore rendered and in money and other things of value heretofore furnished and supplied us and upon the further consideration and stipulations to be ? by the parties of the 2nd party namely H. R. Jackson, Cornelius Galloway Jackson and Mary J. (sic)"C") Jackson and Eliza Jane Jackson have bargained sold and conveyed granted and confirmed subject to life estate of the grantors herein named which is expressly reserved and retained from this conveyance and the operation of this deed to the said H. R. Jackson, C. Galloway Jackson, Eliza Jane Jackson and Mary C. Jackson and their heirs and assigns. Not equally or jointly but in the manner hereinafter more particularily set out. - the following described lands and real estate lying and being in said state and county in Honeycutts Township adjoining the lands of J. W. Reynolds, Matt Strickland, Wm Butler, M. T. Reynolds and others bounded as follows.

"Beginning at a stake on the east side and near the run of Bearskin swamp, Griffith Wise's corner and running thence the dividing line North 85 E 191 poles to a stake on the back line Reynold's corner, thence So 90 poles to a stake, thence S 87 W 171 poles to a stake on the run of Beaskin, thence up the run of said Bearskin to the beginning containing one hundred (100) acres more or less---that is to say the said H. R. Jackson is to have 37 1/2 acres of the above described land lying on Bearskin swamp, C. Galloway Jackson is to have 37 1/2 acres lying on the east side of the said tract of $100) acres adjoining J. W. Reynolds and Wm Butler and M. T. Reynolds. Eliza Jane Jackson is to have the House known as Dunghill of (15) acres and the other grantee, Mary C. Jackson is to have the remaining (10) ten acres --- to have and to hold the said described tract of (100) one hundred acres of land to them the said H. R. Jackson, C.

Galloway Jackson, Eliza J. Jackson and Mary C. Jackson and their heirs, separately in the respective proportions as above set out -- of (37 1/2) thirty seven and one half acres each to the two boys as above indicated and of fifteen and ten (15) (10) acres to the two girls, Eliza J. and Mary C. Jackson as likewise above indicated and pointed out. And the above named grantees shall give and decide among themselves where the said dividing lines shall run as they may call in a disinterested committee of three neighbors and let them fix where the said dividing lines shall run so as to give to the two boys... the remainder of twenty five (25) acres in the proportion of (15) fifteen acres to the girl, Eliza Jane including the house and dwellings and to Mary C. Jackson the other (10) acres and the parties of the 1st part covenant and agree that they are seized and possessed of said lands above described in fee simple and have the right to convey the same ...."

It is said that two of Wiley Calvin's grandchildren, Joseph Paul Jackson and his sister, Susannah Jackson, visited an uncle who lived on property near Crumpler's Mill Pond on the road now known as Crumpler Mill Road. I have been unable to identify this man, but it is said he had a dark complexion and was a brother of Joseph (Joel) Jackson who willed his farm to Alger Rose Holland for services rendered to him, his wife and their daughter, for several years before their deaths. Robertha (Roberta) Holland, daughter of Alger Rose married Oscar Davis Jackson, another grandson of Wiley Calvin. Records support the fact that Wiley Calvin and Joseph (Joel) Jackson were brothers.

Aunt Mattie Ruth Jackson Parker Holland told me about 1998 that Wiley Calvin Jackson and Mary Jane Royal had two other children, Tom (Tommy) and Patience Lee who died young. I can find no record of either of these children. They could have been born and died between census records. Another son, Wiley B. Jackson named one of his children "Thomas Franklin Jackson." Thomas Franklin Jackson did not die young. I have learned that "young" did not necessarily mean the person died as a child and "Uncle" and "Aunt" also were used to show respect for someone dear to you who could have been someone other than an actual Uncle or Aunt.

In transcribed deed books of Sampson-Duplin County, North Carolina, a note is written at the bottom of page 70 in Deed Book 4: "On the 15 day of April 1849 the great Snow fell in Sampson County, North Carolina and every thing (sic) Destroyed. Fruit trees all Vegetation without Distinction the snow upon a Dead level was Seven Inches Deep. Let this Be long Remembered. Ed Vail Transcriber. July 12, 1849."

Wiley Calvin Jackson and Mary Jane were buried in his Family Cemetery, Honeycutts Township, Sampson County, North Carolina, USA.[39] Mary Jane "nee Royal" Jackson was buried on the 13 May 1935.[40] Wiley Calvin Jackson and Mary Jane Royal were married on 12 February 1861 in Clinton, Sampson County, North Carolina by John D. Herring, Esq.[41] The 1850 and 1860 Federal Census records of Sampson County, North Carolina, The spelling of the name of Mary Jane's father was found as "Gabrial" and "Gabriel."

A granddaughter tells that Mary Jane died while scrubbing her back porch with lye. A great-granddaughter says she died during her sleep after going to the back door the evening before and saying she wanted to see the sun set for the last time. Mary Jane's Certificate of Death states: "Worn out" for her cause of death. Her funeral was held on the porch of her home. She was 94 and her health must have improved somewhat after she applied for reclassification of her pension.

One great-granddaughter tells that her mother told her Mary Jane enjoyed dancing and could dance with a glass of water on her head and not spill a drop. When she was a young lady, a man kissed her on the dance floor right in front of everyone. She reached up, jerked out some of his beard and threw it on the floor. He cried, but didn't try to kiss her again. She did not want to disgrace the man and his family and refused to reveal his name.

It has been mentioned that Wiley Calvin treated her badly and her family very much wanted her to leave him, but she refused to do so.

On 15 July 1875 Mary Jane sold to James H. Turlington for $80, her claim and interest in a certain piece or parcel of land that formerly belonged to her mother, Sarah Royal, deceased. The land was bounded on the north by Haywood Crumpler's land, on the west by J. R. Mathews land, on the south by Benjamin Butler's land and on the east by Harvil Butler's land. Acreage wasn't given. Deed Registered 23 July 1875. (Compiler's note: Was "Harvil" actually "Hartwell" Butler?)

The Wiley Calvin Jackson property is now owned by a Butler Family. A few years ago, the old house was still standing and could be seen from Bearskin Road. The last time I visited relatives in Sampson County in 2002, the house was still standing, but large chicken or turkey barns blocked the view of the run-down house and the land was fenced in. The owner of the property was not home and we could not visit the cemetery. On an earlier trip, another old home was between the Wiley Calvin Home Place and Bearskin Road in the area where the large barns now stand. One of his sons may have lived in this house at one time.

Children of Wiley Jackson and Mary Royal are:

27   i.   Millard Cicero Jackson[42], born About 1862 in Sampson County , North Carolina[42]; died Bef. 1908.

         Millard C. Jackson most likely is 'Millard Cicero Jackson.' This writer was told by a close family member that Haburn Rice Jackson had a brother named 'Cicero' who died young. Millard C. Jackson is probably buried in the Wiley Calvin Jackson Family Cemetery. Wiley Cavin Jackson is the only one who has a tombstone and his cannot legally be destroyed because of his service in the Civil War. Mattie Ruth Jackson Parker Holland said there were other tombstones there at one time.

         Millard Cicero is an unusual name and has not been used in the descendants of Wiley Calvin and so far in my research, I have not found it in the ancestors or relatives of Mary Jane; very little is known about the ancestors of Wiley Calvin. Millard (Milard) is found several years later in one family who lived nearby.

You could infer from the few facts we know about Millard's father, Wiley Calvin Jackson, that Wiley was cantankerous and was inclined to displease others. Was it his rebellious attitude that led Wiley Calvin to give the name of "Millard Cicero" to his first son or was this an elusive name of an ancestor that actually gives us the name of his father or grandfather? Did Mary Jane or Wiley Calvin know that the origin of "Millard" (Millar) is English? It is derived from the Old English words "mylen" and "weard," meaning mill and guardian. The name was given to those who ran mills. There were certainly many grist mills and sawmills in the country at that time which leads to another question: why wasn't the name used more often? Of course we only find this for Cicero: (Marcus Tullius) 106-43 B.C; Rom. statesman, orator, & philosopher.

The Wiley Calvin Jackson homeplace is now owned by a Butler family.

+ 28   ii.   Wiley B. Jackson, born 25 November 1864 in Sampson County, North Carolina; died 04 January 1947 in Honeycutts Township, Sampson County, North Carolina.

+ 29   iii.   Eliza Jane Jackson, born February 1866 in Sampson County, North Carolina; died 29 August 1935 in Honeycutts Township, Sampson County, North Carolina.

   30   iv.   Randall Y. Jackson[43], born December 1869[43].

His name is also listed as Randall T. Jackson.

+ 31   v.   Flora Lee Jackson, born 19 August 1872 in Sampson County, North Carolina; died 22 December 1947 in Sampson County, North Carolina.

+ 32   vi.   Ewell Sanford Jackson, born January 1875 in Honeycutts Township, Sampson County, North Carolina; died 19 April 1954 in Honeycutts Township, Sampson County, North Carolina.

+ 33   vii.   Jemima Jewel Jackson, born 29 November 1877 in Honeycutts Township, Sampson County, North Carolina; died 21 January 1959 in Honeycutts Township, Sampson County, North Carolina.

+ 34   viii.   Haburn Rice Jackson, born 22 November 1878 in Honeycutts Township, Sampson County, North Carolina; died 24 September 1968 in Honeycutts Township, Sampson County, North Carolina.

   35   ix.   Patience Lee Jackson[44].

Patience died young. Her name was given to me by my aunt, a granddaughter of Wiley C. Jackson and Mary Jane Royal.

   36   x.   Tommy Jackson[44].

Tommy died young. His name was given to me by my aunt, a granddaughter of Wiley C. Jackson and Mary Jane Royal. No other information is known about Tommy and his sister Patience Lee.

37   xi.   Cornelius Galloway Jackson[45], born February 1882 in Sampson County, North Carolina[46]; died 17 May 1912 in Cumberland County, North Carolina[47].

On September 21, 1908, W. C. Jackson and Mary J. Jackson divided 100 acres of their land between H. R. Jackson, CORNELIUS GALLOWAY JACKSON and Mary C. Jackson and Eliza Jane Jackson.
Deed book 209, pages 306-309 records a deed in Sampson County, North Carolina from John R. and his wife, Mary McLamb to C. G. Jackson and his brother, E. S. Jackson.

In Sampson County, North Carolina, deed book 183, pages 5-7 records a deed dated 2 November 1909 from Kelly Royal and wife (Minnie Royal) to C. G. Jackson. This C. G. Jackson was "Cornelius Galloway Jackson, son of Wiley Calvin Jackson and Mary Jane Royal who was the daughter of Gabriel Royal and Sarah Crumpler. Mary Jane Royal was a sister of Gabriel Royal, Jr., Kelly's father. Kelly and Minnie sold Cornelius 8 1/2 acres for $75.00 in fee simple. Land was near the edge of Bearskin to .... Kelly Royal's line. Deed received in courthouse on 2 November 1909 and was recorded 6 November 1909

Other than the 1900 and 1910 census records, this is the only information about this Cornelius Galloway Jackson. He apparently was the Cornelius G. Jackson who died on 17 May 1912.

+   38   xii.   Mary Catherine Jackson, born 30 July 1888 in Sampson County, North Carolina; died 28 November 1955 in Sampson County Memorial Hospital, Clinton, North Carolina.

17.   Mary A.[5] **Jackson** (Hayburn[4], Hayburn[3], Unidentified[2], Unknown[1])[48] was born about 1846[48]. She married **John Strickland**[49] 29 October 1865 in Sampson County, North Carolina[50]. He was born about 1844 in Illinois[51].

Mary A. Jackson and her two younger brothers, appear to have been born after Hayburn Jackson, Jr. died; however, Hayburn Jackson, Sr., may have been married twice and it could have been Hayburn, Sr. who died in 1842 and Hayburn, Jr's work. may have kept him away from home most of the time. Mary A. Jackson was listed as 4 years under Mary Jackson in 1850; in 1860 she was listed as 12 years old. She was not listed under Mary Jackson in 1870. I believe she is the "Mary J. Stricklin" listed in the Will of her sister, Amma E. (Amy,

Amey) and Amma's husband, "T. P. (Talbert B., Tolbert B) Royal that was probated in 1899.

I believe she may have been the second wife of John Strickland and possibly he was her second spouse. John Strickland and Mary Jackson were married on 29 October 1865 in Sampson County, North Carolina.[52]

Children of Mary Jackson and John Strickland are:

39   i.   Maglenia Strickland[53], born about 1867[53].

40   ii. George A. Strickland[53], born September 1869[53].

18. Joseph E.[5] Jackson (Hayburn[4], Hayburn[3], Unidentified[2], Unknown[1])[54,55] was born About 1849 in Sampson County , North Carolina[56], and died 06 December 1928 in Sampson County , North Carolina[57]. He married **Hepsie Branch**[58] 1893[59], daughter of Jonas Branch and Sallie Hudson. She was born About 1864 in Sampson County , North Carolina[60], and died 12 August 1924 in Sampson County , North Carolina[61].

In the 1850 Federal Census, Joseph was listed as one year old under Mary Jackson; in 1860, Joseph E. Jackson was listed as 10 years under Mary J. Jackson; in 1870, Joseph F. Jackson was listed as 19 under Mary Jackson. He was listed as brother, "Joseph E. Jackson" in the Will of his sister, Amy and her husband.

His name was also listed as "Joel" in Sampson County, North Carolina, deed and one descendant of Alger Rose told me that his name was "Joel," not "Joe." Of course, census records for 1850-1880 show his name as "Joseph (E.) Jackson. The 1900 census was the first to list him as "Joal"(sic) and he and Hepsie were living near Jonah (Jonas) Branch, born January 1854 and Mary (wife of Jonas), born September 1871. Joseph and Hepsie are buried by their daughter, Sally, who appears to have had health problems and died by age 25.

Sometime around August 1920, Joseph (Joel) asked Alger Rose Holland and his wife, Tomzil, whether they and their family would like to move into his home and care for him, his wife, Hepsie, and their daughter, Sallie. Alger Rose and Tomzil agreed and inherited Joseph's farm. Alger Rose's mother, Nancy Elizabeth Hudson, and Hepsie were first cousins. Alger Rose was the informant on the Certificate of Death for "Joe Jackson." Dr. D. M. Royal listed Senility for the cause of death for Joe and about 82 for his age. No parents were listed for Joe. Alger Rose listed "Joe Jackson" for the husband of Hepsie, "Jonas Branch" for her father and "Sallie Hudson" for her mother. Both Hepsie and Joe were buried in a family cemetery; it is unclear what family cemetery. Deeds show that Joe and Hepsie owned additional land that was adjacent to the farm they gave to Alger Rose and Tomzil and that part of the land they owned was left to Helpsie by her mother, Salle Ann (nee Hudson.) Part of the land may have been part of an old Branch and/or Hudson farm. See this deed described below.

Grandpa Alger Rose Holland signed the Certificate of Death for Joseph, but apparently, he did not know the date of birth for Joseph. Of course, there is the possibility that I have linked Joseph E. incorrectly with Wiley Calvin Jackson, but tradition leads me to believe they were either whole or half-brothers and that Joseph E. was called "Joel" (Joal?) and data strongly support the relationahip between Joseph E. and of Wiley Calvin It is said that two of Wiley Calvin's grandchildren would visit with an older man who lived in a small house next door to the farm of Joseph E. Jackson (Joseph gave his farm to Alger Rose Holland) and the children called the older man "Uncle." The name of this "Uncle" has not been determined.

Other deeds:

On the 24 October 1905, J. A. (John Allen) Beaman and wife, Elizabeth (Hepsie's sister), in consideration of $135 sold to Joel (Joseph) Jackson two tracts of land. "First tract beginning at a stake in the edge of Juniper Branch on the Turlington line and runs S.86 E.88 poles to the run of Bear Skin Swamp, thence up the run of said Bear Skin about 44 poles to the mouth of Crumpler's Mill race, thence up the mill race about 68 poles to the mouth of a small ditch, thence up the said ditch as it meaders about 31 poles to the crook of ditch, thence up the south edge of branch 18 poles to the beginning containing about 32-1/2 acres.

"Second tract being lot # 4 in the division of the lands of Sarah A. Branch deceased and drawn by Betsy Simmons. Beginning at a black-gum at high water mark of the Crumpler Mill Pond and runs 88 poles to a stake on the old line, thence S 85, E. 34-1'2 poles to a Juniper of Lucian Branch's corner, thence his line down the old ditch to the run of Bear Skin, thence up the run or mill race about 34 poles to mill house sheets. Thence up the lower side of mill dam S.46 W. 4 poles to end of dam, thence (?) South Side of Mill pond at high water mark to the first station containing 33 acres more or less." Elizabeth was examined on the same day to determine whether she had voluntarily executed the deed.

Deed was received by the Register of Deeds on 19 Octobr 1912 and recorded 21 October 1912.

The deed above provides the clue that Hepsie's sister, Elizabeth (Betsy) married a Simmons and a Beamon.

On the 23rd day of November 1905 Joel Jackson and wife, Hepsy (Hepsie) Jackson ... sold 40-1/2 acres of land to M. J. Crumpler for $70. This land "Beginning at a large sweet-gum on the west side of the old Blewing Crumpler mill pond at high water mark and runs S.23 W. 46 poles to an old field pine at the old cross way of the Juniper Branch on the south side, thence up the south side of said branch about 36 poles to a stake in the old line, thence with said old line S. 86 E. 88 poles to the run of Bear Skin Swamp, thence up the run of said swamp 44 poles to the mouth of Crumpler's Mill race, thence up said mill race about 102 poles to the mill house sheets. Thence up the south side of mill dam S.46 W 4 poles to end of dam. Thence N. 40 W.3 poles to a large sweet gum the beginning corner,..." Hepsey (Hepsie) was examined on the same day to acknowledge she had voluntarily signed the deed. This deed was not recorded until 1912. This land appears to have been the small farm my parents, Oscar

Davis Jackson and Roberta (Holland) Jackson, rented for 2-3 years; my sister was born there in 1943. The land adjoined the land that Joseph (Joel) Jackson and Hepsie (nee Branch) Jackson left to my grandparents, Alger Rose Holland and Tomzel (Holland) Holland.

The mill mentioned above was the one between the farm of my paternal grandparents on what is now "The Avenue" and where my parents lived by the mill now known as the Stacy Crumpler Mill. The old Blewing (Bluman) Crumpler Mill was on Bearskin Swamp and Stacy Crumpler's Mill (built by Stacy's father, Micajah Thomas) was on a tributary of Bearskin. Several times when I was between the ages of five and eight, my dad and I walked across what remained of the Old Blewing Crumpler Mill. Until I reread the above deed and connected it with the route I walked, I had no idea the boards I so carefully walked across above the fast running water were from a mill that was probably about 100 years old. An aunt who is only 12 years older than me tells that she and her sister walked a road that was below the dam only a few years before my dad and I walked that route. Did the road wash away or did my dad take the scary route across those boards because it was shorter?

The Juniper Branch mentioned in the above deed may be the one mentioned in other deeds and I have been unable to determine where it was or, more likely, it was only one "Juniper Branch" that is mentioned in old Sampson County, North Carolina, deed.

Deed dated 22 September 1913: Joel (Joseph) Jackson gave to his spouse, Hepsie A. Jackson, in consideration of one dollar and love and affection to him, two tracts of land; one containing 18 acres and the other 25 acres. The first tract joined the lands of James McKenzie and Charlie Pope; the second tract joined the lands of M. T. Crumpler and E. T. Turlington. Deed was filed on 1 October 1913 and recorded 10 October 1913. Full description can be found in the Registry of Sampson County in Deed Book 227, page 253.

On 18 August 1920, this same land, was part of 63 acres deeded by Hepsie and Joel to Alger (Rose) Holland and wife. First tract.

Bounded "on the North by the lands of John Royal, on the East by the lands of A. S. Lockerman, on the South by the lands of John McKenzie and P. B. Lockerman, on the West by the lands of Mrs. Gussie Rachels containing 43 acres more or less. Second tract: Bounded as follows; on the North by the lands of Tom Crumpler, on the East by the lands of said Tom Crumpler, on the West by the land of A. S. Lockerman containing 25 acres of land, more or less. On the same day Hepsie was examined to determine whether she freely and voluntarily signed the deed! Deed was filed on 3 September 1920 and Recorded on 7 September 1920.

On 23 September 1921 Joel J. Jackson, Hepsie Jackson, A. R. Holland and Thomsal (Tomzil) Holland sold to Augusta Rachels two acres of land for $100. This land began at "a stake on the run of "Little Bear Skin" in the Currie line just above the Bridge at the Rachel overflow and runs S. 25, W. 46 poles to a stake in the Rachel line, thence S. 65, E. 8 poles to a stake, thence N. 25, E. 46 poles to the run of said Little Bear Skin, thence up the run of of the said Bear Skin to the beginning corner." Both wives were examined on 26 September 1921 to determine whether they voluntarily signed the deed. Deed was filed January 25, 1923 and Recorded 29 January 1923.

Joseph Jackson and Hepsie Branch were married in 1893[62]

Child of Joseph Jackson and Hepsie Branch is:

41   i.   Sallie J. Jackson[63,64], born September 1897[65].

> Sallie J. Jackson was buried in woods at edge of field across from pond on Crumpler Mill Road, Sampson County, North Carolina

19. Elisha Moore[5] Jackson (Hayburn[4], Hayburn[3], Unidentified[2], Unknown[1])[66,67] was born May 1853 in North Carolina[68], and died 24 November 1913 in Sampson County, North Carolina[68]. He married **Levinnie Cannady**[68,69], daughter of Hardy Cannady and Anny Jane Faircloth. She was born 10 June 1861 in Sampson County, North Carolina[70,71], and died 03 December 1933 in Sampson County, North Carolina[72,73].

Elisha Moore Jackson is buried in Piney Green Baptist Church Cemetery in Sampson County, North Carolina[74]

Levinnie is also spelled 'Levina,' Levinia,' 'Vinney,' and 'Leviney.' She is buried in Piney Green Baptist Church Cemetery in Sampson County, North Carolina[74] and she also has a marker at Calvary PFWB Church, near Kitty Fork, Sampson County, North Carolina.
In 1920 she was living with her son, Noah Washington Jackson. One family Bible lists her as "Lee Vina."

Children of Elisha Jackson and Levinnie Cannady are:

+ 42 i. Osway W. Jackson, born 07 May 1881 in Sampson County, North Carolina; died 27 October 1958 in Sampson County Memorial Hospital, Clinton, North Carolina.

+ 43 ii. James Trulove Jackson, born 08 February 1889 in Honeycutts Township, Sampson County, North Carolina; died 02 June 1941 in Honeycutts Township, Sampson County, North Carolina.

+ 44 iii. Hosea Moore Jackson, born 29 September 1890 in Sampson County , North Carolina; died 23 September 1988 in Sanford, Lee County, North Carolina.

+ 45 iv. Noah Washington Jackson, born February 1892 in Sampson County, North Carolina; died 1943.

+ 46 v. Alice Jane Jackson, born April 1894 in Sampson County , North Carolina.

+ 47 vi. Lula Mae Jackson, born June 1895 in Sampson County , North Carolina.

+ 48 vii. Amy Lee Jackson, born 01 September 1898 in Sampson County, North Carolina; died 17 January 1968 in Sampson County, North Carolina.

+ 49 viii. Pearl Austin Jackson, born 04 July 1901 in Sampson County , North Carolina; died 02 June 1990 in Dunn, North Carolina.

+ 50 ix. Nina Metherbell Jackson, born 17 March 1904 in Sampson County , North Carolina; died 24 September 2000 in Sampson County, North Carolina.

Generation No. 4

21. Soloman[6] **Godwin** (Aley[5] Jackson, Hayburn[4], Hayburn[3], Unidentified[2], Unknown[1])[75] was born About 1852[76]. He married **(1) Mary A. Brown**[77] 16 June 1872 in Fayetteville, Cumberland County,

North Carolina[77]. She was born about 1854[77]. He married **(2)**
Elizabeth M. Stewart[77] after 1881. She was born about 1864[77].

Children of Soloman Godwin and Mary Brown are:

+	51	i.	Britton A. Godwin, born May 1870.
	52	ii.	Hector Godwin[77], born about 1876[77].
	53	iii.	Alia Godwin[78], born about 1878[79]. She is listed as "Alia" in 1880.
	54	iv.	Rebecca Frances Godwin[79], born 16 May 1881[79].

22.   Saul[6] **Godwin** (Aley[5] Jackson, Hayburn[4], Hayburn[3],
Unidentified[2], Unknown[1])[80] was born May 1853[80]. He married
Eliza Unknown[81]. She was born about 1857[81].

Saul Godwin was listed as "Said" in the 1870 census.

Child of Saul Godwin and Eliza Unknown is:

55	i.	Charles Godwin[81], born about 1874.

23.   Simeon[6] **Godwin** (Aley[5] Jackson, Hayburn[4], Hayburn[3],
Unidentified[2], Unknown[1])[82] was born about 1856[83], and died 22 June
1902[84]. He married **Spicey Jackson**[85] 01 February 1871 in Sampson
County, North Carolina[86,87], daughter of Henry Jackson and Nancy
Strickland. She was born about 1851 in Sampson County, North
Carolina[88].

Simeon Godwin was listed as "Simeon" in the 1860 census and as
"Simon" in 1870. He was buried in Mt. Zion Church Cemetery
on Hwy 13 eight miles west of Spivey's Corner, Sampson County,
North Carolina

Simeon Godwin and Spicey Jackson were married on 01 February
1871 in Sampson County, North Carolina[89,90]

Child of Simeon Godwin and Spicey Jackson is:

56   i.   Ella Jane Godwin[91], born 12 July 1889[91]; died 06 September 1962 in Dunn, Harnett County, North Carolina[91]. She married Anson Bright Page[91]; born 30 April 1881[91]; died 24 September 1950[91].

Ella Jane Godwin was a grade school teacher.

28. Wiley B.[6] **Jackson** (Wiley Calvin[5], Hayburn[4], Hayburn[3], Unidentified[2], Unknown[1])[92] was born 25 November 1864 in Sampson County, North Carolina[93], and died 04 January 1947 in Honeycutts Township, Sampson County, North Carolina[93]. He married **Mollie Anna Lockamy**[94,95] 20 December 1899 in Sampson County, North Carolina[96], daughter of Thomas Lockamy and Martha Parker. She was born 25 August 1875 in Sampson County, North Carolina[97], and died 17 October 1938 in Highsmith Hospital, Cumberland County, North Carolina[98].

It is said that the "B" in Wiley B., was just a "B" and not an initial for a full middle name.

Wiley B. Jackson was buried on 05 January 1947 in a Lockamy Cemetery in Honeycutts Township in Sampson County, North Carolina[99]

The 1910 Federal Census for Honeycutts Township, Sampson County, North Carolina, notes what looks like 'Anna' for Mollie's middle name. Her cause of death: Carcinoma of uterus. She is buried in Sampson County, North Carolina

Wiley B. Jackson and Mollie Lockamy were married on 20 December 1899 in Sampson County, North Carolina[100]

Children of Wiley Jackson and Mollie Lockamy are:

+   57   i.   Randall B. Jackson, born 17 May 1900 in Sampson County, North Carolina; died 20 December 1965 in Honeycutts Township, Sampson County, North Carolina.
+   58   ii.   Tommy Franklin Jackson, born 02 August 1902 in Honeycutts Township, Sampson County, North Carolina; died 22 October 1972 in Honeycutts Township, Sampson County, North Carolina.

+ 59   iii. Effie Jane Jackson, born 29 October 1905; died 03 November 1968.
  60   iv. Wiley Calvin Jackson[101], born 09 October 1907 in Sampson County, North Carolina[102]; died 30 January 1995 in Mary-Gran Nursing Center, Clinton, North Carolina[103]. He married Mollie Lee Parson[104] 24 December 1933[105]; born 13 September 1917 in Johnston County, North Carolina[106]; died 02 December 1980 in Sampson County Memorial Hospital, Clinton, North Carolina[107].

  Wiley Calvin Jackson's nickname was 'Tuck.' W. C. 'Tuck' Jackson is on his tombstone. He and Mollie were married on 24 December 1933.
  Cause of death: pneumonia. He and Mollie Lee were buried in Spell-Tyndall Grove Cemetery near Clinton, North Carolina[108]

  61   v. Maggie V. Jackson[109,110], born about 1911[111]. She married Robert Hobbs[11] who died about 1989[113].

  Robert Hobbs is buried in Faison Cemetery, Faison, North Carolina

+ 62   vi. William C. Jackson, born 22 October 1914 in Sampson County, North Carolina; died 08 December 1966 in Sampson County, North Carolina.

29. Eliza Jane[6] Jackson (Wiley Calvin[5], Hayburn[4], Hayburn[3], Unidentified[2], Unknown[1])[114,115] was born February 1866 in Sampson County, North Carolina[116], and died 29 August 1935 in Honeycutts Township, Sampson County, North Carolina[117].

It has been mentioned that Eliza Jane and Minnie lived their later years in the County Home in Clinton, Sampson County, North Carolina.

Eliza Jane Jackson was buried on 30 August 1935 in a Family Cemetery, Honeycutts Township, Sampson County, North Carolina[118,119]

Child of Eliza Jackson and Unknown Father is:

  63   i. Minnie Jackson[120], born May 1887 in Sampson County , North Carolina[121]; died 04 August 1945 in Clinton, Sampson County, North Carolina[122].

Minnie Jackson had Hypertension and apoplexy (stroke.) Clinton, North Carolina was listed as her place of death meaning that she probably was living in the County Home. In the 1910 and 1920 Federal Censuses for Sampson County, North Carolina, she was listed as the granddaughter of Mary Jane; her Certificate of Death indicates that she was the daughter of Mary Jane and Wiley Calvin.

Minnie Jackson was buried on 04 August 1945 in the Wiley Calvin Jackson Family Cemetery, Sampson County, North Carolina[122]

31. Flora Lee[6] **Jackson** (Wiley Calvin[5], Hayburn[4], Hayburn[3], Unidentified[2], Unknown[1])[123,124] was born 19 August 1872 in Sampson County, North Carolina[125], and died 22 December 1947 in Sampson County, North Carolina[125]. She married **John Martin Lockamy, Jr.**[126] Bef. 1899, son of John Lockamy and Milbrey Reynolds. He was born 28 February 1853 in Sampson County, North Carolina[127], and died 06 February 1933 in Sampson County, North Carolina[128].

Flora Lee Jackson died of Degenerative Heart Disease due to arteriosclerosis for 15 years. She was buried in a Lockamy Cemetery near Kitty Fork, Sampson County, North Carolina[129]

John Martin Lockamy, Jr. was listed as aged 23 in the 1880 Federal Census for Honeycutts Township, Sampson County, North Carolina, and was living with his mother. Elizabeth and Mary A., his sisters were also noted with their mother. Also listed in that census is a daughter with the name of 'Margaret A.', aged 8. Milbrey (Milbry), the mother was listed as age 60. It is highly unlikely that she was the mother of Margaret A.

Since John Martin Lockamy was 21 years older than Flora Lee Jackson, was she his second wife?

Descendants say that John Martin owned a lot of land and was a wealthy man. He and Flora Lee were well known for their hospitality and folks knew they were always welcome in their home near Owens Grove PFW Baptist Church. The minister, his wife and other folks would have Sunday dinner with them and many times stay through supper. Martin was also known as a stingy man. He bought cheese once each year, generally after he sold his first bale of cotton. He would cut up the cheese and dip it in his coffee while saying he had to save money for "the boy," meaning his son, John Allen. He would take one bucket of water to four or five cows and made sure each cow drank only their share.

Flora Lee (called Flar Lee) wore her dresses to her ankles. At the time of her death, she was staying with Fred and her daughter, Mittie Lee (Sissy) Owens. She died of a cerebral hemmorhage. She and Martin Lockamy, Jr. were buried in a Lockamy Cemetery near Kitty Fork, Sampson County, North Carolina[129]

Children of Flora Jackson and John Lockamy are:

64   i.   Mary B. Lockamy[130], born 06 July 1899 in Sampson County , North
             Carolina[131]; died 03 February 1919 in Sampson County , North
             Carolina[131].   She married William Almond Honeycutt[131] about
             October 1917; William Almond was born about 1881 in Sampson
             County , North Carolina[131] and died 27 January 1919 in Sampson
             County , North Carolina[131].

             Both Mary B. and William Almond died of influenza pneumonia
             during the bad flu epidemic of 1918-1919.   Mary and William
             Almond had been married about 15 months and she was pregnant
             when she and William Almond died. Family tried to keep his death a
             secret from her, but shortly before she died she said that she had seen
             Almond at the window and he had come for her.   It is said that the
             William Almond's family did not approve of his marriage to Mary.
             Almond played the fiddle and would leave Mary B. some nights and
             play at dances. He would get 25-50 cents a night. His sister, Josie
             Honeycutt, played the banjo. The dances, called sprees, were held at
             different houses.

             Mary's obituary written by Mrs. Callie Herring and published in the
             newspapre in 1919:
             "Death of Mrs. Mary B. Honeycutt.
             "It is with sadness that I write of the death of Mrs. Mary B. Honeycutt,
             who passed from this world into another, on February 3, 1919. She
             was the daughter of Mr. and Mrs. Martin Lockamy and had been
             married about 15 months to Mr. W. A. Honeycutt, who died just one
             week before she did; both died with influenza pneumonia.
             "She was 19 years old. She leaves a father, mother, four sisters, two
             brothers and many relatives and friends to mourn her death.
             "Mary B. was a good girl and loved by many. She was a faithful
             member of the Free Will Baptist Church at Owen Grove. She was

sanctified and had the Holy Ghost and lived a sweet Christian life. She always had a kind word for everybody. She loved her church and will be greatly missed in Sunday School and prayer meeting, from which she was never absent, unless sickness prevented.

"During her sickness she often said that she was ready to meet her Savior. All was done for her that could be, but Jesus had a place for her, where no sickness, troubles, or trials will ever come. She died praising her Savior. So weep not father and mother, for we feel that your dear one is happy on the other shore. She was laid to rest in the family burying ground. May the Lord comfort the bereaved ones in this sad hour, and may they strive to meet Mary B. some sweet day in a home beyond the skies, where no parting will ever come.

" She is gone; but not forever
 will this separation be,
 For beside the crystal river,
 She is waiting there for me."

Mary B. Lockamy was buried in a Lockamy Family Cemetery near Kitty Fork, Sampson County, North Carolina, and William Almond Honeycutt was buried in the Honeycutt Cemetery not far from the Lockamy Family Cemetery. At the time he and Mary B. died, the Honeycutt Cemetery was behind the house where they lived; today it is on Highway 421 in Sampson County.

William Almond's obituary:
"In memory of W. A. Honeycutt.
"Sunday p.m. at 3:30 o'clock the death angel visited the home of Mr. W. A. Honeycutt and bore him from this world of sorrow and pain. He had been sick only one week with influenza and then pneumonia.
"Almond was about thirty eight years old. Having been married about one year and three months to Miss Mary B. Lockamy who was seriously ill at the time of his death.
"He will be greatly missed by his many friends and neighbors. He was a kind friend, good neighbor, dutiful son and loving husband. It was hard to part with him but we must all submit to God's will, who never commits an error. He leaves to mourn their loss a loving wife, father, mother and two sisters. Besides a host of relatives and friends.
"He was tenderly laid to rest in the family burial ground the following day.
"May God be with and comfort the bereaved ones in their hour of grief.
"A.M.L."

+ 65   ii. Mittie Lee Lockamy, born 27 October 1900 in Sampson County , North Carolina; died 07 April 1993 in Sampson County , North Carolina.

+ 66   iii. Hattie Stella Lockamy, born 22 November 1902; died 14 January 1974.

+   67   iv.   David Martin Lockamy, born 05 August 1904; died 10 October 1966.

+   68   v.   Beulah Jane Lockamy, born 28 June 1907 in Sampson County, North Carolina; died 22 October 1990 in Sampson County, North Carolina.

+   69   vi.   Lizzie Adeline Lockamy, born 08 June 1909; died 01 February 1988.

      70   vii.   John Allen Lockamy[132], born 08 December 1911 in Sampson County, North Carolina[133]; died 20 September 1955[134].

John Allen Lockamy never married. After his discharge from service in 1946, he stayed with his sister, Mittie (Sissy) and her husband, Fred Owens and died in the swing at their home. He served in WW II as a TEC4-COB-724-Military Police-B.N. While at sea, he was eating ice cream when a torpedo hit the ship and cut it in half.

Apparently, he was nice when he was sober, but many people were afraid of him when he was drinking. He spent most of his adult life fishing, drinking and serving time in prison before and after service in the U. S. Army. When his father died in 1933, he received his inheritance and none of it was left by 1938. He would go to Fayetteville in his 1937 Ford convertible , pick up several girls, ride around and drink and it was on one of these trips that he beat up one girl and locked her in the rumble seat; that earned him six months in jail. After his discharge from the Army, he wrote bad checks which earned him a second prison term. Apparently, the prison was in Fayetteville, North Carolina. He cooked while in prison and would pay off the guards, visit taverns in downtown Fayetteville, drink and return to the prison in time to cook the next meal.

It is said he would come home after drinking and make so much noise, the family could not sleep. One night he was singing nd cursing so loudly, his nephew, McKinley hit him with a tobacco stick, but did not hurt him.

John Allen Lockamy was buried in the Lockamy Cemetery near Kitty Fork, Sampson County, North Carolina[135]

32.   **Ewell Sanford[6] Jackson** (Wiley Calvin[5], Hayburn[4], Hayburn[3], Unidentified[2], Unknown[1])[136] was born January 1875 in Honeycutts Township, Sampson County, North Carolina[137,138], and died 19 April 1954 in Honeycutts Township, Sampson County, North Carolina[139,140]. He married **Ada Ann Strickland**[141] in Clinton, Sampson County, North Carolina[141], daughter of William Strickland and Louisa Branch. She was born November 1892[142,143], and died 1965 in Honeycutts Township, Sampson County, North Carolina[144].

Ewell Sanford Jackson's nickname was Sant. Wiley Calvin served in the Civil War and most likely, the name of "Ewell" comes from Confederate Brigadier-General Richard S. Ewell. Mary Jane's brother, Henry H. Royal(s) also had a son named "Sanford." In the 1910 Federal Census for Sampson County, North Carolina, Ewell Sanford is listed in the household with his mother and his name looks like "Santicco;" but it is difficult to read.

One of Ewell's nieces tells that his and Ada's home was located at the back edge of the Bearskin Missionary Baptist Church Cemetery in Sutton Town.

On 29 October 1909, Kelly Roy and his wife, Minnie Royal sold 15 acres to Ewell for the sum of $157 in fee simple. Received in courthouse in Sampson County, North Carolina, on 2 November 1909 and recorded 6 November 1909. Kelly Royal was a nephew of Ewell's mother, Mary Jane Royal.

On the 11 December 1911, John R. McLamb and Mary McLamb sold 16 1/2 acres of land to Ewell Sanford Jackson and his brother Cornelius Galloway Jackson for $500 in fee simple. Land in Honeycutts Township, Sampson County, North Carolina, beginning at a stake near the end of John Reynolds' line. Deed recorded 16 Dec 1911.

I found a marriage date of October 1914, but this could be an error; records show that they were married in Clinton, Sampson County, North Carolina[145]

Ewell Sanford Jackson and his wife, Ada Ann were buried in McGee United Methodist Church Cemetery, Sampson County, North Carolina[144]

Children of Ewell Jackson and Ada Strickland are:

71   i.   Cornelius Mathew Jackson[146], born 17 November 1914 in Honeycutts Township, Sampson County, North Carolina[147]; died October 1981 in Sampson County, North Carolina[148].

Cornelious never married and he was named after his uncle, Cornelius Galloway Jackson. His nickname was 'Sapp.' Perry Scott Jackson and Ruby Doris Jackson Lee confirmed that this "Cornelious" did lose his hair overnight, after a car wreck. I can find no tombstone for Cornelious Mathew at McGee United Methodist Church Cemetery in Sampson County, North Carolina[149]
where he is said to be buried.

Family members say another son, Samuel Jackson, was called "Sapp."

72   ii.   Stillborn Jackson[150], born 17 November 1914[150].

A Certificate of Death for a stillborn infant was dated the same as for Cornelious Mathew Jackson. Apparently, they were twins.

73   iii. Samuel Jackson[151].

Descendants say Samuel Jackson was a son of Ewell Sanford and Ada Ann and say he was known as "Sapp." Others say that it was "Cornelious Mathew," another son of Ewell, who was known as "Sapp."

+   74   iv.   Andrew Davis Jackson, born 28 May 1916 in Honeycutts Township, Sampson County, North Carolina; died 16 December 1990 in Sampson County Memorial Hospital, Clinton, North Carolina.

+   75   v.   Fleet Martin Jackson, born 06 September 1920 in Sampson County, North Carolina; died 08 August 1978.

+   76   vi.   Felton Lee Jackson, born 12 June 1927; died 09 June 1976.

77   vii. Fannie Roe Jackson[152], born 29 December 1937 in Sampson County, North Carolina[152]; died 04 May 1938 in Sampson County, North Carolina[152].

Fannie Roe Jackson was buried in McGee United Methodist Church Cemetery[152]

33. Jemima Jewel⁶ Jackson (Wiley Calvin⁵, Hayburn⁴, Hayburn³, Unidentified², Unknown¹)[153,154,155] was born 29 November 1877 in Honeycutts Township, Sampson County, North Carolina[156,157], and died 21 January 1959 in Honeycutts Township, Sampson County, North Carolina[158,159]. She married **James Thomas Lockamy**[160,161] son of Thomas Lockamy and Martha Parker. He was born 20

April 1876 in Honeycutts Township, Sampson County, North Carolina[162,163], and died 11 December 1947 in Honeycutts Township, Sampson County, North Carolina[164,165].

Jemima Jewel Jackson' first name is found in the Bullard family, but not in a direct line; Wiley Calvin's paternal grandfather married a "Bullard." Jewel Jackson was known as "Mimi" and as 'Jute.' In the Family Bible of her brother, Haburn Rice Jackson, he wrote her name as Jemime Jewel Jackson and the date she died. Of course, he probably did not know the correct spelling. Gregory Bryan Dixon's research indicates that Jemima Jewel was her name.

Jemima Jewel Jackson and James Thomas Lockamy were buried in Owens Grove Pentecostal FWB Church Cemetery in Sampson County, North Carolina[166,167,168,169]

Children of Jemima Jackson and James Lockamy are:

+ 78   i.   James Lee Lockamy, born 29 August 1901; died 07 December 1985 in Sampson County , North Carolina.
+ 79   ii. Lula Bee Lockamy, born 25 September 1903 in Honeycutts Township, Sampson County, North Carolina; died 16 May 1993 in Sampson County , North Carolina.
+ 80   iii. Robert C. Lockamy, born 29 March 1906 in Sampson County , North Carolina; died 18 January 1988 in Sampson County , North Carolina.
+ 81   iv. Flora Della Lockamy, born 05 October 1907 in Sampson County , North Carolina; died 19 June 1984 in Sampson County , North Carolina.
  82   v.   William Quince Lockamy[170], born 1909 in Sampson County , North Carolina[170]; died 1970 in Sampson County , North Carolina[170].

           William Quince Lockamy never married. He was buried in Owens Grove Pentecostal FWB Church Cemetery in Sampson County, North Carolina[170]

+ 83   vi. Martha Anna Lockamy, born 30 September 1915 in Sampson County , North Carolina; died 18 February 1995.

34. Haburn Rice[6] Jackson (Wiley Calvin[5], Hayburn[4], Hayburn[3], Unidentified[2], Unknown[1])[171] was born 22 November 1878 in

Honeycutts Township, Sampson County, North Carolina[172], and died 24 September 1968 in Honeycutts Township, Sampson County, North Carolina[172]. He married **(1) Molsey Eveline Naylor**[173] 17 October 1908 in Clinton, North Carolina[174], daughter of William Naylor and Vestina Cannady. She was born December 1883 in Honeycutts Township, Sampson County, North Carolina[175], and died 13 August 1925 in Honeycutts Township, Sampson County, North Carolina[176]. He married **(2) Joanna Naylor**[177,178] 01 February 1929 in Clinton, Sampson County, North Carolina, USA[179], daughter of William Naylor and Vestina Cannady. She was born 12 March 1880 in Sampson County, North Carolina, USA[180], and died 11 March 1970 in Sampson County, North Carolina, USA[180].

Haburn is the correct spelling of the first name of Grandfather Haburn Rice Jackson. The index for births in 1918 for Sampson County, North Carolina lists his name as "Habron R. Jackson," father of "Elmer Sikes Jackson." (Roll #: B-CO87-66001, Volume: 4, page 397.) However, "Haburn" has been recorded and transcribed so many different ways over the years, starting with very early deeds and grants of Duplin/Sampson County, North Carolina, I cannot determine the actual spelling of the given name of the earliest Hayburn (Habon) Jackson.

Grandfather Haburn's WW I draft registration card lists 1879 for his year of birth and blue for the color of his eyes; most of the writing is difficult to read. I remember him as tall and wiry.

Mary Royal, Bettie Royal and Estie Royal witnessed his marriage to Molsey at the residence of S. A. Royal. "Halburn R. Jackson" was listed for his name when he and "Joann" were married and perhaps he attempted to spell "Hayburn." Sherman Andrew (S.A.) Royal may have married them and his wife, Mary was probably a witness, but I cannot determine the relationship of Bettie and Estie.

Grandpa "Habe" told that when he worked for a neighbor, collecting rosin from pine trees, he walked barefooted and after walking for a time from tree to tree, the rosin and pine straw would stick to his feet and make it uncomfortable to walk. I can surmise that he walked barefooted to save his shoes and wonder how often he had to stop to remove the mess stuck to his feet.

In October of 1948, Haburn Rice gave each of his three sons about 17 acres of land when he found out that Oscar and Roberta were giving serious thought to buying a farm east of Clinton, North Carolina. My father, Oscar Jackson, and Uncle Elvin could not support their families with what they could earn from 17 acres and they had to work off the farm to supplement their income. After we moved to the house my parents built on their land, I had to walk past Grandpa Habe (Haburn) and Grandma (Aunt) Jo's on school days to meet the bus. I found excuses to stop and talk with them on the way home from the bus stop. About two years later the bus route was extended and I no longer had an excuse for not arriving home on time after getting off the bus.

It is said that Haburn was a "homebody" and didn't drink alcohol or use tobacco in any form. Cause of death: renal failure, general arteriosclerosis. He also fractured his hip on 17 September 1968.

Haburn Rice Jackson died in Sampson County Memorial Hospital, Clinton, North Carolina and he was buried in Sunrise memorial Gardens, Salemburg, North Carolina, USA[180]

Molsey Eveline Naylor's first name has been spelled 'Maulsey', 'Malsey', 'Malsy', 'Maulsy', 'Malcy', etc. and her tombstone shows it as "Maulcy E. Jackson." She must have been named after her Aunt 'Molsey A.' This aunt also had her name spelled 'Malcyanna.' On Haburn Rice Jackson's registration card for World War I, her name was listed "Malsy Adeline Jackson" or "Malsy 'Adelella' Jackson." A daughter says she was called "Tiny."

She died from Bright's Disease (Nephritis), an inflammation of the kidney. Her son, Oscar stated that she bled to death in a wagon on the way to the hospital in Fayetteville, North Carolina. At another time he stated that she called him to her death bed and asked him to look after his sister, Mary. Cause of death listed on Certificate of Death is Chronic nephritis. Weak kidneys and exposure. Was this exposure due to the heat during a day in August? It is said that she suffered from kidney problems most of her life.

Descendants tell that Grandma Molsey did not like her in-laws and this led Grandpa Haburn to sell the property and the home he had built on land his father had given him.

Transcribed cemetery records show 1891 for her year of birth; this appears to be incorrect. Census records of 1900 listed her age as 16. Family Bible shows December 1883.

The Naylors are said to have had "nubby" fingers and toes --- short wide thumbs that have very narrow nails, and we see this in a few of Haburn and Molsey's descendants.

Molsey Eveline Naylor was buried on 14 August 1925 in Piney Green Baptist Church Cemetery in Sampson County, North Carolina[181,182, 183]

Joanna Naylor first married Daniel Butler, and possibly during the time she and Daniel were married, she worked as a midwife and would stay with families after the baby's birth. The one dollar left to her by Daniel probably made it necessary for her to continue to work as a midwife after his death. She and her sister, Melvina, apparently also lived with familes and helped them with domestic chores during an illness.
She was a boarder with her sister, Rovene, and brother-in-law, Albert Lynn Lockamy in 1900.

Of course, Grandma Molsey died before I was born, but I fondly remember visiting Grandpa Habe (Haburn) and "Grandma Jo," (Aunt Jo) before he divided his farm among his three sons in 1948. Two of the tallest pear trees I have ever seen grew in their back yard and the pears were large also. I still remember the great taste of those pears and the stinging insects that buzzed around the trees and pears on the ground. Aunt Jo and I sampled the sauerkraut right from the jars in the smokehouse. She kept perishables cool in the water by the spring near the house and later, that spring fed a nice pond dug by my Uncle Elvin on the south side of the house. The dam for the pond was eventually destroyed by a tornado, but I remember someone mentioned that it was repaired a few years ago. Grandma Jo kept watermelons cool under her bed. I have often wished I had a rosebush as beautiful as the pink one by the front steps that she called "Seven Sisters."

I've been told that she had a nasty temper which she must have controlled when I was nearby.

Cause of death: Cardiac arrest. Senility. She was buried on 13 March 1970, in Sunrise Memorial Gardens, Salemburg, North Carolina, USA[184]

Children of Haburn Jackson and Molsey Naylor are:

+ 84   i.   Oscar Davis Jackson, born 19 July 1909 in Honeycutts Township, Sampson County, North Carolina; died 02 September 1986 in Jacksonville, Onslow County, North Carolina.

+ 85   ii.   Willard Paul Jackson, born 19 January 1911 in Honeycutts Township, Sampson County, North Carolina; died 14 November 1967 in Sampson County Memorial Hospital, Clinton, North Carolina.

+ 86   iii.   Mattie Ruth Jackson, born 01 September 1912 in Honeycutts Township, Sampson County, North Carolina; died 18 May 2006.

+ 87   iv.   Mary Jane Jackson, born 09 April 1915 in Honeycutts Township, Sampson County , North Carolina; died 20 April 1999 in Sampson County , North Carolina.

+ 88   v.   Elvin Sikes Jackson, born 30 September 1918 in Honeycutts Township, Sampson County, North Carolina; died 14 March 1987 in Honeycutts Township, Sampson County , North Carolina.

38.   Mary Catherine[6] **Jackson** (Wiley Calvin[5], Hayburn[4], Hayburn[3], Unidentified[2], Unknown[1])[186,187] was born 30 July 1888 in Sampson County, North Carolina[188], and died 28 November 1955 in Sampson County Memorial Hospital, Clinton, North Carolina[188]. She married **James Trulove Jackson**[189] after 1919, son of Elisha Jackson and Levinnie Cannady. He was born 08 February 1889 in Honeycutts Township, Sampson County, North Carolina[190], and died 02 June 1941 in Honeycutts Township, Sampson County, North Carolina[190].

Mary Catherine Jackson was called "Capper" by some family members and "Cat (Kat) by others. One older family member said she is buried in the Lockamy Cemetery near Owens Grove FWB Church in an unmarked grave. Cause of death: Hypertensive cardic vascular disease for 1 year. Family tradition says that data entered for Mary Catherine is correct. I was told that she and James Trulove eventually married after the death of his first wife, Minnie. They are either buried next to each other, or at least have stones next to each other at Owens Grove Pentecostal FW Baptist Church Cemetery [191].

In 1920, James Trulove was living with his mother and his brother, Noah, who was listed as head of household. Cause of death: Coronary thrombosis.

Children of Mary Catherine Jackson and James Trulove Jackson are:

89 i. Joseph Paul Jackson[193], born 25 March 1919 in Honeycutts Township, Sampson County, North Carolina[194]; died 03 February 1978 in Sampson County, North Carolina[195]. He married Eva Register[196]; born 07 April 1898[197]; died 24 December 1985[197].

It has been mentioned that Joseph (Josey) Paul and his sister, Susannah are both buried at the Wiley C. Jackson homeplace. They are not buried there. The property was already owned by someone else many years before Susannah died and Joseph is buried at Owen's Grove PFWB Church Cemetery in Sampson County, North Carolina.

Eva Register was buried in Trinity Methodist Church Cemetery, Magnolia, North Carolina

90 ii. Susanna Jackson[199], born 14 August 1921[200]. She married Archie Wimbley[201].

On Susanna's Certificate of Birth, her name was written "Sarah Ann." This was crossed out and "Susanna" written above it.

42. Osway W.[6] **Jackson** (Elisha Moore[5], Hayburn[4], Hayburn[3], Unidentified[2], Unknown[1])[202,203] was born 07 May 1881 in Sampson County, North Carolina[204], and died 27 October 1958 in Sampson County Memorial Hospital, Clinton, North Carolina[205]. He married **Katie Lee Strickland**[206,207] 1916, daughter of William Strickland and Louisa Branch. She was born 15 October 1899 in Sampson County, Clinton, North Carolina[208], and died 01 September 1979 in Sampson County Memorial Hospital, Clinton, North Carolina[208].

Osway Jackson's nickname was 'Auzzie' and his middle name was probably 'Washington,' as that name is found in his descendants. He was buried on 29 October 1958 in Piney Green Baptist Church Cemetery at intersection of Highway 242 and High House Road, Sampson County, North Carolina.[209] \ One source has different dates for several of Osway's children.

Katie Lee was buried on 04 September 1979 in Piney Green Baptist Church Cemetery at intersection of Highway 242 and High House Road, Sampson County, North Carolina.[210]

Children of Osway Jackson and Katie Strickland are:

+ 91   i. Willie Osway Jackson, born 10 October 1916; died 25 April 1984.

   92   ii. Hosea Almond Jackson[211,212], born 04 October 1918 in Honeycutts Township, Sampson County, North Carolina[213,214]; died 18 August 1941[215].

> Certificate of Birth for Hosea Almond spells middle name as "Alomon." Tombstone notes Hosea Almond Jackson, son of O. W. and Katie Lee Jackson. Lincoln MacDonald (Mack) Jackson, Hosea Almond Jackson's brother, told me that Hosea was on leave from service and was killed soon after he arrived home. A log truck hit his car. 'Hosea Almond Jackson' is on his tombstone. He was buried in Owens Grove Pentecostal FWB Church Cemetery, Sampson County, North Carolina[216]

+ 93   iii. Addie May Jackson, born 25 March 1920 in Honeycutts Township, Sampson County, North Carolina; died Aft. 2001.

94   iv. Wilbert Lee Jackson[217], born 07 July 1921 in Honeycutts Township, Sampson County, North Carolina[217]; died 15 December 1921 in Honeycutts Township, Sampson County, North Carolina[217]. My notes from vital records in Sampson County, North Carolina indicate, his full name was Wilbert Lee Jackson and the cause of death was Spinal meningitis. He was buried at Piney Green Baptist Church Cemetery at intersection of Highway 242 and High House Road, Sampson County, North Carolina[217]

95   v. David Fulton Jackson[218,219], born 10 January 1923 in Sampson County, North Carolina[220]; died 22 May 1999 in Charlotte, Mecklenburg County, North Carolina[220]. He married Christine Pope[221]; born 11 August 1926[222]; died 11 July 1993 in Charlotte, Mecklenburg County, North Carolina[222].
David Fulton Jackson's nickname was 'PECK' He was killed in 1999 in Charlotte, North Carolina. The Birth Index of Sampson County, North Carolina may list June 10, 1923 for his date of birth.

+ 96   vi. Leon Calvin Jackson, born 01 September 1924 in Sampson County, North Carolina; died 04 August 1986 in Sampson County, North Carolina.

+ 97   vii. Lattie Pearl Jackson, born 07 March 1926 in Sampson County, North Carolina.

98   viii. Earl Lee Jackson[223], born 28 September 1928 in Sampson County, North Carolina[224]; died 06 January 1968 in Sampson County, North Carolina[224]. He married Louise Huffman[225]; born Aft. 1930.

Earl Lee Jackson's nickname was 'Jay Bird.' He died while serving in the Vienam War. He was buried in Owens Grove Pentecostal FWB Church Cemetery, Sampson County, North Carolina[226]

99   ix. Raymond D. Jackson[227], born 08 January 1931 in Sampson County, North Carolina[228]; died 23 February 1994 in Sampson County Memorial Hospital, Clinton, North Carolina[228].

Raymond D. never married. Cause of death: Acute respiratory failure from Chronic obstructive pulmonary disease. He was buried in Spell-Tyndall Grove Cemetery near Clinton, North Carolina[228]

100   x. John Thomas Jackson[229], born 12 December 1932 in Sampson County, North Carolina[230]; died 19 September 1985 in Clinton, Sampson County, North Carolina[230].

John Thomas Jackson never married. He was buried on 21 September 1985 in Owens Grove Pentecostal FWB Church Cemetery in Sampson County, North Carolina[230]

101   xi. Henry M. Jackson[231], born December 1934 in Honeycutts Township, Sampson County, North Carolina[232]; died 08 January 1935 in Honeycutts Township, Sampson County, North Carolina[233].

Henry M. Jackson was buried on 09 January 1935 in a Family Cemetery in Honeycutts Township, Sampson County, North Carolina[233]

+ 102   xii.   Mollie Louise Jackson, born 29 May 1936 in Sampson County, North Carolina.
+ 103   xiii.   Lincoln MacDonald Jackson, born 04 April 1938.
   104   xiv.   Astor Washington Jackson[234], born 30 July 1943[234]. He married Rebecca Bryant[234]; born 01 April 1953[234].

43.   **James Trulove[6] Jackson** (Elisha Moore[5], Hayburn[4], Hayburn[3], Unidentified[2], Unknown[1])[235] was born 08 February 1889 in Honeycutts Township, Sampson County, North Carolina[236], and died 02 June 1941 in Honeycutts Township, Sampson County, North Carolina[236]. He married **(1) Minnie Unknown**[237] Bef. 1919. He married **(2) Mary Catherine Jackson**[238,239] Aft. 1919, daughter of Wiley Jackson and Mary Royal. She was born 30 July 1888 in Sampson County, North Carolina[240], and died 28 November 1955 in Sampson County Memorial Hospital, Clinton, North Carolina[240].

James Trulove served in World War I. In 1920, he was living with his mother and his brother Noah was listed as head of household. This may have been after James Trulove lost his first wife. He died from Coronary thrombosis and was buried on 03 June 1941 in Owens Grove Pentecostal FWB Church Cemetery, Sampson County, North Carolina[241]

He second wife was called "Capper" by some family members and "Cat (Kat) by others. One older family member said she is buried in the Lockamy Cemetery near Owens Grove FWB Church in an unmarked grave. Cause of death: Hypertensive cardic vascular disease for 1 year. I was told that she and James Trulove eventually married after the death of his wife, Minnie. James Trulove and Mary Catherine are either buried next to each other, or at least have stones next to each other, at Owens Grove Pentecostal FW Baptist Church Cemetery. Mary Catherine was buried on 30 November 1955.

Child of James Jackson and Minnie ?? is:

+ 105   i. James Leslie Jackson, born 30 April 1934.

Children of James Trulove and Mary Catherine are listed above under (38) Mary Catherine Jackson.

44.   Hosea Moore[6] Jackson (Elisha Moore[5], Hayburn[4], Hayburn[3], Unidentified[2], Unknown[1])[243] was born 29 September 1890 in Sampson County , North Carolina[244], and died 23 September 1988 in Sanford, Lee County, North Carolina[244]. He married **Allene Hunt**[245] 24 June 1930. She was born in Moore County, North Carolina.

The data in the source was submitted by Hosea Moore Jackson. Hosea attended Benson High School, 1910-1913 and from 1914-1915, he attended The University of North Carolina. After serving in World War I, he studied law at Valparaiso University in Indiana and "earned his LL.B. degree from University of North Carolina Law School in 1920." After passing the bar examination , he finished his liberal arts education at Wake Forst College in 1921 and moved to Sanford on 5 September 1921.

Child of Hosea Jackson and Allene Hunt is:

+ 106   i. George Moore Jackson, born 20 October 1941; died November 1987 in Bridgeton, Craven County, North Carolina.

45.   Noah Washington[6] Jackson (Elisha Moore[5], Hayburn[4], Hayburn[3], Unidentified[2], Unknown[1])[246] was born February 1892 in Sampson County, North Carolina[247,248], and died 1943[249]. He married **Mary Lizzie Ellis**[249,250] Bef. 1930, daughter of Marion Ellis and Lou Stallings. She was born 1908[251], and died 1983[251].

In 1920, he was living with his mother and was listed as head of household. James Trulove, Pearl, and Nina were also listed with him. Noah Washington Jackson and Mary Lizzie were buried in Owens

Grove Pentecostal FWB Church Cemetery, Sampson County, North Carolina[251]

Children of Noah Jackson and Mary Ellis are:

+   107   i.   Lucille Jackson, born 06 October 1930.
+   108   ii.   Almoye W. Jackson, born 26 March 1933.
+   109   iii.   J. B. Jackson, born 02 November 1935.

46. Alice Jane[6] **Jackson** (Elisha Moore[5], Hayburn[4], Hayburn[3], Unidentified[2], Unknown[1])[252] was born April 1894 in Sampson County , North Carolina[252]. She married **James Noah Wise**[253] Bef. 1912. He was born 02 September 1885[254], and died 16 March 1945[254].

Alice Jane Jackson Wise died when her last child was about two months old. Family says her date of birth was 2 September 1895. The 1900 census lists April 1894 for her and June 1894 for her sister, Lula Mae. James Noah Wise was buried in Owens Grove Pentecostal FWB Church Cemetery, Sampson County, North Carolina.

Children of Alice Jackson and James Wise are:

     110   i.   Mary Wise[255]. She married Unknown Grant[256].
+   111   ii.   Elsie Lee Wise, born 26 January 1911; died 13 August 1971 in Clinton, North Carolina.
+   112   iii.   James Franklin Wise, born 23 April 1913 in Sampson County , North Carolina; died January 1978.
+   113   iv.   Celester Wise, born 02 January 1916; died 28 October 1990.
+   114   v.   Annie Kathleen Wise, born 10 October 1917; died 09 May 1993.
+   115   vi.   Janie Wise, born Aft. 1917 in Erwin, North Carolina.

47. Lula Mae[6] **Jackson** (Elisha Moore[5], Hayburn[4], Hayburn[3], Unidentified[2], Unknown[1])[256] was born June 1895 in Sampson County , North Carolina[256]. She married **Robbie Thornton**[256,257].

Children of Lula Jackson and Robbie Thornton are:

116   i.   Hardy Thornton[258], born in Unknown. He married Alease Edwards[258] Unknown

117   ii.   Mott Thornton[258]. He married Betty Unknown[259]

          Moth Thornton and Betty had two children; names unknown

48. Amy Lee[6] Jackson (Elisha Moore[5], Hayburn[4], Hayburn[3], Unidentified[2], Unknown[1])[260] was born 01 September 1898 in Sampson County, North Carolina[261], and died 17 January 1968 in Sampson County, North Carolina[261]. She married **William Harvey Pope**[262,263] 10 January 1915 in Sampson County, North Carolina.[264], son of Unknown Pope and Mary Unknown. He was born 22 October 1896 in North Carolina[264], and died 21 February 1970 in North Carolina[265].

On Amy Lee Jackson and W. H. Pope's marriage license, she is listed as "Annie Lee Jackson". Amy Lee Jackson was buried in Owens Grove Pentecostal FWB Church Cemetery, Sampson County, North Carolina[266]

William Harvey Pope is said to have been buried at Shady Grove FWB Church Cemetery, but records indicate that he was either buried in, or he has as tombstone in Owens Grove Pentecostal FWB Church Cemetery, Sampson County, North Carolina[266]

Children of Amy Jackson and William Pope are:

118   i.   Alice Pope[267], born in Sampson County, North Carolina. She married Dillon Daniels[268].

119   ii.   Sudie L. Pope[269], born About 1920 in Sampson County, North Carolina. She married Curt Blackburn[269].

120   iii.   Paul Pope[270], born 24 August 1925 in North Carolina[270]. He married Grace Westbrook[270].

121   iv.   William Harvey Pope. Jr.[271], born 13 January 1927 in Sampson County, North Carolina[271]; died 18 August 1927 in Sampson County, North Carolina[272].

William Harvey Pope. Jr. was buried in Owens Grove Pentecostal FWB Church Cemetery, Sampson County, North Carolina[273]

122   v.   Gaynelle Pope[274], born 09 August 1928 in North Carolina[275]; died 20 May 1998[276]. She married Berlye L. Mazingo[277,278]; born 01 January 1929[279].

Gaynelle Pope was buried in Owens Grove Pentecostal FWB Church Cemetery, Sampson County, North Carolina[280]

123   vi.   Amos Coland Pope[281], born 25 March 1931 in Sampson County, North Carolina[281]; died 18 June 1932 in Sampson County, North Carolina[281].

Amos Coland Pope was buried in Owens Grove Pentecostal FWB Church Cemetery, Sampson County, North Carolina[282]

+ 124   vii. Preston Carr Pope, born 16 February 1935 in Sampson County, North Carolina.

   125   viii. William Robert Pope[283], born 01 June 1939 in Sampson County, North Carolina[284]; died 01 June 1939 in Sampson County, North Carolina[285].

William Robert Pope was buried in Owens Grove Pentecostal FWB Church Cemetery, Sampson County, North Carolina[285]

49. Pearl Austin[6] Jackson (Elisha Moore[5], Hayburn[4], Hayburn[3], Unidentified[2], Unknown[1])[286] was born 04 July 1901 in Sampson County , North Carolina, and died 02 June 1990 in Dunn, North Carolina. He married **Madge Elizabeth Hall**[287] About 1930[288], daughter of Lalice Hall and Dona Tew. She was born 22 June 1905[288], and died 29 January 2002 in Dunn, North Carolina[288].

Pearl Austin Jackson's middle name was also spelled "Ostin." Minister. One source mentions he and Madie had eleven children, six unknown.

Pearl was living with his brother, Noah, and his mother in 1920.

Children of Pearl Jackson and Madge Hall are:

126   i.   Pearl E. Jackson[289], born 1928 in Harnett County, North Carolina[289].

127   ii.   Fonza Elizabeth Jackson[290], born 18 May 1932 in Harnett County, North Carolina[291]; died 07 December 1998 in Dunn, North Carolina[291].

128   iii. F. D. Jackson[292].

129   iv.   Marie Jackson[292].

130   v.   Elizabeth Jackson[292].

50.   Nina Metherbell[6] **Jackson** (Elisha Moore[5], Hayburn[4], Hayburn[3], Unidentified[2], Unknown[1])[293] was born 17 March 1904 in Sampson County , North Carolina[294], and died 24 September 2000 in Sampson County, North Carolina[295]. She married **Robert Owen Lockamy**[296] 26 September 1925 in Sampson County, Clinton, North Carolina[297], son of John Lockamy and Onie Holland. He was born 02 September 1904 in Sampson County, North Carolina[298], and died 01 July 1966 in Sampson County, North Carolina[298].

Robert Owen Lockamy went by the nickname "Buddy". He and Nina Metherbell Jackson were buried in Owens Grove Pentecostal FWB Church Cemetery, Sampson County, North Carolina[299]

Children of Nina Jackson and Robert Lockamy are:

+   131   i.   Astraudia Brown Lockamy, born 14 September 1926 in Sampson County, North Carolina; died 21 December 1995 in Sampson County, North Carolina.

    132   ii.   James Roland Lockamy[303], born 28 March 1928[304]; died October 2006[305]. He married Flora Jane Hall[306]; born in Sampson County , North Carolina.

Generation No. 5

51.   Britton A.[7] **Godwin** (Soloman[6], Aley[5] Jackson, Hayburn[4], Hayburn[3], Unidentified[2], Unknown[1])[307] was born May 1870[307]. He married **Mary F. Young**[307]. She was born About 1874[307].

Children of Britton Godwin and Mary Young are:

+   133   i.   Carson Blaine Godwin, born 14 July 1908 in Sampson County, North Carolina; died 1966 in Wallum Lake, Rhode Island.

134	ii.	John E. Godwin[307], born August 1898[307]; died 1910[307].
135	iii.	Herman Lain Godwin[307], born 18 November 1903[307]; died October 1970 in Boston, Massachusetts[307].
136	iv.	Living Godwin[307].
137	v.	Eschol Sherman Godwin[307], born 11 November 1910[307]; died January 1975 in Durham, North Carolina[307].

57. Randall B.[7] Jackson (Wiley B.[6], Wiley Calvin[5], Hayburn[4], Hayburn[3], Unidentified[2], Unknown[1])[308,309] was born 17 May 1900 in Sampson County, North Carolina[310], and died 20 December 1965 in Honeycutts Township, Sampson County, North Carolina[310]. He married **Bannie Clyde Lockamy**[311] 20 June 1922 in Clinton, Sampson County, North Carolina[312], daughter of William Lockamy and Fannie Honeycutt. She was born 29 April 1905 in Sampson County, North Carolina[313], and died 20 November 1969 in Sampson County, North Carolina[313].

Randall B. Jackson was buried on 21 December 1965; he and Bannie Clyde were buried in Owens Grove Pentecostal FWB Church Cemetery, Sampson County, North Carolina[314]

It is said that in the 1930's, Bannie's father, William Solomon, built a store about a mile from Kitty Fork for her and her husband, Randall Jackson. The story was later run by William Solomon's daughter, Emily, and her husband, Jerry Gallagher. Bannie and Randall later built a smaller store beside the first one and made the larger store into their home.

Children of Randall Jackson and Bannie Lockamy are:

138	i.	Warren Stancil Jackson[317], born 24 March 1923 in North Carolina[318]; died 24 February 1986 in Sampson County, North Carolina[318]. He married Lora Warren[319]; born 08 May 1920 in Honeycutts Township, Sampson County, North Carolina[319,320].
		Warren Stancil Jackson was buried in Grandview Memorial Gardens, Clinton, Sampson County, North Carolina

+ 139   ii. William B. Jackson, born 06 November 1925 in Sampson County, North Carolina; died 31 January 1995 in Sampson County Memorial Hospital, Clinton, North Carolina.
+ 140   iii. Claudia Priscilla Jackson, born 01 November 1938 in Sampson County, North Carolina.
+ 141   iv. J. W. Jackson, born 08 October 1942.

58.   Tommy Franklin[7] Jackson (Wiley B.[6], Wiley Calvin[5], Hayburn[4], Hayburn[3], Unidentified[2], Unknown[1])[321] was born 02 August 1902 in Honeycutts Township, Sampson County, North Carolina[322], and died 22 October 1972 in Honeycutts Township, Sampson County, North Carolina[322].   He married **Carrie Lee Simmons**[323] 05 November 1921 in North Clinton Township, Clinton, North Carolina[324], daughter of William Simmons and Mary Lockamy. She was born 1903 in Sampson County, North Carolina[325], and died 1984 in Sampson County, North Carolina[325].

Tommy Franklin Jackson's tombstone reads 'E' for his middle initial. Apparently this was incorrect.

His Certificate of Birth shows 9 September 1922 for his date of birth. His Certificate of Death indicates 9 October 1922 for his birth and that he was buried in Lockamy Family Cemetery, but cemetery records list him in the Spell-Tyndall Cemetery. He listed "Tom Jackson" for his name when he and Carrie Simmons were married in Clinton, Sampson County, North Carolina. He was buried on 24 October 1972; he and Carrie Lee were buried in Spell-Tyndall Grove Cemetery near Clinton, North Carolina[326,327]

Children of Tommy Jackson and Carrie Simmons are:

+ 142   i.   Ester Jackson, born About 1922; died About 1943.
+ 143   ii. Callie Estelle Jackson, born 24 August 1924 in Sampson County, North Carolina; died 13 March 2006.
+ 144   iii. Edna Lee Jackson, born 04 August 1928; died 31 December 1966.
+ 145   iv. Bernice Franklin Jackson, born 26 October 1931 in Sampson County, North Carolina; died 11 December 2003.
   146   v.   Wiley Leoner Jackson[329], born 12 April 1935 in Sampson County, North Carolina[330]; died 14 April 1935[331].

> Wiley Leoner Jackson was buried at "Old Sauls Place." This cemetery is probably either off or near an old road that is now named "McKenzie Road".

+ 147   vi.   William Robert Jackson, born 08 August 1938.
+ 148   vii. Thomas A. Jackson, born 30 November 1944 in Sampson County, North Carolina.

59. Effie Jane[7] Jackson (Wiley B.[6], Wiley Calvin[5], Hayburn[4], Hayburn[3], Unidentified[2], Unknown[1])[332,333] was born 29 October 1905[334], and died 03 November 1968[334]. She married **Benjamin Franklin Tyndall, Sr.**[335] 16 August 1923[336], son of Joshua Tyndall and Jane Butler. He was born August 1896 in Sampson County , North Carolina[336,337], and died 12 April 1965[338].

A relative has indicated to this writer that Effie and Benjamin had one daughter. Transcribed cemetery records shows 14 August 1905(?) for Benjamin's birth.

Effie Jane Jackson and Benjamin Franklin Tyndall, Sr. were buried in Calvary Tabernacle PFB Church Cemetery, 1 mile from intersection of Hwy 242 and High House Road, Sampson County, North Carolian

Children of Effie Jackson and Benjamin Tyndall are:

+ 149   i.   Donnie Pittman Tyndall, born 23 June 1926 in Honeycutts Township, Sampson County, North Carolina; died 10 June 1968 in Clinton, North Carolina.
+ 150   ii.   Benjamin Franklin Tyndall, Jr., born 14 June 1933; died 26 March 1984.
  151   iii. Lawrence B. Tyndall[339,340], born 1937[340]; died 1984[340].

> Lawrence B. Tyndall was buried in Calvary Tabernacle Pentecostal FW Baptist Church Cemetery, on High House Road one mile west of Highway 242, Sampson County, North Carolina

62. William C.[7] Jackson (Wiley B.[6], Wiley Calvin[5], Hayburn[4], Hayburn[3], Unidentified[2], Unknown[1])[341] was born 22 October 1914 in Sampson County, North Carolina[341,342], and died 08 December 1966 in Sampson County, North Carolina[342]. He married **Lattie Pearl Jackson**[343], daughter of Osway Jackson and Katie Strickland. She was born 07 March 1926 in Sampson County, North Carolina[343].

William C. Jackson was known as Sambo Jackson. I have never found a full middle name and doubt that the name "Calvin" would have been given for a second time, but it was not unusual for the same middle name to be given to children, at the time. Cicero was the middle name of an uncle.

William C. Jackson was buried in a Lockamy Cemetery near Kitty Fork, Sampson County, North Carolina[344]

Lattie Pearl personally told me that she and William C. Jackson were first cousins. I have been told that her mother and William C's mother were sisters. However, William's mother was a Lockamy. Her mother, Katie Lee Strickland, was a sister to Ada Ann Strickland, spouse of Ewell Sanford Jackson, William's uncle. I have found nothing to confirm that Lattie Pearl and William C. were first cousins through the Strickland line; that kinship had to have been through the Jackson line (through their paternal grandfather. Of course, they were related through the Strickland line, but they were not first cousins.

Children of William Jackson and Lattie Jackson are:

152	i.	Bobby Ray Jackson[345], born 23 August 1953[345].
+ 153	ii.	Wanda Faye Jackson, born 23 August 1953.

65. Mittie Lee[7] Lockamy (Flora Lee[6] Jackson, Wiley Calvin[5], Hayburn[4], Hayburn[3], Unidentified[2], Unknown[1])[346,347] was born 27 October 1900 in Sampson County , North Carolina[348], and died 07 April 1993 in Sampson County , North Carolina[348]. She married **Fred Owens**[349,350] 24 August 1921 in Unknown[351], son of Thomas Owens and Minnie Lockamy. He was born 02 October 1897 in

Kitty Fork, Sampson County, North Carolina[351], and died 13 October 1996 in Kitty Fork, Sampson County, North Carolina[351].

Mittie Lee and Fred Owens were buried in Owens Grove Pentecostal FWB Church Cemetery, Sampson County, North Carolina[351]

It is mentioned in "Footprints From Kitty Fork" that Fred grew up in a house with no windows, but had shutters to open for light. The chimney was made of clay and sticks and Fred remembered the sticks catching fire once. Fred went to three different schools in Sampson County. At about six years of age, he started to attend Skeeter Hill School that was located on what is now High House Road and when it closed around 1910, he then attended Belvoir School on Beaverdam Road (now called Belvoir School Road.) Teachers at Belvoir were Miss Royal and Miss Lucy Herring who encouraged Fred to board at her family's house and attend a larger school. Not able to afford to attend the larger school, he then attended Carver Dale School, named for Alex Carver where he was taught by Miss Nollie, daughter of Joe Nollie. He had to teach her how to work arithmetic problems. After one month, he left school to help his father on the farm.

Miss Sannie Smith taught all grades for four months out of the year---November-February at Skeeter Hill School, a one room frame building that was heated by a wood burning stove in the center of the room. Belvoir School was near Harrells Store. Carver Dale School was in front of the Archie Newman home place near Kitty Fork in Sampson County, on land owned by John Robert Lockamy (Fred's Uncle) and his wife, Onie Holland Lockamy. It was named after Alexander Royal Carver, grandson of Reason Royal and son of Edith B. Royal and David Carver, Jr. Teachers there were Mrs. Effie Butler, Mrs. Maude Malpass Parker and Mrs. Ioa Matthis. Around 1921, John Robert Lockamy decided he wanted the Carver Dale School out of his field and moved the building to where Owens Grove Church Cemetery is now located. The school remained open for about three years; students then attended the new Herring School built about 10 miles north of Clinton on Highway 421.

Children of Mittie Lockamy and Fred Owens are:

154   i.   William McKinley Owens[352], born 19 June 1924 in Kitty Fork, Sampson County, North Carolina[352]; died 17 February 2007 in Sampson County , North Carolina[353]. He married Clarice Cannady[354] 25 December 1947[355]; born 27 July 1929 in Bonnetsville, Sampson County, North Carolina[355]; died 21 February 2007 in Sampson County , North Carolina[356].

Notes for William McKinley Owens:
William McKinley and Clarice lived near Kitty Fork in Sampson County, North Carolina. He died at Carrol S. Roberson Hospice Center in Fayetteville, North Carolina.

William McKinley and Clarice Owens were buried in Owens Grove Pentecostal FW Baptist Church Cemetery near Kitty Fork in Sampson County, North Carolina. Clarice was living at Southwood Nursing and Retirement Center in Clinton, North Carolina, when she died.

+ 155   ii.   Eunice Mae Owens, born 18 June 1935 in Honeycutts Township, Sampson County, North Carolina.

66. Hattie Stella[7] Lockamy (Flora Lee[6] Jackson, Wiley Calvin[5], Hayburn[4], Hayburn[3], Unidentified[2], Unknown[1])[358,359] was born 22 November 1902[359], and died 14 January 1974[360]. She married **Perdie Hall**[361], son of James Hall and Sallie Sessoms. He was born 17 September 1900 in Sampson County , North Carolina[362], and died 24 May 1978[362].

Hattie Stella Lockamy Hall and Perdie Hall were buried in a Hall Family Cemetery on Perdie Hall Road, Sampson County, North Carolina

Children of Hattie Lockamy and Perdie Hall are:

156   i.   Flora Jane Hall[363], born in Sampson County , North Carolina. She married James Roland Lockamy[364]; born 28 March 1928[365]; died October 2006[366].

157   ii.   Gerald Hall[367]. He married Blanche Nolen[367]; born About 1908[367]; died 11 November 1997[367].

Blanche Nolen Hall was buried in a Hall Family Cemetery on Perdie Hall Road, Sampson County, North Carolina

+ 158   iii. Lossie Mae Hall, born 26 September 1923; died 28 August 1987.

159   iv. Dorothy Hall[367], born About 1925[367]; died 25 May 1999[367]. She married William A. Wooldridge[367]; died 02 February 2005[367].

Dorothy Hall had two children.

160   v. David Hall[367].

David Hall never married.

67. David Martin[7] **Lockamy** (Flora Lee[6] Jackson, Wiley Calvin[5], Hayburn[4], Hayburn[3], Unidentified[2], Unknown[1])[368] was born 05 August 1904[369,370], and died 10 October 1966[371]. He married **Hattie Elizabeth Tyndall**[372,373] 25 December 1933[374], daughter of L. Tyndall and Venie Unknown. She was born 12 August 1913 in Dismal Township, Sampson County, North Carolina[374,375], and died 13 April 1994[376].

Hattie Elizabeth died in a car accident. She and David Martin Lockamy were buried in a Lockamy Cemetery near Kitty Fork, Sampson County, North Carolina[376]

Children of David Lockamy and Hattie Tyndall are:

+ 161   i. Edna Lee Lockamy, born 13 September 1934.
+ 162   ii. Wiley Martin Lockamy, born 01 January 1937.
+ 163   iii. Alice Faye Lockamy, born 28 November 1941.
+ 164   iv. William David Lockamy, born 23 August 1951; died 22 June 1996.

68. Beulah Jane[7] **Lockamy** (Flora Lee[6] Jackson, Wiley Calvin[5], Hayburn[4], Hayburn[3], Unidentified[2], Unknown[1])[377,378] was born 28 June 1907 in Sampson County, North Carolina[379], and died 22 October 1990 in Sampson County, North Carolina[379]. She married **Raymond Gray Lockamy**[380] 22 February 1936[381], son of William Lockamy and Fannie Honeycutt. He was born 22 May 1900 in

Sampson County, North Carolina[382], and died 24 November 1966 in Sampson County, North Carolina[382].
Beulah Jane Lockamy and Raymond Gray Lockamy were buried in Owens Grove Pentecostal FWB Church Cemetery, Sampson County, North Carolina[382]

Child of Beulah Lockamy and Raymond Lockamy is:

+   165   i.   Fannie Lee Lockamy, born 05 August 1941.

69.   Lizzie Adeline[7] Lockamy (Flora Lee[6] Jackson, Wiley Calvin[5], Hayburn[4], Hayburn[3], Unidentified[2], Unknown[1])[384,385,386] was born 08 June 1909[387], and died 01 February 1988[387]. She married **William Elmer McLamb**[388]. He was born 03 October 1906[389], and died 23 May 1973 in Sampson County , North Carolina[389].

"Almer" is also listed for the middle name of William Elmer. He and Lizzie Adeline Lockamy were buried in Owens Grove PFWB Church Cemetery, Sampson County, North Carolina.

Children of Lizzie Lockamy and William McLamb are:

+   166   i.   Doris Allese McLamb, born 10 March 1930 in Herrings Township, Sampson County, North Carolina.
     167   ii.   Edith Gray McLamb[390], born 22 August 1936[390]; died 22 December 1962[390]. She married Darrel Gunter[390].

                   Edith Gray McLamb was buried in Owens Grove Pentecostal FWB Church Cemetery, Kitty Fork, Sampson County, North Carolina

     168   iii.   Sophronie Lee McLamb[390], born 06 November 1937[390]; died 06 November 1937[390].

                   Sophronie Lee McLamb was buried om a Lockamy Family Cemetery near Kitty Fork, Sampson County, North Carolina

74. Andrew Davis[7] Jackson (Ewell Sanford[6], Wiley Calvin[5], Hayburn[4], Hayburn[3], Unidentified[2], Unknown[1])[391] was born 28 May 1916 in Honeycutts Township, Sampson County, North Carolina[392], and died 16 December 1990 in Sampson County Memorial Hospital, Clinton, North Carolina[393]. He married **Georgia Long**[394,395], daughter of Ammie Long and Laura Lockamy. She was born 02 March 1918[396,397], and died 28 November 1986 in Sampson County, North Carolina[398].

Andrew Davis Jackson was a carpenter and was known as "Boot." Cause of death: Acute pulmonary infection resulting from aspiration and cerebral vascular accident. Other factor: Severe Peripheral vascular disease.

The Birth Index of Sampson County, North Carolina records a birth for Fannie Ray, born 29 December 1937 and gives her father as Andrew D. Jackon

Andrew Davis Jackson and Georgia (Georgianna) were buried in McGee United Methodist Church Cemetery, Sampson County, North Carolina[399]

Children of Andrew Jackson and Georgia Long are:

169   i.   Ruby Doris Jackson[401], born 11 September 1940 in Sampson County, North Carolina[401]. She married Johnny Lee[401] 24 December 1959[401]; born 13 May 1937[402]; died 12 November 1975.

Johnny Lee was buried in McGee United Methodist Church Cemetery[403]

+ 170   ii. Joyce Ann Jackson, born 1945; died 01 March 2001 in Holly Springs, Wake, North Carolina.

+ 171   iii. Larry Davis Jackson, born 13 January 1946 in North Carolina.

+ 172   iv. Hilda Grey Jackson, born 17 March 1947 in North Carolina.

+ 173   v. Perry Scott Jackson, born 26 September 1949 in North Carolina.

174   vi. Johnny Mac Jackson[405], born 05 June 1950[405]. He married Ruthie Sessoms[405].

Johnny Mac Jackson has old pictures of the family.

+ 175   vii. Brenda Faye Jackson, born 27 May 1951.

75. Fleet Martin[7] **Jackson** (Ewell Sanford[6], Wiley Calvin[5], Hayburn[4], Hayburn[3], Unidentified[2], Unknown[1])[406] was born 06 September 1920 in Sampson County, North Carolina[407], and died 08 August 1978[407]. He married **Peggy Starling**[408], daughter of Ed Starling.

Fleet Martin Jackson was buried in Burial: McGee United Methodist Church Cemetery in Sampson County, North Carolina[409]

Peggy Starling was from Maryland.

Children of Fleet Jackson and Peggy Starling are:

176	i.	Ray Jackson[410].
177	ii.	Sharon Jackson[410].

76. Felton Lee[7] **Jackson** (Ewell Sanford[6], Wiley Calvin[5], Hayburn[4], Hayburn[3], Unidentified[2], Unknown[1])[410] was born 12 June 1927[411], and died 09 June 1976[412]. He married **Sadie Elizabeth Faircloth**[413].

Felton Lee Jackson owned a nursery and landscaping businesss. Cousins mention that Jimmy, his son, is still in business. A business: Jimmy Jackson Landscaping, Kar-Hea Nursery, Inc., was listed as a business on Hwy 24, Stedman, North Carolina. The name, "Kar-Hea" is, most likely, influenced by the Great Coharie and Little Coharie Rivers. I have unable to reach his children.

Felton Lee Jackson and Sadie Elizabeth were buried in Oak Grove Pentecostal FWB Cemetery, Stedman, North Carolina[414]

Children of Felton Jackson and Sadie Faircloth are:

178	i.	James Andrew Jackson, born 26 May 1951 in Cumberland County, North Carolina[415].
179	ii.	Michael Jackson[415].

180   iii.   Donald Wayne Jackson[415], born 16 May 1955[416]; died 26 October 1997[416].

Donald Wayne Jackson was buried in Oak Grove Pentecostal Free Will Baptist Church Cemeteryon Oak Grove Church Road, near Stedman, North Carolina

181   iv.   Deborah Joy Jackson, born 19 April 1952 in Cumberland County, North Carolina[417].

I found a Debbie Jackson, but was unable to reach her.

182   v.   Elizabeth Marcelle Jackson[417,418], born 17 March 1959 in Fayetteville, North Carolina[418]. She married Dennis Clay Matthews[418]; born 16 February 1955.

Dennis Clay Matthews was born in Fayetteville, North Carolina[418]

78. James Lee[7] Lockamy (Jemima Jewel[6] Jackson, Wiley Calvin[5], Hayburn[4], Hayburn[3], Unidentified[2], Unknown[1])[419] was born 29 August 1901[419,420], and died 07 December 1985 in Sampson County , North Carolina[420,421]. He married Leona Hairr[422,423], daughter of Isaiah Hairr and Ella J. Tyndall. She was born 30 August 1905 in North Carolina[424], and died 05 February 1998[424].

James Lee and Leona were buried in Owens Grove Pentecostal FWB Church Cemetery, Sampson County, North Carolina[424,425]

Child of James Lockamy and Leona Hairr is:

+   183   i.   James Houston Lockamy, born 12 February 1924; died 30 December 1997 in Sampson County , North Carolina.

79. Lula Bee[7] Lockamy (Jemima Jewel[6] Jackson, Wiley Calvin[5], Hayburn[4], Hayburn[3], Unidentified[2], Unknown[1])[427] was born 25 September 1903 in Honeycutts Township, Sampson County, North Carolina[428], and died 16 May 1993 in Sampson County , North Carolina[429]. She married Spence B. Hairr[430], son of Isaiah Hairr and Ella J. Tyndall. He was born 29 July 1900 in Sampson County ,

North Carolina[431], and died 23 November 1961 in Sampson County , North Carolina[431].

Lula Bee sang in a group with her sisters, Flora Della Martha Ann and brother, Robert C.; Marth Ann played guitar. Spence B. and Lula Bee were buried in Owens Grove Pentecostal FWB Church Cemetery, Sampson County, North Carolina[432]

Children of Lula Lockamy and Spence Hairr are:

184   i. Bruce Hairr[434], born About 1924[435]. He married (1) Edith Unknown[436]; born [436]. He married (2) Geneva Hall[436].

Bruce Hairr is deceased.

+ 185   ii. Floyd Lutrell Hairr, born 01 November 1928 in Sampson County , North Carolina.

80.   **Robert C.[7] Lockamy** (Jemima Jewel[6] Jackson, Wiley Calvin[5], Hayburn[4], Hayburn[3], Unidentified[2], Unknown[1])[437] was born 29 March 1906 in Sampson County , North Carolina[438], and died 18 January 1988 in Sampson County , North Carolina[438]. He married **Minnie Lee Dixon**[439]. She was born 10 May 1911 in Sampson County , North Carolina[440], and died 31 May 1976 in Sampson County , North Carolina[440].

Robert C. sang in a group with his sisters, Flora Della, Lula Bee and Martha Ann; Martha Ann played guitar.

Robert C. and Minnie Lee were buried in Owens Grove Pentecostal FWB Church Cemetery, Sampson County, North Carolina[440]

Children of Robert Lockamy and Minnie Dixon are:

+ 186   i. Willa Dean Lockamy, born 06 November 1931 in Sampson County , North Carolina.
+ 187   ii. Thomas Daniel Lockamy, born 14 August 1935.

81.   Flora Della[7] **Lockamy** (Jemima Jewel[6] Jackson, Wiley Calvin[5], Hayburn[4], Hayburn[3], Unidentified[2], Unknown[1])[441,442] was born 05 October 1907 in Sampson County, North Carolina[443], and died 19 June 1984 in Sampson County , North Carolina[443]. She married **Ralph Edward Flynn**[444]. He was born 15 April 1916[445], and died 13 March 1977[445].

Flora Della Lockamy sang in a group with her sisters, Lula Bee, Martha Ann and brother Robert (Rob) C. She and Ralph Edward were divorced. Flora Della was buried in Owens Grove Pentecostal FWB Church Cemetery, Sampson County, North Carolina[446]
Ralph Edward Flynn was buried in Grandview Memorial Gardens in Clinton, North Carolina.

Child of Flora Lockamy and Ralph Flynn is:
> 188   i.   Henry Edward Flynn[447], born 24 September 1939[448]; died 13 February 1991[449].
>
> Henry Edward Flynn was buried in Grandview Memorial Gardens, Clinton, Sampson County, North Carolina[451]

83.   Martha Anna[7] **Lockamy** (Jemima Jewel[6] Jackson, Wiley Calvin[5], Hayburn[4], Hayburn[3], Unidentified[2], Unknown[1])[452] was born 30 September 1915 in Sampson County , North Carolina[453,454], and died 18 February 1995[455,456]. She married **Leburn William Dixon**[457]. He was born 24 May 1915[458,459], and died 23 June 1983[460,461].

Martha Anna Lockamy played guitar and sang with her sisters, Flora Della, Lula Bee, and brother, Robert C.

Martha Anna and her husband Leburn William Dixon were buried in Turkey Baptist Church Cemetery, Turkey, North Carolina

Children of Martha Lockamy and Leburn Dixon are:
> +   189   i.   William Glenn Dixon, born 26 December 1936 in Turkey, North Carolina.

+   190   ii.   Velva Jewell Dixon, born 10 October 1944 in Sampson County ,
             North Carolina.

84.   Oscar Davis[7] Jackson (Haburn Rice[6], Wiley Calvin[5],
Hayburn[4], Hayburn[3], Unidentified[2], Unknown[1])[462,463] was born 19 July
1909 in Honeycutts Township, Sampson County, North Carolina[463],
and died 02 September 1986 in Onslow County, Jacksonville, North
Carolina[464].   He married **(1) Roberta Holland**[465] 29 May 1929 in
Clinton, Sampson County, North Carolina[465], daughter of Alger
Holland and Ella Howell.   She was born 01 September 1910 in
Bladen County, North Carolina[465], and died 22 January 1985 in
Sampson County Memorial Hospital, Clinton, North Carolina[466,467].
He married **(2) Betty Ezzell**[468] Aft. January 1985. She was born 01
September 1907 in Duplin County, North Carolina[468], and died 14
October 1988 in Clinton, Sampson County , North Carolina.

It is said that my father, Oscar Davis Jackson, left home when he
was about 16. This could have been shortly after his mother died in
1925 when his mother's sister, Aunt Joanna Naylor, moved into the
household to help care for the children. Apparently, Dad boarded
with Clarence Hubbard Butler and Bettie Allen Autry; he never
mentioned this event of his life. A close relative stated that Mr.
Butler financed a car for him and treated him like a son. It is unclear
how long he stayed with them, but on 29 May 1929, he and mother
were married. I was unable to find a copy of their marriage records
in Sampson County; they are listed in the marriage index.

For a few years starting about 1942, my parents, Oscar Davis Jackson
and Roberta Holland rented a farm from James Crumpler, brother
of Stacy Crumpler. The small, unpainted three room, tenant house,
still standing today, is now on land owned by a Strickland family and
is situated across the road from Crumpler Grist Mill on the road
that is today known as Crumpler Mill Road. My sister, Jackie, was
born in 1943 in this house and although we were not living there in
1933, my sister Betty Carolyn, who lived only about 24 hours after
she was born in February 1933 was buried near the house in a small
cemetery. This cemetery is at the edge of a field on land owned by

descendants of a sister of my mother. A small pond is now by the house, but in earlier years there was an older pond and a mill a little farther south of the house and the present ponds.

While we lived in the tenant house described above, my maternal grandparents lived a short distance from us and the shortest route to my paternal grandparents who lived on the road now known as "The Avenue," included paths through the woods, narrow roads at the edge of fields and over what may have been the few old boards of the supporting structure for either the older mill mentioned above or a bridge over Bearskin Swamp. I hated walking across these old boards as it was necessary to look down in order to step safely from one board to another to avoid falling into the murky water which flowed swiftly at times. A sister of my mother tells that she and another sister walked this short route to visit James Senter Holland, their older brother and his wife, Vernita Simmons, who rented a house from Grandpa Haburn Rice Jackson, my father's father and they walked on a bridge to cross over the water without fearing for their safety. I remember how the water frightened me later each time I walked to my paternal grandparents with my dad.

Between BearSkin Swamp and The Avenue were two farms that Dad and I passed each time we walked the short route to his parents. James Senter Holland and John Wesley Holland, older brothers of my mother, courted and married two Simmons sisters who lived on the first farm. The second farm was owned by a Mr. Holden, a son of my father's great aunt.

Oscar David had diabetes and heart problems. After a stroke, he remained in a coma for a few months in a nursing home in Jacksonville, North Carolina, before he died. He remarried after my mother's death and unfortunately, I was unable to go to my father's funeral.

Oscar Davis Jackson was buried on 04 September 1986 in Grandview Memorial Gardens, Clinton, North Carolina[469]

Roberta Holland died from Cardiac Arrest due to Ischemic Heart Disease for 2 years and diabetes mellitus for several years. A permanent pacemaker was placed in her chest a few years before her death.

In an "old" Family Bible that Roberta had, "Robertha" is written in pencil on page 291. I believe this old Bible probably belonged to her mother, Ella Jane Howell, and a few notes in the Bible indicate that it may have belonged to Ella Jane's mother.

She listed "Robertha" for her name when she and Oscar Davis Jackson were married. This, most likely was her name, but she used "Roberta" more often and it is found on other records. Her nickname was Robert (pronounced "Rowbert"). Registration of birth was not a requirement in Bladen County, North Carolina, when she was born.

"Daniel P. Holland Born 10 September 1900" was also written in the old Bible mentioned above. Lonnie Perry Holland was Alger's son by his first wife and this note indicates that his name may have been "Daniel P(erry) rather than Lonnie Perry Holland.

"George Beatty Sikes born 07 October 1850" is a notation we also found in this old Carter or Howell Bible. I have not determined his relationship to the Carters, Howells or Hollands? "George B. Sikes," aged 10 can be found in the 1860 census for Lisbon Township, Sampson County, North Carolina. He was the son of Charles M. Sikes who was born about 1825 and Ann M. Herring, born about 1832. Ann M. Herring was the daughter of Washington Herring and Margaret Spell. Dr. Gibson Lewis Sikes (Sykes) practiced medicine in Salemburg, North Carolina.

"April 29 and 30 1860 cold, rainy and very stormy," is another note in the Bible. This tells us that this "old Bible" was around in April 1860. Apparently, the Bible was passed down to Ella Jane Howell, Roberta's mother, and the notation about the weather in 1860 indicates it probably belonged to Ella Jane Howell's grandparents: either John Carter (1818) and his wife Charlotte Averitt (born about 1827) or David Howell (born about 1809) and his wife, Rox

A. (maiden name unknown), born about 1830. The cover and a few pages are missing from the Bible. The Bible is now in the care of Jackie, my sister, Roberta's youngest daughter.

Mother had birthmarks under her arm that looked like blueberries, and she believed they resulted from her mother's craving for blueberries during her pregnancy.

Roberta Holland was buried on 25 January 1985, in Grandview Memorial Gardens, Clinton, North Carolina[469]

Betty Ezzell was first married to a 'Dail.' She had ten children by her first husband. She was buried in Grandview Memorial Gardens, Clinton, North Carolina

Children of Oscar Jackson and Roberta Holland are:

191   i. Betty Carolyn Jackson[471], born February 1933 in Honeycutts Township, Sampson County, North Carolina[471]; died February 1933 in Honeycutts Township, Sampson County, North Carolina[472].

        Betty Carolyn lived 24 hours. She had webbed hands and feet and was buried in an unmarked grave across from the Crumpler Mill owned by Stacy Crumpler now on Crumpler Mill Road near the boundary of the property owned, at that time, by Roberta's parents. The Cemetery may have been an old Branch, Hudson or Jackson Family Cemetery. Records show that Hepsie Branch, daughter of Sallie Ann Hudson and Jonas Branch may have inherited a portion of the property from her mother. Hepsie married Joseph E. Jackson who was known as Joel. Hepsie and Joel gave the property to Alger Rose Holland and his second wife, Tomzil Clyde Holland for services Alger and Tomzil provided for them during their old age and for their daughter, Sallie, who died young.

+ 192   ii. Nancy Eveline Jackson, born 21 April 1936 in Honeycutts Township, Sampson County, North Carolina.

193   iii. Elon Adel Jackson[473], born 08 May 1938 in Honeycutts Township, Sampson County, North Carolina[474]; died 21 February 2002 in Rocky Mount Hospital, Nash County, North Carolina[475]. He married Sudie Mae Pruitt[476] 21 December 1960 in Sampson County, Clinton, North Carolina[477]; born 14 August 1942 in Elkin, North Carolina[477].

Adel was a Machinist (repaired knitting machines in a sock plant.) Retired in 1999. He served as a PFC in the Army from 27 November 1961 to 26 November 1963 (E-1.)

He liked gardening and old cars. In the spring of 2000 the doctors urged him to have an angiogram, but he was concerned about dying during the procedure and refused. His health problems continued to get worse and he finally had the angiogram in early October 2000 and had open heart surgery on 19 October 2000. About two weeks later, he was rushed to the emergency room and one and 3/4 liters of fluid were removed from his lungs. He continued to have breathing problems and at times could not finish shaving.

For several years before his death, the pain in his legs and shortness of breath resulting from his heart problems and diabetes made it impossible for him to walk very far without resting. He was buried on 24 February 2002 in Grandview Memorial Gardens, Clinton, North Carolina[478]

+   194   iv.   Jackie Olene Jackson, born 09 February 1943 in Honeycutts Township, Sampson County, North Carolina.

85.   Willard Paul[7] Jackson (Haburn Rice[6], Wiley Calvin[5], Hayburn[4], Hayburn[3], Unidentified[2], Unknown[1])[480] was born 19 January 1911 in Honeycutts Township, Sampson County, North Carolina[480], and died 14 November 1967 in Sampson County Memorial Hospital, Clinton, North Carolina[480]. He married **Callie Estelle Jackson**[481] About 1937, daughter of Tommy Jackson and Carrie Simmons. She was born 24 August 1924 in Sampson County, North Carolina[481], and died 13 March 2006[482].

Aunt Mattie Ruth Jackson Parker Holland told me in 1996 that Williard Paul Jackson died from complications resulting from a spinal tap. Certificate of Death shows malignant hypertension for 2 months. He was buried on 15 November 1967 in Corinth Baptist Church Cemetery, Honeycutts Township, Sampson County, North Carolina[483]

Callie Estelle Jackson was listed as "Callie Lee" in the Birth Index of Sampson County, North Carolina. One of Callie's sons is called "Abe." She was buried in a Spell - Tyndall Grove Cemetery, on Tyndall Grove Road, Sampson County, North Carolina

Children of Willard Jackson and Callie Jackson are:

195   i.   David B. Jackson[484], born 14 January 1938 in Sampson County, North Carolina[484]; died 08 June 2007 in Sampson County, North Carolina[485].

         David B. Jackson never married.
196   ii. Thurman Earl Jackson[486], born 19 January 1942 in Sampson County, North Carolina[486]. He married Edith Knowles[486].
197   iii. Annette Carrie Jackson[486], born 08 August 1943 in Sampson County, North Carolina[486]. She married Leon Hayes[486].
198   iv. Billy Ray Jackson[486], born 28 September 1945 in Sampson County, North Carolina[486].

         Billy Ray Jackson is single.

86.   Mattie Ruth[7] **Jackson** (Haburn Rice[6], Wiley Calvin[5], Hayburn[4], Hayburn[3], Unidentified[2], Unknown[1])[487] was born 01 September 1912 in Honeycutts Township, Sampson County, North Carolina[487], and died 18 May 2006[488]. She married **(1) Miles Simpson Parker**[489], son of Gustavus Parker and Mary Tyndall. He was born 30 October 1910 in Sampson County , North Carolina[489,490], and died 08 September 1958 in Sampson County , North Carolina[491,492]. She married **(2) Stephen Senter Holland, Jr.**[493] Aft. 1959, son of Stephen Holland and Nancy Hudson. He was born 08 February 1898 in Honeycutts Township, Sampson County, North Carolina[493], and died 19 February 1978 in Honeycutts Township, Sampson County, North Carolina[493].

Mattie Ruth and Miles Simpson were buried in Corinth Baptist Church Cemetery on Corinth Church Road (SR 1326), Sampson County, North Carolina

Stephen Senter Holland, Jr. was called 'Bud(d).' Cause of death: ASHD with Fibrilation (5 years). He was buried on 21 February 1978 in Salemburg Cemetery, Salemburg, North Carolina.

Children of Mattie Jackson and Miles Parker are:

+ 199   i.   Sallie Reneonia Parker, born 12 March 1932 in Honeycutts Township, Sampson County, North Carolina; died 18 February 1997 in North Carolina.

  200   ii. Delmus Habron Parker[496], born 30 August 1934 in Honeycutts Township, Sampson County, North Carolina[497]; died 15 March 1953 in Maryland[497].

       Delmus Habron died in an automobile accident. He was buried in Corinth Baptist Church Cemetery near Bearskin, Sampson County, North Carolina[497]

+ 201   iii. Margaret Ann Parker, born 02 October 1935 in Honeycutts Township, Sampson County, North Carolina.

+ 202   iv. Miles Joel Parker, born 30 July 1939 in Honeycutts Township, Sampson County, North Carolina.

+ 203   v.   Rena Florence Parker, born 09 January 1941.

+ 204   vi. Glenn Truman Parker, born 06 May 1945 in Honeycutts Township, Sampson County , North Carolina.

87. Mary Jane[7] Jackson (Haburn Rice[6], Wiley Calvin[5], Hayburn[4], Hayburn[3], Unidentified[2], Unknown[1])[498] was born 09 April 1915 in Honeycutts Township, Sampson County , North Carolina[499], and died 20 April 1999 in Sampson County , North Carolina[500]. She married **James W. Long**[501,502], son of Ammie Long and Laura Lockamy. He was born 13 January 1914[502], and died 19 July 1981 in Sampson County , North Carolina[502].

Mary Jane and James W. Long were buried in McGee United Methodist Church Cemetery near Bearskin, Sampson County, North Carolina[502]

Children of Mary Jackson and James Long are:

+ 205   i.   William Craven Long, born 17 May 1936.
+ 206   ii. Floyd Vernon Long, born 26 May 1938; died 07 April 1989.
+ 207   iii. Charles Levon Long, born 18 October 1943 in North Carolina; died 01 January 1998 in North Carolina.
+ 208   iv. Robert Earl Long, born 11 February 1947; died 24 January 1998 in Sampson County , North Carolina.

88.   Elvin Sikes[7] Jackson (Haburn Rice[6], Wiley Calvin[5], Hayburn[4], Hayburn[3], Unidentified[2], Unknown[1])[503] was born 30 September 1918 in Honeycutts Township, Sampson County, North

Carolina[504], and died 14 March 1987 in Honeycutts Township, Sampson County , North Carolina[505]. He married **Virginia Lee Horne**[506] 30 September 1944 in Dillon, South Carolina[507], daughter of William Horne and Lillie Unknown. She was born 30 September 1928 in Salemburg, Sampson County, North Carolina[508].

Elvin Sikes Jackson had diabetes. He died from a heart attack while taking a walk in the woods across the road from his home. It is said that he only had one kidney and apparently was born with only one. He was buried on 16 March 1987 in a Jackson Family Cemetery on The Avenue in Honeycutts Township, Sampson County, North Carolina[509]

Elvin Jackson and Virginia Horne were divorced.

Children of Elvin Jackson and Virginia Horne are:

+ 209   i.   James Elvin Jackson, Sr., born 02 January 1946 in Roseboro, Sampson County , North Carolina.
+ 210   ii.   Lorenda Kaye Jackson, born 14 January 1947 in Sampson County , North Carolina.
+ 211   iii.   Heidi Jane Jackson, born 18 September 1948 in Sampson County , North Carolina.
   212   iv.   Cornelia Ann Jackson[511], born 09 May 1950[512]. She married Lewis Randall Fite[513] 06 May 1988 in York, South Carolina[514]; born 21 January 1948[515].
+ 213   v.   Terry Lynn Jackson, born 28 February 1954 in Sampson County , North Carolina.
+ 214   vi.   William Latham Jackson, born 02 May 1964 in Sampson County , North Carolina.

91.   **Willie Osway**[7] **Jackson** (Osway W.[6], Elisha Moore[5], Hayburn[4], Hayburn[3], Unidentified[2], Unknown[1])[517] was born 10 October 1916[518], and died 25 April 1984[518]. He married **Nancy Eleanor Carter**[519,520]. She was born 12 October 1916[521,522], and died 02 May 1990[523].

Willie Osway Jackson and Nancy Eleanor were buried in Grandview Memorial Gardens, Clinton, Sampson County, North Carolina[523]

Nancy Eleanor Carter must have remarried after her first husband, Willie Osway Jackson died. Her tombstone notes the name: Eleanor Jackson Nunnery with the remark: Wife of Willie O. Jackson. She is also buried by her first husband. On page 326 in "The Descendants of Abraham Naylor and John Baggett of Sampson County, North Carolina," by John C. Rosser, Jr., it notes Nancy Eleanor Carter's first name as "Mary."

Children of Willie Jackson and Nancy Carter are:

215 i. Robert Ashley Jackson[524], born 25 July 1947[525,526]; died 25 July 1947[526,527].

    Robert Ashley Jackson was buried in Owens Grove Pentecostal FWB Church Cemetery, Sampson County, North Carolina[528]

216 ii. Linda Eileen Jackson[529], born 06 July 1948 in Honeycutts Township, Sampson County, North Carolina[529]. She married Oscar Kenneth Boone[529]; born 30 September 1946 in Honeycutts Township, Sampson County, North Carolina[529].

    Linda Eileen Jackson was married to a "Hunter" prior to her marriage to Oscar Kenneth Boone.

217 iii. Sharon Kaye Jackson[530,531], born 30 September 1955 in Clinton, Sampson County, North Carolina. She married (1) James Croom[532]. She married (2) Oscar Thomas Fann[533,534] 17 July 1978 in Roseboro, Sampson County, North Carolina; born 12 November 1953 in Clinton, Sampson County, North Carolina[535].

    Oscar Thomas Fann and Evelyn Idell Holland divorced in June 1978.

93. Addie May[7] Jackson (Osway W.[6], Elisha Moore[5], Hayburn[4], Hayburn[3], Unidentified[2], Unknown[1])[536] was born 25 March 1920 in Honeycutts Township, Sampson County, North Carolina[537], and died Aft. 2001. She married **Almon Beasley**[538]. He was born 12 October 1924[538].

Children of Addie Jackson and Almon Beasley are:

+ 218 i. Larry Edward Beasley, born 16 January 1946.
+ 219 ii. Ethel Katie Beasley, born 22 November 1948.

+   220   iii.   Thelma Dean Beasley, born 16 July 1951.

96.   Leon Calvin[7] Jackson (Osway W.[6], Elisha Moore[5], Hayburn[4], Hayburn[3], Unidentified[2], Unknown[1])[539] was born 01 September 1924 in Sampson County, North Carolina[539], and died 04 August 1986 in Sampson County, North Carolina[540]. He married **Callie Estelle Jackson**[541] About 1957, daughter of Tommy Jackson and Carrie Simmons. She was born 24 August 1924 in Sampson County, North Carolina[541], and died 13 March 2006[542].

My research notes that the middle name of Leon Jackson was 'Calvin.' This is interesting and may also support a kinship between Wiley Calvin Jackson who was born in 1837 and Osway (Auzzie) Jackson.

Leon Calvin Jackson and Callie Estelle were buried in Spell-Tyndall Grove Cemetery near Clinton, North Carolina

Callie Estelle Jackson is listed as "Callie Lee" in the Birth Index of Sampson County, North Carolina. One of Callie's sons is called "Abe."

Children of Leon Jackson and Callie Jackson are:

221   i.   Bobby Lynn Jackson[543], born 15 October 1958[543].
222   ii. Larry Fulton Jackson[543], born 17 January 1960[543].

97. Lattie Pearl[7] Jackson (Osway W.[6], Elisha Moore[5], Hayburn[4], Hayburn[3], Unidentified[2], Unknown[1])[544] was born 07 March 1926 in Sampson County, North Carolina[544]. She married **William C. Jackson**[544], son of Wiley Jackson and Mollie Lockamy. He was born 22 October 1914 in Sampson County, North Carolina[544,545], and died 08 December 1966 in Sampson County, North Carolina[545].
Lattie Pearl personally told me that she and William C. Jackson were first cousins and I have been told that her mother and William C's mother were sisters. However, William's mother was a Lockamy.

Her mother, Katie Lee Strickland, was a sister to Ada Ann Strickland, spouse of Ewell Sanford Jackson, William's uncle. I have found nothing to confirm that Lattie Pearl and William C. were first cousins through the Strickland line; that kinship had to have been through the Jackson line (through their paternal grandfather. Of course, they were related through the Stricklands, but not first cousins.

William C. Jackson was known as Sambo Jackson. I have never found a full middle name and doubt that the name "Calvin" would have been given for a middle name twice by Wiley Jackson and Mollie; however, it was done by families at that time. Cicero was the middle name of an uncle.

William C. Jackson was buried in a Lockamy Cemetery near Kitty Fork, Sampson County, North Carolina[545]

Children are listed above under (62) William C. Jackson.

102.   Mollie Louise[7] Jackson (Osway W.[6], Elisha Moore[5], Hayburn[4], Hayburn[3], Unidentified[2], Unknown[1])[546] was born 29 May 1936 in Sampson County, North Carolina[546]. She married **(1) L. G. Carter**.   She married **(2) Melvin Lyons**[546].

Mollie Louise Jackson was known as 'Mallie.'

Child of Mollie Jackson and L. Carter is:

223   i.   Unknown Carter, born Unknown.

103. Lincoln MacDonald[7] Jackson (Osway W.[6], Elisha Moore[5], Hayburn[4], Hayburn[3], Unidentified[2], Unknown[1])[547] was born 04 April 1938[548]. He married **Margaret Elizabeth Bryant**[548]. She was born 09 January 1945[548].
Lincoln MacDonald (Mack) Jackson and Margaret Elizabeth Bryant are separated

Children of Lincoln Jackson and Margaret Bryant are:

224   i. Donald Mack Jackson[549], born 17 March 1965[550].
225   ii. Glenn Jackson.

105. James Leslie[7] Jackson (James Trulove[6], Elisha Moore[5], Hayburn[4], Hayburn[3], Unidentified[2], Unknown[1])[551] was born 30 April 1934[552]. He married **Eleanora Colohan**[553]. She was born About 1935[554].

James Leslie Jackson lived with his Aunt Nina and her husband until he was about 16 years of age and was named Ted (Theadore) Lockamy. It is said that he later changed his name to Theadore Jackson.

Child of James Jackson and Eleanora Colohan is:

226   i. Jack Jackson[555].

106. George Moore[7] Jackson (Hosea Moore[6], Elisha Moore[5], Hayburn[4], Hayburn[3], Unidentified[2], Unknown[1])[556] was born 20 October 1941[557], and died November 1987 in Bridgeton, Craven County, North Carolina[557]. He married **Frances Hatcher**[558].

Children of George Jackson and Frances Hatcher are:

227   i. Elizabeth Jackson[558].
228   ii. Frances Jackson[558].

107. Lucille[7] Jackson (Noah Washington[6], Elisha Moore[5], Hayburn[4], Hayburn[3], Unidentified[2], Unknown[1])[559,560,561] was born 06 October 1930[562]. She married **Minson Sessoms**[563,564], son of Henry Sessoms and Emma Johnson. He was born 26 October 1929[565,566].

Either Minson's first or middle name may be "Fletcher."

Children of Lucille Jackson and Minson Sessoms are:

229   i.   Deborah Sessoms[566], born in Unknown. She married Gary Wayne
               Hall[566]; born Unknown in Unknown.
230   ii. Dianne Sessoms[567].

108. Almoye W.[7] Jackson (Noah Washington[6], Elisha Moore[5], Hayburn[4], Hayburn[3], Unidentified[2], Unknown[1])[568,569] was born 26 March 1933[570,571]. He married **Bonnie Maxine Gilchrist**[571,572]. She was born 24 September 1935[573].

Children of Almoye Jackson and Bonnie Gilchrist are:

+   231   i.   Pamela Mae Jackson, born 03 December 1958 in Clinton, North
                  Carolina.
+   232   ii. Robyn Lisa Jackson, born 13 September 1962 in Unknown.
+   233   iii. Robert Alan Jackson, born 27 October 1971 in Unknown.

109. J. B.[7] Jackson (Noah Washington[6], Elisha Moore[5], Hayburn[4], Hayburn[3], Unidentified[2], Unknown[1])[573] was born 02 November 1935[574]. He married **Faye Smith**[575].

Child of J. Jackson and Faye Smith is:

+   234   i.   Kimberly Jackson.

111. Elsie Lee[7] Wise (Alice Jane[6] Jackson, Elisha Moore[5], Hayburn[4], Hayburn[3], Unidentified[2], Unknown[1])[576] was born 26 January 1911[577], and died 13 August 1971 in Clinton, North Carolina. She married **(1) Challie Clem Fisher**[578], son of Charlie Fisher and Mollie Sessoms. He was born 08 August 1906[579], and died 09 April 1943 in Fayetteville, North Carolina[579]. She married **(2) Leon Williams, Sr.**[579] Bef. 1954, son of William Williams and Willie Hall. He was born 12 July 1909[579], and died 25 May 1975 in Fayetteville, North Carolina[579].

Elsie Wise's nickname was 'Nini."

Challie Clem Fisher is listed as "Shallie Clem Fisher" in transcribed cemetery records. He was buried in Fisher Cemetery 2.5 miles from Autryville Road (SR 1233), Sampson County, North Carolina

Children of Elsie Wise and Challie Fisher are:

235	i.	Hughlon Fisher[580].
236	ii.	Margaret Fisher[581]. She married Jackie L. Hardison[582].
237	iii.	Doris Fisher[582582].
238	iv.	Cranford Fisher[582].
239	v.	Colon Fisher[582].

Child of Elsie Wise and Leon Williams is:

| 240 | i. | Ernestine Williams[583], born 06 February 1954 in Roseboro, North Carolina[583]. |

> Ernestine Williams was Stillborn. She was buried in William Redin Williams Family Cemetery, Sampson County, North Carolina

112. James Franklin[7] Wise (Alice Jane[6] Jackson, Elisha Moore[5], Hayburn[4], Hayburn[3], Unidentified[2], Unknown[1])[584] was born 23 April 1913 in Sampson County , North Carolina[584], and died January 1978[585]. He married **Otha Florence Tyndall**[586,587,588,589] About 1937, daughter of Fredrick Tyndall and Lillie Lockamy. She was born 03 October 1916[590,591], and died 07 February 2006[591].

James Franklin Wise was buried in Grandview Memorial Gardens, Clinton, Sampson County, North Carolina[592]

In "Cannady Family History", Atha Florence Tyndall's first name is spelled 'Otha.' Otha Florence Tyndall Wise also has a tombstone at Grandview Memorial Gardens Cemetery and apparently will be buried there.

Children of James Wise and Otha Tyndall are:

+ 241   i.   David Franklin Wise, born 1938.
   242   ii. James Frederick Wise[593], born 29 March 1937[593]; died 29 March 1937[593].

          James Frederick Wise was buried in Owens Grove Pentecostal FWB Church Cemetery, Sampson County, North Carolina[593]

+ 243   iii. Robert Howell Wise, born 26 October 1939 in Honeycutts Township, Sampson County, North Carolina.
   244   iv. Alice Florence Wise[594], born April 1941 in Sampson County, North Carolina[595]; died April 1941 in Sampson County, North Carolina[595].

          Alice Florence Wise was buried in Owens Grove Pentecostal FWB Church Cemetery, Sampson County, North Carolina[595]

113.   Celester[7] Wise (Alice Jane[6] Jackson, Elisha Moore[5], Hayburn[4], Hayburn[3], Unidentified[2], Unknown[1])[596] was born 02 January 1916[596], and died 28 October 1990[596]. She married **Roland Sessoms**[597], son of Eddie Sessoms and Mollie Williams. He was born 23 April 1915[598], and died 16 September 1978[598].

Celester Wise Sessoma and Roland Sessoms were buried in Mt. Carmel Church of God Cemetery near Autryville, North Carolina[598]

Children of Celester Wise and Roland Sessoms are:

+ 245   i.   Bobby Lee Sessoms, born 01 August 1939; died 02 April 2001.
+ 246   ii. Billy Roland Sessoms, born 14 May 1942 in Roseboro, North Carolina.
+ 247   iii. Jackie Lester Sessoms, born 27 October 1944 in Roseboro, North Carolina.
+ 248   iv. Brenda Sessoms, born 16 November 1946.

114.   Annie Kathleen[7] Wise (Alice Jane[6] Jackson, Elisha Moore[5], Hayburn[4], Hayburn[3], Unidentified[2], Unknown[1])[599] was born 10 October 1917[599], and died 09 May 1993[599]. She married **Carvie Thomas Bass**[599,600]. He was born 09 February 1914[601], and died 05 June 1993[602].

Annie Kathleen and Carvie Thomas Bass were buried in Owens Grove PFWB Church Cemetery near Kitty Fork, Sampson County, North Carolina

Children of Annie Wise and Carvie Bass are:

+   249   i.   Margie Geraldene Bass, born 19 April 1937.
        250   ii.   Jane Gwendylene Bass[603], born 01 August 1940[603].

115. Janie[7] **Wise** (Alice Jane[6] Jackson, Elisha Moore[5], Hayburn[4], Hayburn[3], Unidentified[2], Unknown[1])[604] was born Aft. 1917 in Erwin, North Carolina. She married **Thomas Williams**[604], son of Lora Jane Williams. He was born About 1915.

Children of Janie Wise and Thomas Williams are:

        251   i.   Jimmy Stokes Williams[604].
        252   ii.   Helen Stokes Williams[604].
        253   iii.   Richard Williams[604].

124. Preston Carr[7] **Pope** (Amy Lee[6] Jackson, Elisha Moore[5], Hayburn[4], Hayburn[3], Unidentified[2], Unknown[1])[605] was born 16 February 1935 in Sampson County, North Carolina[605]. He married **(1) Helen Sinclair**[605] Bef. 1959, daughter of John Sinclair and Eva Gautier. She was born 03 February 1939 in Herrings Township, Sampson County, North Carolina[606]. He married **(2) Sandra Earl Jernigan**[607] 19 December 1974[607]. She was born 28 November 1944 in Westbrooks Township, Sampson County, North Carolina[607,608].

Helen Sinclair Pope married second, Richard Hairr, Jr. Helen and Richard have no children.

Children of Preston Pope and Helen Sinclair are:

254   i.   Terry Preston Pope[609], born 19 August 1959 in Sampson County, North Carolina[609]; died 02 February 1976 in Sampson County, North Carolina[609].

+ 255   ii.   Tammy Lynnette Pope, born 12 June 1964 in Clinton, Sampson County, North Carolina.

131.   Astraudia Brown[7] Lockamy (Nina Metherbell[6] Jackson, Elisha Moore[5], Hayburn[4], Hayburn[3], Unidentified[2], Unknown[1])[610] was born 14 September 1926 in Sampson County, North Carolina[611], and died 21 December 1995 in Sampson County, North Carolina[611]. She married **Wyatt Allen Adams**[612] 21 January 1949 in Owens Grove Pentecostal FWB Church, Sampson County, North Carolina[613]. He was born 22 January 1924 in Angier, Harnett County, North Carolina[614,615], and died 23 November 1972 in Angier, Harnett County, North Carolina[616].

Wyatt Adams service information on his tombstone: North Carolina Sgt COM 1 Inf. WW II

Astraudia Brown and Wyatt Allen Adams were buried in Owens Grove Pentecostal FWB Church Cemetery, Sampson County, North Carolina

Children of Astraudia Lockamy and Wyatt Adams are:

+ 256   i.   Robert Wayne Adams, born 28 February 1950 in Dunn Hospital, North Carolina.

257   ii.   Margie Joanne Adams[618], born 21 October 1952 in Sampson Memorial Hospital, Clinton, Sampson County, North Carolina[618]. She married (1) Maxwell Ivey Minnich[619] 10 June 1972[620]. She married (2) Michael Ramsey Aft. 1972; born Unknown in Unknown.

Margie Joanne Adams and Maxwell Ivey Minnich separated in 1974 and she assumed her maiden name.

Generation No. 6

133. Carson Blaine[8] Godwin (Britton A.[7], Soloman[6], Aley[5] Jackson, Hayburn[4], Hayburn[3], Unidentified[2], Unknown[1])[621] was born 14 July 1908 in Sampson County, North Carolina[621], and died 1966 in Wallum Lake, Rhode Island[621]. He married **Madaline Benson**[621]. She was born 25 December 1904 in Johnston County, North Carolina[621], and died 1962 in Erwin, Harnett County, North Carolina[621].

Children of Carson Godwin and Madaline Benson are:

> 258   i. David Ottis Godwin[621], born 26 July 1927 in Erwin, Harnett County, North Carolina[621]. He married Elizabeth Kent Holmes[621]; born 02 October 1931 in Council, North Carolina[621].
>
> David Ottis and Elizabeth had four children.

> 259   ii. Living Godwin[621].
> 260   iii. Garland Homer Godwin[621], born 02 June 1936 in Erwin, Harnett County, North Carolina[621].

139. William B.[8] Jackson (Randall B.[7], Wiley B.[6], Wiley Calvin[5], Hayburn[4], Hayburn[3], Unidentified[2], Unknown[1])[622,623] was born 06 November 1925 in Sampson County, North Carolina[623], and died 31 January 1995 in Sampson County Memorial Hospital, Clinton, North Carolina[623]. He married **Joyce Mae Ellis**[624], daughter of B. Ellis and Mayne Pope. She was born 30 March 1934 in Sampson County, North Carolina[624].

William B. was buried in Owens Grove Pentecostal FWB Church Cemetery, Sampson County, North Carolina

Child of William Jackson and Joyce Ellis is:

> + 261   i. William Ellis Jackson, born 03 July 1957.

140. Claudia Priscilla[8] **Jackson** (Randall B.[7], Wiley B.[6], Wiley Calvin[5], Hayburn[4], Hayburn[3], Unidentified[2], Unknown[1])[625] was born 01 November 1938 in Sampson County, North Carolina[626]. She married **(1) Norwood Clyde Honeycutt**[627] 25 February 1958 in Home of The Rev. Hubert Byrd, Sampson County, North Carolina[628], son of Wiley Honeycutt and Alice Williams. He was born 05 April 1934 in Sampson County , North Carolina[629], and died 20 December 1987[629]. She married **(2) Alfred G. Nickolson**[630] 28 April 1976.   She married **(3) Paul Fields**[631] 14 August 1984[631].

Claudia Priscilla provided the data on her family. She and Norwood Honeycutt were married in the home of Rev. Hubert Byrd, Sampson County, North Carolina[631]

Children of Claudia Jackson and Norwood Honeycutt are:

262   i.   Karen Denise Honeycutt[632], born 01 September 1960 in Aberdeen Proving Ground in Maryland[632]; died 03 September 1960 in Aberdeen Proving Ground in Maryland[632].

263   ii.   Deborah Lynn Honeycutt[633], born 17 September 1962 in Ft. Eutis, Virginia[634]. She married Mitchell Drew Rivenbark[635] 15 July 1983 in Bear Marsh Baptist Church, Duplin County, North Carolina[636]; born 04 January 1955[637].

+   264   iii.   Rodney Keith Honeycutt, born 30 April 1965 in Ft. Benning, Georgia.

141. J. W.[8] **Jackson** (Randall B.[7], Wiley B.[6], Wiley Calvin[5], Hayburn[4], Hayburn[3], Unidentified[2], Unknown[1])[639] was born 08 October 1942[639]. He married **(1) Joyce Faircloth**[639] About 1962. She was born 22 October 1942[640], and died 12 February 2005[640]. He married **(2) Linda Diane Johnson**[641] 12 June 1982[642]. She was born 05 February 1948[643].

J. W. Jackson and Joyce Faircloth are divorced.

Joyce Faircloth was buried on 17 February 2005 in Peniel Pentecostal Holiness Church Cemetery, North Carolina.

Children of J. Jackson and Joyce Faircloth are:

<table>
<tr><td>+</td><td>265</td><td>i.</td><td>Randall Franklin Jackson, born 19 July 1963.</td></tr>
<tr><td>+</td><td>266</td><td>ii.</td><td>Andrew Jackson, born 21 August 1964.</td></tr>
<tr><td></td><td>267</td><td>iii.</td><td>Brian Keith Jackson[645], born 20 August 1968[646].</td></tr>
<tr><td></td><td>268</td><td>iv.</td><td>Lori Ann Jackson[647], born August 1970.</td></tr>
</table>

142.   Ester[8] Jackson (Tommy Franklin[7], Wiley B.[6], Wiley Calvin[5], Hayburn[4], Hayburn[3], Unidentified[2], Unknown[1])[648] was born About 1922, and died About 1943. She married **James Beasley**[649].

Ester Jackson was buried in a Lockamy Family Cemetery near Kitty Fork, Sampson County, North Carolina

Child of Ester Jackson and James Beasley is:
269   i.   Reva Beasley[649], died 1998[649].

143.   Callie Estelle[8] Jackson (Tommy Franklin[7], Wiley B.[6], Wiley Calvin[5], Hayburn[4], Hayburn[3], Unidentified[2], Unknown[1])[650] was born 24 August 1924 in Sampson County, North Carolina[650], and died 13 March 2006[651]. She married **(1) Willard Paul Jackson**[652] About 1937, son of Haburn Jackson and Molsey Naylor. He was born 19 January 1911 in Honeycutts Township, Sampson County, North Carolina[652], and died 14 November 1967 in Sampson County Memorial Hospital, Clinton, North Carolina[652]. She married **(2) Sonny Smith** About 1947. She married **(3) Leon Calvin Jackson**[653] About 1957, son of Osway Jackson and Katie Strickland. He was born 01 September 1924 in Sampson County, North Carolina[653], and died 04 August 1986 in Sampson County, North Carolina[654].

Callie Estelle Jackson is listed as "Callie Lee" in the Birth Index of Sampson County, North Carolina. One of Callie's sons is called "Abe."

Callie Estelle and Leon Calvin are buried in Spell - Tyndall Grove Cemetery, on Tyndall Grove Road, Sampson County, North Carolina

Aunt Mattie Ruth Jackson Parker Holland told me in 1996 that Williard Paul Jackson died from complications resulting from a spinal tap. Certificate of Death shows malignant hypertension for 2 months.

Willard Paul Jackson was buried on 15 November 1967 in Corinth Baptist Church Cemetery, Honeycutts Township, Sampson County, North Carolina[655]

My research notes that the middle name of Leon Jackson was 'Calvin.' This is interesting! Was he named after his Uncle Wiley Calvin Jackson whom some say was not related to Osway?

Children of Callie and Willard Paul Jackson are listed above under (85) Willard Paul Jackson.

Children of Callie Jackson and Sonny Smith are:

270	i.	Lucille Smith[656], born 23 November 1948[656].
271	ii.	Emma Smith[656], born 28 December 1950[656].
272	iii.	William Almond Smith[656], born 08 July 1953[656]; died 14 February 1956 in Sampson County, North Carolina[657].

The middle name for William Almond Smith is also given as "Alman."

William Almond Smith was buried in a Lockamy Cemetery near Kitty Fork, Sampson County, North Carolina[658]

273	iv.	Katie Grey Smith[659], born About 1951. She married Tony Hedgepeth[660].

Children of Callie and Leon Calvin Jackson are listed above under (96) Leon Calvin Jackson.

144. Edna Lee[8] Jackson (Tommy Franklin[7], Wiley B.[6], Wiley Calvin[5], Hayburn[4], Hayburn[3], Unidentified[2], Unknown[1])[661] was born 04 August 1928[662], and died 31 December 1966[662]. She married

William Bivens[662]. He was born 21 January 1920[662], and died 28 June 1985[662].

Edna Lee and William Bivens were buried in a Lockamy Family Cemetery near Kitty Fork, Sampson County, North Carolina

Children of Edna Jackson and William Bivens are:

274   i. Randy B. Lee Bivens[662], born 1959[662]; died 1983[662].

           Randy B. Lee Bivens was buried in a Lockamy Family Cemetery near Kitty Fork, Sampson County, North Carolina

275   ii. William Bivens, Jr.[662].

145. Bernice Franklin[8] **Jackson** (Tommy Franklin[7], Wiley B.[6], Wiley Calvin[5], Hayburn[4], Hayburn[3], Unidentified[2], Unknown[1])[663,664] was born 26 October 1931 in Sampson County, North Carolina[665,666], and died 11 December 2003[667]. He married **Pauline M. Case**[668]. She was born 12 January 1935[669].

Bernice Franklin Jackson was buried in Grandview Memorial Park Cemetery, Sampson County, Clinton, North Carolina[670]

Children of Bernice Jackson and Pauline Case are:

276   i. B. Leon Jackson[672], born 04 November 1952[673]; died 04 October 1975[673].

           B. Leon Jackson was buried in Grandview Memorial Gardens, Clinton, North Carolina[674]

+ 277   ii. Marie J. Jackson.
    278   iii. Linda J. Jackson[675]. She married Unknown Spell[676].

147. William Robert[8] **Jackson** (Tommy Franklin[7], Wiley B.[6], Wiley Calvin[5], Hayburn[4], Hayburn[3], Unidentified[2], Unknown[1])[677] was born 08 August 1938[678]. He married **Inez Dudley**[678]. She was born 17 May 1939[678].

Children of William Jackson and Inez Dudley are:

+   279   i.   William Franklin Jackson, born 11 December 1957; died 20 March 1999.

+   280   ii. Barbara Ellen Jackson, born 17 May 1963.

148. Thomas A.[8] Jackson (Tommy Franklin[7], Wiley B.[6], Wiley Calvin[5], Hayburn[4], Hayburn[3], Unidentified[2], Unknown[1])[679] was born 30 November 1944 in Sampson County, North Carolina[679]. He married **Dwanda Rose Tyndall**[679] 04 July 1968 in Clinton, North Carolina[679], daughter of Troy Tyndall and Ophila Unknown. She was born 17 March 1950 in Sampson County, North Carolina[679].

The 'A' in Thomas' name is just an 'A.'

Children of Thomas Jackson and Dwanda Tyndall are:

+   281   i.   Thomas Jerome Jackson, born 03 March 1970 in Sampson County, North Carolina.

+   282   ii. Stephanie Denice Jackson, born 07 January 1973.

+   283   iii. Teresa Rose Jackson, born 11 October 1975.

149. Donnie Pittman[8] Tyndall (Effie Jane[7] Jackson, Wiley B.[6], Wiley Calvin[5], Hayburn[4], Hayburn[3], Unidentified[2], Unknown[1])[680] was born 23 June 1926 in Honeycutts Township, Sampson County, North Carolina[680], and died 10 June 1968 in Clinton, North Carolina[680]. He married **Mavis Matthews**[680], daughter of Lattie Matthews and Anna Williams. She was born 24 November 1925 in Dismal Township, Sampson County, North Carolina[680], and died 09 April 1999[681].

Donnie Pittman and Mavis Tyndall were buried in Union Grove Baptist Church Cemetery on SR 1438 one mile west of Rebel City, Sampson County, North Carolina

Children of Donnie Tyndall and Mavis Matthews are:

    284   i. Larry Don Tyndall[682], born 13 October 1955 in Roseboro, North Carolina[682]. He married Judy Gail House[682].

    285   ii. Johnny Lynn Tyndall[682].

150.   Benjamin Franklin[8] **Tyndall, Jr.** (Effie Jane[7] Jackson, Wiley B.[6], Wiley Calvin[5], Hayburn[4], Hayburn[3], Unidentified[2], Unknown[1])[683] was born 14 June 1933[683], and died 26 March 1984[683]. He married **Iris Oxendine**[683] 30 March 1956[683]. She was born 25 August 1937[683].

Benjamin Franklin Tyndall, Jr. was buried in Calvary Tabernacle PFB Church Cemetery, one mile from intersection of Hwy 242 and High House Road, Sampson County, North Carolina.

Child of Benjamin Tyndall and Iris Oxendine is:

    286   i. Gail Tyndall.

153.   Wanda Faye[8] **Jackson** (William C.[7], Wiley B.[6], Wiley Calvin[5], Hayburn[4], Hayburn[3], Unidentified[2], Unknown[1])[684] was born 23 August 1953[684]. She married **David Milligan**[684].

Wanda Faye Jackson and David Milligan are divorced.

Children of Wanda Jackson and David Milligan are:

+ 287   i. Tina Michelle Milligan, born Unknown.

    288   ii. Heather Milligan[684], born Unknown. She married Unknown McCray[685].

155.   Eunice Mae[8] **Owen** (Mittie Lee[7] Lockamy, Flora Lee[6] Jackson, Wiley Calvin[5], Hayburn[4], Hayburn[3], Unidentified[2], Unknown[1])[686] was born 18 June 1935 in Honeycutts Township, Sampson County, North Carolina[686]. She married **Lonnie Jackson Bass, Sr.**[686] 14 January 1956 in Owens Grove PFW Baptist Church,

Kitty Fork, North Carolina[686], son of Lonnie Bass and Tempie Jackson. He was born 06 July 1931 in North Clinton Township, Sampson County, North Carolina[686].

Children of Eunice Owen and Lonnie Bass are:

> 289   i.   Deborah Rose Bass[686], born 25 November 1956 in Clinton, Sampson County, North Carolina[686]. She married John Wesley Thompson[687].
>
> 290   ii.   Lonnie Jackson Bass, Jr.[688], born 09 October 1960 in Clinton, Sampson County, North Carolina[688].
>
> + 291   iii.   Lora Lynn Bass, born 29 December 1965 in Clinton, Sampson County, North Carolina.

158. Lossie Mae[8] Hall (Hattie Stella[7] Lockamy, Flora Lee[6] Jackson, Wiley Calvin[5], Hayburn[4], Hayburn[3], Unidentified[2], Unknown[1])[689] was born 26 September 1923[689], and died 28 August 1987[689]. She married **Jimmy Jones**[689].

Lossie Mae Hall was buried in a Hall Family Cemetery on Perdie Hall Road, Sampson County, North Carolina.

Children of Lossie Hall and Jimmy Jones are:

> 292   i.   Linda Carol Jones[689], born 29 August 1946[689]; died 07 September 1996[689].
>
>   Linda Carol Jones was buried in a Hall Family Cemetery on Perdie Hall Road, Sampson County, North Carolina.
>
> 293   ii.   Robert Glenn Jones.

161. Edna Lee[8] Lockamy (David Martin[7], Flora Lee[6] Jackson, Wiley Calvin[5], Hayburn[4], Hayburn[3], Unidentified[2], Unknown[1])[690] was born 13 September 1934. She married **Hershall Merel McLaurin**[690,691] 03 September 1977[692,693]. He was born 19 January 1930[693], and died 20 September 1992[693].

Children of Edna Lockamy and Hershall McLaurin are:

+ 294   i.   Rose Marie McLaurin, born 10 March 1957.
+ 295   ii.   Elizabeth Mae McLaurin, born 09 January 1960.
+ 296   iii.   David Merel McLaurin, born 04 June 1967.
   297   iv.   Franklin Lee McLaurin[695], born 15 May 1968. He married Jennifer Dale McLean[695] 01 October 1993[695].

162. Wiley Martin[8] **Lockamy** (David Martin[7], Flora Lee[6] Jackson, Wiley Calvin[5], Hayburn[4], Hayburn[3], Unidentified[2], Unknown[1])[696] was born 01 January 1937[697]. He married **(1) Nanette Wallace**[697] About 1960. He married **(2) Nan Hairr**[697] About 1963. He married **(3) Yolanda Gonzalez**[697] Bef. 1969.

Child of Wiley Lockamy and Nanette Wallace is:

   298   i.   Martin Scott Lockamy[697], born 18 June 1961[697].

Child of Wiley Lockamy and Nan Hairr is:

+ 299   i.   Yvonne Lockamy, born 06 January 1964.

Children of Wiley Lockamy and Yolanda Gonzalez are:

+ 300   i.   Kimberley Valentina Lockamy, born 25 March 1969.
   301   ii.   Tonya Elizabeth Lockamy, born 30 September 1970.

163. Alice Faye[8] **Lockamy** (David Martin[7], Flora Lee[6] Jackson, Wiley Calvin[5], Hayburn[4], Hayburn[3], Unidentified[2], Unknown[1])[697] was born 28 November 1941[697]. She married **Tracy Teague Hackney**[697] 02 August 1964.

Children of Alice Lockamy and Tracy Hackney are:

+ 302   i.   Jessica Lockamy Hackney, born 03 November 1968.
   303   ii.   Camilla Blythe Hackney[697], born 12 June 1973[697].
   304   iii.   Tracy Teague Hackney, Jr.[697], born 08 August 1976[697].

164. William David[8] **Lockamy** (David Martin[7], Flora Lee[6] Jackson, Wiley Calvin[5], Hayburn[4], Hayburn[3], Unidentified[2], Unknown[1])[697] was born 23 August 1951[697], and died 22 June 1996[697]. He married **Linda Jones**[698]. died [698].

William David Lockamy retired retired from the U.S. Navy and enrolled in the Medical University of South Carolina Occupational Therapy Program. He was buried in James Island Presbyterian Church Cemetery, James Island, South Carolina

Child of William Lockamy and Linda Jones is:

> 305   i.   Patrick David Lockamy[699].

165. Fannie Lee[8] **Lockamy** (Beulah Jane[7], Flora Lee[6] Jackson, Wiley Calvin[5], Hayburn[4], Hayburn[3], Unidentified[2], Unknown[1]) was born 05 August 1941. She married **Kenneth Reed Williams** 13 January 1968, son of Angus Williams and Lillie Unknown. He was born 11 May 1942 in Clinton, Sampson County , North Carolina.

Child of Fannie Lockamy and Kenneth Williams is:

> + 306   i.   Regina Gray Williams, born 17 October 1969 in Sampson County , North Carolina.

166. Doris Allese[8] **McLamb** (Lizzie Adeline[7] Lockamy, Flora Lee[6] Jackson, Wiley Calvin[5], Hayburn[4], Hayburn[3], Unidentified[2], Unknown[1])[700] was born 10 March 1930 in Herrings Township, Sampson County, North Carolina[700]. She married **Clarence Johnson Bass**[701], son of Lonnie Bass and Tempie Jackson. He was born 27 May 1924 in North Clinton Township, Sampson County, North Carolina[702].

Children of Doris McLamb and Clarence Bass are:

> + 307   i.   Barbara Gail Bass, born 26 July 1950 in Clinton, Sampson County, North Carolina.

+ 308 ii. Steven Johnson Bass, born 02 October 1955 in Clinton, Sampson County, North Carolina.
+ 309 iii. Edith Joan Bass, born 14 March 1963 in Clinton, Sampson County, North Carolina.

170. Joyce Ann[8] Jackson (Andrew Davis[7], Ewell Sanford[6], Wiley Calvin[5], Hayburn[4], Hayburn[3], Unidentified[2], Unknown[1])[703] was born 1945[704], and died 01 March 2001 in Holly Springs, Wake, North Carolina[704]. She married **(1) Freddie Britt**. She married **(2) J. C. Ashworth**[705].

Child of Joyce Jackson and Freddie Britt is:

310 i. Lois Ann Britt[706], born 23 April 1961[706]; died 16 September 1962[706].

Lois Ann Britt was buried in McGee United Methodist Church Cemetery[706]

Children of Joyce Jackson and J. Ashworth are:

+ 311 i. Jeffrey Ashworth.
312 ii. Pam Ashworth[707].

171. Larry Davis[8] Jackson (Andrew Davis[7], Ewell Sanford[6], Wiley Calvin[5], Hayburn[4], Hayburn[3], Unidentified[2], Unknown[1])[708] was born 13 January 1946 in North Carolina[708]. He married **Beatrice Sessoms**[708].

Children of Larry Jackson and Beatrice Sessoms are:

313 i. Linda Fay Jackson[708], born 16 September 1969[708]. She married Carlton Honeycutt[708].
314 ii. Larry Don Jackson[708], born 10 May 1975[708].

172. Hilda Grey[8] Jackson (Andrew Davis[7], Ewell Sanford[6], Wiley Calvin[5], Hayburn[4], Hayburn[3], Unidentified[2], Unknown[1])[708] was born 17 March 1947 in North Carolina[708]. She married **(1) Thomas Coats**[708]. She married **(2) Fred Sessoms**[709].

Children of Hilda Jackson and Thomas Coats are:

315   i.   Tony Wayne Coats[710]. He married Sherry Edge[710].

316   ii.   Donna Grey Jackson Coats[710].

Child of Hilda Jackson and Fred Sessoms is:

317   i.   Freddie Sessoms[711].

173. Perry Scott[8] Jackson (Andrew Davis[7], Ewell Sanford[6], Wiley Calvin[5], Hayburn[4], Hayburn[3], Unidentified[2], Unknown[1])[712] was born 26 September 1949 in North Carolina[713]. He married **(1) Treva Elaine Murphey**[714,715] 1968. He married **(2) Kim Jernigan**[716] Aft. 1987. She was born 13 July 1962[716].

Children of Perry Jackson and Treva Murphey are:

318   i.   Carol Ann Jackson[716], born 29 September 1968[717]. She met Jimmy McCullen 1988.

                 Carol Ann Jackson and Jimmy McCullen are divorced.

319   ii.   Andy Scott Jackson[718], born 02 January 1976[719]. He married Christy Hawley[720].

175. Brenda Faye[8] Jackson (Andrew Davis[7], Ewell Sanford[6], Wiley Calvin[5], Hayburn[4], Hayburn[3], Unidentified[2], Unknown[1])[721] was born 27 May 1951[721]. She married **(1) Ronald Wayne Fowler**[721], son of Willie Fowler and Thelma Lockamy. He was born 07 November 1947[722], and died 01 March 1983[722]. She married **(2) William Spicer**. He was born Unknown. She married **(3) Albert Sullivan** 07 July 2000.

Brenda Faye Jackson and Ronald Wayne Fowler were divorced. He was buried in Grandview Memorial Gardens, Clinton, North Carolina[722]

Child of Brenda Jackson and Ronald Fowler is:

320   i.   Cristal Gail Fowler[723]. She married Unknown Smith[724].

183. James Houston[8] **Lockamy** (James Lee[7], Jemima Jewel[6] Jackson, Wiley Calvin[5], Hayburn[4], Hayburn[3], Unidentified[2], Unknown[1])[725] was born 12 February 1924[726,727], and died 30 December 1997 in Sampson County , North Carolina[728,729]. He married **Revah Spell**[729,730] 25 May 1942 in Dillon, South Carolina[731], daughter of John Spell and Clennie McKenzie. She was born 21 July 1923[731], and died 03 July 2005[732].

James Houston and Revah Lockamy were buried in Grandview Memorial Gardens, Clinton, Sampson County, North Carolina[733]

Children of James Lockamy and Revah Spell are:

+   321   i.   Houston Lee Lockamy, born 25 February 1944.
     322   ii.   Brenda Faye Lockamy[736], born 03 January 1946[736]. She married Darious Woodrow Wilson[736].
+   323   iii.   Omie Kaye Lockamy, born 09 February 1948.
+   324   iv.   Jimmy McThomas Lockamy, born 27 March 1950.
+   325   v.   Jackie Lou Lockamy, born 26 September 1953.

185. Floyd Lutrell[8] **Hairr** (Lula Bee[7] Lockamy, Jemima Jewel[6] Jackson, Wiley Calvin[5], Hayburn[4], Hayburn[3], Unidentified[2], Unknown[1])[737,738] was born 01 November 1928 in Sampson County , North Carolina[739]. He married **Barbara Jean Jordan**[740] 10 November 1957, daughter of Oscar Jordan and Armathia Tew. She was born 04 June 1938 in Sampson County , North Carolina[740].

Children of Floyd Hairr and Barbara Jordan are:

+ 326   i.   Ronald Keith Hairr, born 08 June 1959.
+ 327   ii. Shelia Rose Hairr, born 11 April 1965.

186.   Willa Dean[8] **Lockamy** (Robert C.[7], Jemima Jewel[6] Jackson, Wiley Calvin[5], Hayburn[4], Hayburn[3], Unidentified[2], Unknown[1])[741] was born 06 November 1931 in Sampson County , North Carolina[742]. She married **Thomas Best Jordan**[743] 24 February 1948 in Dillon, South Carolina[743]. He was born 01 October 1927 in Sampson County , North Carolina, and died 31 January 2000 in Sampson County , North Carolina.

Thomas Best Jordan was buried in Grandview Memorial Gardens, Clinton, Sampson County, North Carolina[744]

Children of Willa Lockamy and Thomas Jordan are:

+ 328   i.   Ronnie Best Jordan, born 14 November 1952 in Sampson County , North Carolina.
+ 329   ii. Linda Lee Jordan, born 11 May 1949.
+ 330   iii. William Glenn Jordan, born 19 May 1964.

187.   Thomas Daniel[8] **Lockamy** (Robert C.[7], Jemima Jewel[6] Jackson, Wiley Calvin[5], Hayburn[4], Hayburn[3], Unidentified[2], Unknown[1])[746] was born 14 August 1935[747]. He married **Carla Beatty**[747].

Thomas Daniel Lockamy was called 'Sam.' Sam provided names for his wife and children and date of birth and full name for himself. His children may not be lised in the correct order.

Children of Thomas Lockamy and Carla Beatty are:

331   i.   Sam Michaels Lockamy[748,749], born in Unknown; died 26 April 2002[750]. He married Laurel Moore[750].

332	ii.	Mitchell Thomas Lockamy[751,752].
333	iii.	Jenny Dawn Lockamy[753,754].
334	iv.	Adrian Samatha Lockamy[755,756], born in Unknown. She married (1) Donald Honeycutt[756]; born Unknown in Unknown.

Adrian Sam Lockamy was known as 'Little Sam.'

| + | 335 | v. | Carla Jean Lockamy, born 29 March 1953 in Clinton, Sampson County, North Carolina. |

189. William Glenn[8] Dixon (Martha Anna[7] Lockamy, Jemima Jewel[6] Jackson, Wiley Calvin[5], Hayburn[4], Hayburn[3], Unidentified[2], Unknown[1])[757] was born 26 December 1936 in Turkey, North Carolina[758]. He married **Nan McChrae Wright**[758] 23 February 1958 in Cheraw, South Carolina[758]. She was born 04 January 1939 in Turkey, North Carolina[758].

Children of William Dixon and Nan Wright are:

| 336 | i. | Steven Glenn Dixon[758], born 10 March 1959[758]; died 26 February 2001[758]. |
| 337 | ii. | Gregory Bryan Dixon[758], born 12 February 1962[758]. He married Connie. |

190. Velva Jewell[8] Dixon (Martha Anna[7] Lockamy, Jemima Jewel[6] Jackson, Wiley Calvin[5], Hayburn[4], Hayburn[3], Unidentified[2], Unknown[1])[759] was born 10 October 1944 in Sampson County , North Carolina[760]. She married **James Alison Smith**[761]. He was born 04 August 1943[762].

Children of Velva Dixon and James Smith are:

+	338	i.	Darrin Grey Kennedy, born 30 September 1969.
	339	ii.	Donna Michelle Kennedy[763], born 06 May 1972[764].
	340	iii.	Brandon Dixon Smith[765], born 14 June 1979[766].

192. Nancy Eveline[8] Jackson (Oscar Davis[7], Haburn Rice[6], Wiley Calvin[5], Hayburn[4], Hayburn[3], Unidentified[2], Unknown[1])[767] was born 21 April 1936 in Honeycutts Township, Sampson County, North Carolina[768]. She married **(1) Richard Joseph Pleitt** 18 September 1954 in St. Bonaventure Church, 1615 Diversey

Avenue, Cook County, Chicago, IL[769]. He was born 19 May 1933 in Chicago, Cook County, Illinois[770], and died 29 June 1981 in Mt. Sinai Medical Center, Milwaukee, Wisconsin[771]. She married **(2) Robert Collins** 1983 in Waukegan, Lake County, Illinois. She married **(3) Edwin John Fenner** 09 June 1988 in Waukesha County Courthouse, Waukesha, Wisconsin. He was born 25 March 1925 in Eau Claire, Wisconsin, and died 05 July 2001 in Clearview Nursing Home, Juneau, Dodge County, Wisconsin.

Notes for Nancy Eveline Jackson:
I was born prematurely at seven months; the certificate of birth signed by the midwife, Steller Butler shows I was born at 10 p.m. and the one signed by Dr. W. H. Nelson shows 10:45 p.m. Dr. Nelson, who apparently arrived 45 minutes after I was born, told my parents that I probably would not live long, but advised them to keep a large steel hot water container on one side of me while I would have the heat from my mother's body on the other side. This was my incubator for a few weeks! Considering Dr. Nelson's prediction, I thank God for the 71 years he has given me.

With the exception of a short time my parents lived in the town of Fayetteville, North Carolina, I lived the first 12 years of my life on various tenant farms in Sampson County, North Carolina. In 1948, my paternal Grandfather, Haburn Rice Jackson, gave each of his three boys one third of his small farm. My parents grew tobacco, cotton and what was known at the time in Sampson County as truck crops which for us included tomatoes, cucumbers, peppers, summer squash, lima beans and field peas. At times my dad also worked off the farm in the cotton mills and at other odd jobs to supplement his income. For several weeks at the end of each school year, we started school earlier each day and classes were shortened to allow us to go home earlier to help during the planting season. For several weeks at the start of the school year we had the same short scheduled day to give us time to help with the harvest.

All of us who grew up in Sampson County, North Carolina, know how much we enjoy eating the local grown peas. I wanted to laugh when I found the field pea defined as a strain of the common pea (Pisum sativum var. arventse) with mottled leaves and purplish flowers, grown for forage. I vote for a better dictionary! This definition prompted me to search the internet for "field pea" and there I found more evidence that many university web sites of the Northern States in America present information on how to grow several varieties of field peas for hogs. However, I also found limited interesting information about the field pea grown for humankind!

One web site states that the Field Pea (Pisum sativum L.) originated in India and was among the oldest of cultivated crops and in prehistoric times, seeds were carried to Europe and in the 1600s introduced to the New World.

On the web site of Clemson University Cooperative Extension Service, I found: "Southern peas, black-eyed peas and field peas are all names for the crop known worldwide as cowpeas (Vigna unguiculata ssp. unguiculata). Cowpeas probably originated in Africa and were introduced to the United States during early colonial times. They quickly becama a staple crop in the Southeast.

"There are four types of peas---Field pea: Robust, viny type usually with small seeds that produce a dark liquid when cooked. Crowder pea: Starchy seeded types "crowded" into the pods, normally cooking up dark. Cream pea: Smaller plant type with light colored seeds that cook up light. 'Black-eyed' pea: Intermediate in its plant type and seed cooking characteristics.

"Cultivars. Field-'Iron/Clay,' various heirlooms. Crowder-'Carolina,' 'Colussus 80'. Cream-'Zipper Cream,' 'Carolina Cream.' Black-eye type-'Pinkeye Purple Hull,' 'Dixielee,' 'Santee Early Pinkeye.'"

Other web sites mention additional cultivars (varities) and note that the field peas became a staple food among poor people in the southern United States; the soil in the south was more suitable for its production.

Today, my relatives in Sampson County, North Carolina, grow or buy the Dixielee (Dixie Lee) pea when possible. During my childhood, I looked forward to each summer and those servings of peas seasoned with salt pork or cured ham. My father gave me a pint of these seeds around 1974 and I remember planting some in my vegetable garden in Northern Illinois. We did havest a few green peas, but apparently the season was not long enough; the plants did very poorly.

Most of my childhood was before mechanical cotton pickers were invented. I remember how my body felt after that first day of picking cotton each fall. I had difficulty walking upright for a few days and the sharp pointed burr tips of the cotton boll would prick and scratch my fingers, hands and arms and at least a few minutes during lunch time and in the evening of each day I had to spend time removing the burrs that were embedded in my fingers, hands and arms.

.

On page 553 in "The Heritage of Sampson County, North Carolina, 1784-1984," edited by Oscar M. Bizzell, Mary John Parker gives a good description of how the cotton was weighed at the end of each day and she probably remembers more than I do:

"Somehow a cotton picker could always tell when weighing-up time came. The sun told them when to start picking in the morning and when to quit picking at night. And of course Daddy always showed up about weighing-up time...He would pull the weigh horse that stayed with us so long. Now the weigh horse was a homemade contraption made with a long pole tilted up at one end and fastened in the middle to two wooden legs which held one end up while the other rested on the ground until you were ready to weigh cotton. To do this you lifted up the end off the ground and the other end would go down and pick up a cotton sheet by the long slender iron scales that dangled with a hook used for catching the sheets. Then with a lift upward of the end that was down, the other end went down and the cotton sheet was hooked to the scales and then pulled back up again with the bursting open cotton sheet rising and swaying back and forth. Somehow I always liked to watch Daddy's eyes squint in the sunset and his hand run along those black scales -- tapping and pushing the weights (called "peas') along that told you how much cotton each picker had. Each one had an account page that was added at the end of each week when paying-up time came around. That was when the biggest and loudest part of the humming and singing came, a sign of real 'old-time satisfaction from a hard weeks' work. That was when it was time to stop and rest. it was a known fact that Daddy had about the best cotton pickers around. It was nothing for one to pick several hundred pounds in a single day. In fact, Daddy had such good cotton pickers that he was about the last one to convert over to the mechanical way of picking cotton."

Only on rare occasions did my father, Oscar Jackson, hire cotton pickers. This was a time when we three children sometimes stayed home from school on nice days to pick cotton. One year Dad hired a man with a small plane to fly over and spray the cotton field directly behind our house in order to reduce or kill the boll weevil infestation. We were asked to close our windows and doors during, and for a time after, the spraying. The white cloud of dust, that most likely was DDT, was thick and also settled everywhere near the field. I've asked myself whether my allergies developed as a result of the use of DDT.

A "cotton sheet" most of the time was a sheet made from at least four large burlap bags sewed together. The pickers would empty their bags of cotton onto these sheets during the day. The corners of the sheets were tied together and the hooks on the scales would slip under the knot at weighing-up time.

The adult cotton pickers also used a large burlap bag to stuff the cotton into as they worked along the rows. Children generally had smaller bags.

Mary John Parker also says this: "A cotton sheet had character. ... Not only did it hold the cotton -- it held the babies, too. It was hardly any job at all to convert a cotton sheet into a playpen. You had only to stretch it out between two rows of cotton, tie the corners to cotton stalks, empty a sack or two of cotton in it and there it was, a perfect playpen. Stretch another sheet high up over it and you a sun-proof job."

The cotton stalks were a lot larger when I (Nancy Jackson Pleitt Fenner) was a child and probably even larger when Mary John Parker was a child. Today, It would be almost impossible to find cotton stalks large enough to serve as corners of a playpen. When my sister, Jackie, was an infant, I had the responsibility of watching her one day while my parents picked cotton. We children were at the end of the field where the cotton was emptied on the sheets and one sheet must have been piled high when I placed her on top of the cotton. She rolled off and was hurt and frightened; her screams quickly brought our mother to us and I do know I was punished, but I don't remember how. Usually, she found a switch.

Richard Joseph Pleitt made his first Holy Communion on May 30, 1942 at St. Bonaventure Church, Diversey Parkway and North Marshfield Ave., Chicago, Illinois. Priest, Rev O. (V.?) J. Moran. He entered the Marine Corps very shortly after he turned 18; after he returned from Korea, he was stationed at Camp LeJeune in North Carolina. One Saturday in August 1953, he and two friends decided to drive to Fayetteville, North Carolina, to find some servicemen from Fort Bragg to harass, but made a stop in Rose's Dime Store in Clinton where I was working. Richard wanted a small book in which he could enter telephone numbers for the girls they also hoped to meet in Fayetteville. They never made it to Fayetteville and from August until he was discharged in May 1954, he and some of his friends found their way to Clinton on most weekends.

Witnesses for the marriage of Nancy Jackson and Richard Pleitt were a Pleitt family friend, Earl R. McClaughry, and Richard's Aunt Rose Seiler, his mother's sister. A reception was held in the evening at the home of Richard's parents, Margaret F. (nee Waclawek) and Joseph Edward Pleitt.

Starting in 1955, Richard attended Roosevelt Univerity, DePaul University and then while working full-time, he pursued a Doctorate in Physics at Illinois Institute of Technology on a part-time basis, but after moving to work in Pennsylvania and South Carolina, we returned to Illinois and he decided not to finish his doctorate.

Richard Joseph generously seasoned the food on his plate with salt; that and hereditary factors contributed to the development of his serious high blood pressure and heart problems. He died at the age of 47 while undergoing open heart bypass surgery and was buried on 03 July 1981 in Resurrection Cemetery, Justice, Illinois[772]

Edwin John Fenner is buried by his first wife in Flora Cemetery, Flora, near Belvidere, Illinois.

Children of Nancy Jackson and Richard Pleitt are:

341 i. Margaret Roberta Pleitt[774], born 21 April 1956 in Illinois Masonic Hospital, Cook County, Chicago, Illinois[775]. She married Keith Allen Clark[776] 18 August 1978 in Church of the Holy Apostles, Wauconda, Lake County, Illinois[777]; born 28 August 1953 in Battle Creek, Michigan[778].

Both Margaret and Keith graduated from Indiana University, Bloomington, Indiana. He is a teacher in the Monroe County Scools and she works at Indiana University.

342 ii. Baby Girl Pleitt[780], born 27 December 1959 in Chicago, Cook County, Illinois[781,782,782]; died 27 December 1959.

Baby Girl Pleitt was buried on 28 December 1959 in Resurrection Cemetery, Justice, Illinois[783,784,784]

+ 343 iii. Joseph Richard Pleitt, born 05 December 1961 in Lutheran General Hospital, Park Ridge, Cook County, Illinois.

+ 344 iv. Anna Bernadette Pleitt, born 13 January 1965 in Holy Family Hospital, Cook County, Illinois.

194. Jackie Olene[8] **Jackson** (Oscar Davis[7], Haburn Rice[6], Wiley Calvin[5], Hayburn[4], Hayburn[3], Unidentified[2], Unknown[1])[785] was born 09 February 1943 in Honeycutts Township, Sampson County, North Carolina[785]. She married **Charles Phillip Smith**[785] 15 August 1959 in Dillon, South Carolina[786], son of Jacob Smith and Fannie Waters. He was born 23 August 1939 in Benton County, Tennessee[787].

When Jackie and Phillip's two older sons, Charles Davis and Michael Edward, were young, they were playing in a mudhole during a storm when lightning struck nearby and they saw a hand and stars come down into the mudhole. The boys didn't understand what happened, but Jackie, Phillip and others understand the Lord kept those boys safe that day.

Children of Jackie Jackson and Charles Smith are:

+ 345   i. Charles Davis Smith, born 03 April 1961 in Clinton, Sampson County, North Carolina.
+ 346   ii. Michael Edward Smith, born 29 May 1962 in Bethel, Pitt County, North Carolina.
+ 347   iii. Jackie Gregory Smith, born 22 April 1966 in Tarboro, North Carolina.

199.   Sallie Reneonia[8] Parker (Mattie Ruth[7] Jackson, Haburn Rice[6], Wiley Calvin[5], Hayburn[4], Hayburn[3], Unidentified[2], Unknown[1])[789] was born 12 March 1932 in Honeycutts Township, Sampson County, North Carolina[790], and died 18 February 1997 in North Carolina[791]. She married **Dave Goodrich**[792].

Children of Sallie Parker and Dave Goodrich are:

348   i. Linda Goodrich, born About 1954. She married Dennis Marshall.
349   ii. Connie Goodrich, born About 1958.

201.   Margaret Ann[8] Parker (Mattie Ruth[7] Jackson, Haburn Rice[6], Wiley Calvin[5], Hayburn[4], Hayburn[3], Unidentified[2], Unknown[1])[793] was born 02 October 1935 in Honeycutts Township, Sampson County, North Carolina[794]. She married **B. J. Gallagher, Jr.**[795]. He was born 05 April 1930[796].

Child of Margaret Parker and B. Gallagher is:

+   350   i.   Clyde Earl Gallagher, born 04 February 1962.

202. Miles Joel[8] Parker (Mattie Ruth[7] Jackson, Haburn Rice[6], Wiley Calvin[5], Hayburn[4], Hayburn[3], Unidentified[2], Unknown[1])[797] was born 30 July 1939 in Honeycutts Township, Sampson County, North Carolina[798]. He married **Janice F. Butler**[799,800] Bef. 1960, daughter of Quinton Butler and Cleo Holland. She was born 25 June 1940 in Guilford County, North Carolina[801], and died 28 August 1984 in Wake County, North Carolina[802].

Janice F. Butler was buried in Corinth Baptist Church Cemetery near Bearskin, Sampson County, North Carolina[803,804]

Children of Miles Parker and Janice Butler are:

+   351   i.   Melanie Joy Parker, born 10 September 1960 in Honeycutts Township,
                       Sampson County, North Carolina.
+   352   ii.   Melina Jill Parker, born 26 December 1964 in Sampson County ,
                       North Carolina.
     353   iii. Millette Jana Parker[805], born 27 December 1967 in Sampson County
                       , North Carolina[805]. She married Freddie West[806].

203. Rena Florence[8] Parker (Mattie Ruth[7] Jackson, Haburn Rice[6], Wiley Calvin[5], Hayburn[4], Hayburn[3], Unidentified[2], Unknown[1])[807,808] was born 09 January 1941[809]. She married **(1) Donnie Ray Honeycutt**[810] About 1958. He was born 13 April 1936[811], and died 05 November 1959[811]. She married **(2) Leonard Paul King**[812] About 1964, son of William King and Jessie Holland. He was born 21 April 1939[813]. She married **(3) Ronnie Bradshaw**[814] Aft. February 1968. He was born 24 May 1947[815].

Rena Florence's first husband is deceased. She and Ronnie Bradshaw are either separated or divorced.

Child of Rena Parker and Donnie Honeycutt is:

+ 354   i. Anthony Ray Honeycutt, born 23 March 1959.

Children of Rena Parker and Leonard King are:

+ 355   i. Leonard Scott King, born 06 March 1965.
+ 356   ii. Timmy Maxwell King, born 26 January 1968.

Child of Rena Parker and Ronnie Bradshaw is:

+ 357   i. Breezy Bradshaw, born 17 July 1977.

204. Glenn Truman[8] **Parker** (Mattie Ruth[7] Jackson, Haburn Rice[6], Wiley Calvin[5], Hayburn[4], Hayburn[3], Unidentified[2], Unknown[1])[816] was born 06 May 1945 in Honeycutts Township, Sampson County, North Carolina[817]. He married **Sadie Catherine Thornton**[818]. She was born 05 November 1946 in Fayetteville, North Carolina[819].

Children of Glenn Parker and Sadie Thornton are:
358   i. Veronica Ann Parker[820], born 17 June 1965 in Clinton, Sampson County, North Carolina[820].
359   ii. Delmus Glenn Parker[820], born 03 May 1966 in Clinton, Sampson County, North Carolina[820].
360   iii. Jeri Maresa Parker[821], born 18 February 1968 in Clinton, Sampson County, North Carolina[822].

205. William Craven[8] **Long** (Mary Jane[7] Jackson, Haburn Rice[6], Wiley Calvin[5], Hayburn[4], Hayburn[3], Unidentified[2], Unknown[1])[823] was born 17 May 1936[824]. He married **(1) Betty Jo Melvin**[825] in Unknown. She was born 02 April 1938[825]. He married **(2) Jean Beaudeaux**[826] in Unknown.
Child of William Long and Betty Melvin is:

361   i. William Craven Long, Jr.[827], born 04 May 1955[828].

Child of William Long and Jean Beaudeaux is:

+   362   i.   Terry Wayne Long, born 22 December 1959.

206. Floyd Vernon[8] **Long** (Mary Jane[7] Jackson, Haburn Rice[6], Wiley Calvin[5], Hayburn[4], Hayburn[3], Unidentified[2], Unknown[1])[829] was born 26 May 1938[830], and died 07 April 1989[831]. He married **Lula Jane Sessoms**[832] 06 August 1960[832].

Floyd Vernon Long had diabetes and high blood pressure died from a heart attack.. He was buried in Newton Grove Cemetery, Newton Grove, North Carolina

Children of Floyd Long and Lula Sessoms are:

363   i.   Floyd Keith Long[832], born About 1961.
364   ii.   Janet Long[833], born About 1963. She married Ronnie Hobbs[834].
365   iii. Christy Long[835], born About 1966. She married Allen Murray[836]; born Unknown in Unknown.
366   iv.   Joni Long[837], born About 1970.

207. Charles Levon[8] **Long** (Mary Jane[7] Jackson, Haburn Rice[6], Wiley Calvin[5], Hayburn[4], Hayburn[3], Unidentified[2], Unknown[1])[838] was born 18 October 1943 in North Carolina[839], and died 01 January 1998 in North Carolina[839]. He married **Emma Louise Jackson**[840].

Child of Charles Long and Emma Jackson is:

367   i.   Sunnie Ann Long[840], born About 1965. She married Timmie Jackson[840].

208. Robert Earl[8] **Long** (Mary Jane[7] Jackson, Haburn Rice[6], Wiley Calvin[5], Hayburn[4], Hayburn[3], Unidentified[2], Unknown[1])[841] was born 11 February 1947[842], and died 24 January 1998 in Sampson County , North Carolina[843]. He married **Jean Ellen Bradshaw**[844]. She was born 17 July 1948[845], and died 06 January 1990[845].

Robert Earl Long Served with the 32nd A. D. Com, Fr. Jackson, South Carolina from ? to 6 March 1968. Specialist 4th Class, E. 4. Also stationed at Fort Dix, New Jersey.

Children of Robert Long and Jean Bradshaw are:

+ 368   i.   Sondra Jean Long, born 07 December 1966 in Sampson County , North Carolina.
+ 369   ii. Charles Franklin Long, born 08 September 1971 in Cumberland County, North Carolina.

209. James Elvin[8] Jackson, Sr. (Elvin Sikes[7], Haburn Rice[6], Wiley Calvin[5], Hayburn[4], Hayburn[3], Unidentified[2], Unknown[1])[846] was born 02 January 1946 in Roseboro, Sampson County , North Carolina[847]. He married **Judy Katherine Barnes**[848] 12 June 1966 in Roseboro, Sampson County, North Carolina[849], daughter of James Barnes and Elizabeth Keene. She was born 11 May 1948 in Clinton, Sampson County, North Carolina[849].

James Elvin Jackson, Sr. is known as "Jimmy." He attended Fayetteville Techical Institute, Fayetteville, North Carolina.

Judy Katherine Barnes has a B.S. from Campbell University, North Carolina.

Children of James Jackson and Judy Barnes are:

+ 370   i.   James Elvin Jackson, Jr., born 21 January 1968 in Raleigh, North Carolina.
+ 371   ii.   John Trent Jackson, born 15 December 1974.
+ 372   iii. Joseph Wayne Jackson, born 15 December 1974.

210. Lorenda Kaye[8] Jackson (Elvin Sikes[7], Haburn Rice[6], Wiley Calvin[5], Hayburn[4], Hayburn[3], Unidentified[2], Unknown[1])[850] was born 14 January 1947 in Sampson County , North Carolina[851]. She married **(1) Samuel Tony Wallace**[852] Bef. 1963. He was born 13 July 1944[853]. She married **(2) R. M. Hayes** Aft. January 1970. She married **(3) Rufus William Carr**[854] 12 December 2000 in Chestham

115

County, Tennessee[855], son of Rufus Carr and Lola West. He was born 30 September 1948 in Raleigh, North Carolina[856].

Children of Lorenda Kaye Jackson and Samuel Wallace are:

> 373   i.   Tony Robinson Wallace[858], born 14 September 1963[859]; died 17 August 1982 in Charlotte, North Carolina[859].
>
>   Tony Robinson Wallace was buried in a Jackson Family Cemetery on The Avenue in Honeycutts Township, Sampson County, North Carolina[860]
>
> 374   ii.   Richard Elvin Wallace[861], born 22 April 1966[861].
> + 375   iii.   Angela Rochelle Wallace, born 14 December 1970.

211.   Heidi Jane[8] Jackson (Elvin Sikes[7], Haburn Rice[6], Wiley Calvin[5], Hayburn[4], Hayburn[3], Unidentified[2], Unknown[1])[862] was born 18 September 1948 in Sampson County, North Carolina[863]. She married **Charles Edwin Tyndall**[864,865] 04 July 1965 in Dillon, South Carolina[866], son of Edwin Tyndall and Lula Autry. He was born 25 October 1944 in Sampson County , North Carolina[866].

Child of Heidi Jackson and Charles Tyndall is:

> + 376   i.   Cheryl Elaine Tyndall, born 13 April 1968 in Clinton, Sampson County, North Carolina.

213.   Terry Lynn[8] Jackson (Elvin Sikes[7], Haburn Rice[6], Wiley Calvin[5], Hayburn[4], Hayburn[3], Unidentified[2], Unknown[1])[867] was born 28 February 1954 in Sampson County , North Carolina[868]. He married **(1) Yong Suk**[869] About 1974.   He married **(2) Jackie Hall**[870] Aft. 1978. She was born 30 April 1952[871].
Terry Lynn Jackson is retired from the US Army. He served in three conflicts from June 15, 1971 - June 15, 1993.

Children of Terry Jackson and Yong Suk are:

| 377 | i. | Sharon Yvette Jackson[872], born 27 January 1976. |
| 378 | ii. | Virginia Lee Jackson[872], born 26 April 1978. |

214. William Latham[8] **Jackson** (Elvin Sikes[7], Haburn Rice[6], Wiley Calvin[5], Hayburn[4], Hayburn[3], Unidentified[2], Unknown[1])[873] was born 02 May 1964 in Sampson County , North Carolina[874]. He married **Diana Lynn Graybeal**[875]. She was born 01 July 1969[876].

Children of William Jackson and Diana Graybeal are:

| 379 | i. | Elizabeth Lynn Jackson[877], born 21 September 1997[878]. |
| 380 | ii. | William Christopher Jackson[879], born 23 June 1999[880]. |

218. Larry Edward[8] **Beasley** (Addie May[7] Jackson, Osway W.[6], Elisha Moore[5], Hayburn[4], Hayburn[3], Unidentified[2], Unknown[1])[881] was born 16 January 1946[881]. He married **Sybil Caspleman**[881]. She was born 10 October 1970[881].

Children of Larry Beasley and Sybil Caspleman are:

381	i.	Larry Andrew Beasley[882].
382	ii.	Charles Allen Beasley[883].
383	iii.	Michael Paul Beasley[883].

219. Ethel Katie[8] **Beasley** (Addie May[7] Jackson, Osway W.[6], Elisha Moore[5], Hayburn[4], Hayburn[3], Unidentified[2], Unknown[1])[883] was born 22 November 1948[883]. She married **(1) Rick Chase**. She married **(2) Lynn**[883]

Children of Ethel Beasley and Lynn are:

384	i.	Wendy Alice Lynn[883], born Unknown.
385	ii.	Melissa Lynn[883], born Unknown.
386	iii.	Raymond Lynn[883], born Unknown.

220. Thelma Dean[8] **Beasley** (Addie May[7] Jackson, Osway W.[6], Elisha Moore[5], Hayburn[4], Hayburn[3], Unidentified[2], Unknown[1])[883] was born 16 July 1951[883]. She married **Ronald Stephon Simkhobitch**[883] in Virginia. He was born About 1948[883].

Children of Thelma Beasley and Ronald Simkhobitch are:

+ 387   i.   Stacy Lynn Simkhobitch, born 16 December 1970.
   388   ii.   Ronald Stephon Simkhobitch, Jr.[883], born 17 December 1974[883].

231. Pamela Mae[8] **Jackson** (Almoye W.[7], Noah Washington[6], Elisha Moore[5], Hayburn[4], Hayburn[3], Unidentified[2], Unknown[1])[884] was born 03 December 1958 in Clinton, North Carolina[884,885]. She married **Jerry Craig Matthews**[886], son of Owen Matthews and Clarise Simmons. He was born 18 December 1957 in Wayne County[887].

Child of Pamela Jackson and Jerry Matthews is:

   389   i.   Alexander Craig Matthews[888], born 07 March 1993[888].

232. Robyn Lisa[8] **Jackson** (Almoye W.[7], Noah Washington[6], Elisha Moore[5], Hayburn[4], Hayburn[3], Unidentified[2], Unknown[1])[888] was born 13 September 1962 in Unknown[889]. She married **Ernest Dwight Avery**[890]. He was born About 1960[891].

Child of Robyn Jackson and Ernest Avery is:

   390   i.   Jackson Dwight Avery[892], born 14 September 1998[892].

233. Robert Alan[8] **Jackson** (Almoye W.[7], Noah Washington[6], Elisha Moore[5], Hayburn[4], Hayburn[3], Unidentified[2], Unknown[1])[892] was born 27 October 1971 in Unknown[893]. He married **Lee Martin Wilson**[894]. She was born 24 July 1972 in Unknown[894].

Children of Robert Jackson and Lee Wilson are:

   391   i.   Catherine Alana Jackson[894], born 08 September 1998[894].

392   ii. Reid Whitfield Jackson[894], born 21 September 2002[894].

234. Kimberly[8] **Jackson** (J. B.[7], Noah Washington[6], Elisha Moore[5], Hayburn[4], Hayburn[3], Unidentified[2], Unknown[1])[894]. She married **Paul Kiel**[894]. He was born Unknown in Unknown.

Child of Kimberly Jackson and Paul Kiel is:

393   i. Joshua Kiel[895].

241. David Franklin[8] **Wise** (James Franklin[7], Alice Jane[6] Jackson, Elisha Moore[5], Hayburn[4], Hayburn[3], Unidentified[2], Unknown[1])[896] was born 1938. He married **Joyce Crumpler**[896].

Children of David Wise and Joyce Crumpler are:

+   394   i. Melanie Wise.
+   395   ii. Wendy Wise.

243. Robert Howell[8] **Wise** (James Franklin[7], Alice Jane[6] Jackson, Elisha Moore[5], Hayburn[4], Hayburn[3], Unidentified[2], Unknown[1])[897] was born 26 October 1939 in Honeycutts Township, Sampson County, North Carolina[897]. He married **Jeanette Tyndall**[898] 11 August 1962 in Honeycutts Township, Sampson County, North Carolina[899], daughter of William Tyndall and Nannie Tyndall. She was born 03 November 1943 in Herrings Township, Sampson County, North Carolina[899].

Children of Robert Wise and Jeanette Tyndall are:

+   396   i. Robert Keith Wise, born 22 November 1964 in Clinton, Sampson County, North Carolina.
     397   ii. Frederick Wise[900]. He married Beverly Hobbs[900].
     398   iii. Gregg Wise[900]. He married Emily Preddy[900].

245. Bobby Lee[8] **Sessoms** (Celester[7] Wise, Alice Jane[6] Jackson, Elisha Moore[5], Hayburn[4], Hayburn[3], Unidentified[2], Unknown[1])[901] was born 01 August 1939[901,902], and died 02 April 2001[903,904]. He married **Oloby May McPhail**[905,906] 29 June 1961[907], daughter of James McPhail and Lessie Honeycutt. She was born 13 May 1942[908,909].

Apparently, county records show 2 Aug 1940 for Bobby Lee's date of birth.

Bobby Lee Sessoms was buried in Union Grove Baptist Church Cemetery on Vander Road one mile west of Rebel City, Sampson County, North Carolina

Child of Bobby Sessoms and Oloby McPhail is:

    399   i.   Jane Michelle Sessoms[911], born About 1965.

246. Billy Roland[8] **Sessoms** (Celester[7] Wise, Alice Jane[6] Jackson, Elisha Moore[5], Hayburn[4], Hayburn[3], Unidentified[2], Unknown[1])[911] was born 14 May 1942 in Roseboro, North Carolina[912]. He married **(1) Elizabeth Armeallia Faircloth**[913,914]. She was born 24 November 1942 in Little Coharie Township, Sampson County, North Carolina[914]. He married **(2) Jeanette Cook**. She was born Unknown.

Children of Billy Sessoms and Elizabeth Faircloth are:

+   400   i.   James Roland Sessoms, born 23 June 1965.
+   401   ii. Karen Celester Sessoms, born About 1968.
+   402   iii. Deana LeeAnn Sessoms, born About 1972.

247. Jackie Lester[8] **Sessoms** (Celester[7] Wise, Alice Jane[6] Jackson, Elisha Moore[5], Hayburn[4], Hayburn[3], Unidentified[2], Unknown[1])[914] was born 27 October 1944 in Roseboro, North Carolina[914]. He married **Margaret Ann Smith**[914]. She was born 04 September 1947[914].

Children of Jackie Sessoms and Margaret Smith are:

+ 403   i.   Kimberly Ann Sessoms, born 01 August 1967.
+ 404   ii.   Melonie Denice Sessoms, born 03 August 1971.

248. Brenda[8] **Sessoms** (Celester[7] Wise, Alice Jane[6] Jackson, Elisha Moore[5], Hayburn[4], Hayburn[3], Unidentified[2], Unknown[1])[915] was born 16 November 1946[915]. She married **Earl Clayton Tanner**[915,916]. He was born 19 February 1947[917].

Children of Brenda Sessoms and Earl Tanner are:

+ 405   i.   Kevin Earl Tanner, born 11 April 1972.
   406   ii.   Shannon Noah Tanner[918], born 24 April 1974[918].
   407   iii.   Brian Clay Tanner[918], born 14 February 1984[918].

249. Margie Geraldene[8] **Bass** (Annie Kathleen[7] Wise, Alice Jane[6] Jackson, Elisha Moore[5], Hayburn[4], Hayburn[3], Unidentified[2], Unknown[1])[919] was born 19 April 1937[919]. She married **James Franklin Dickinson**[919]. He was born 04 August 1935[919].

Children of Margie Bass and James Dickinson are:

   408   i.   James Franklin Dickinson II[919], born 25 April 1963[919]. He married Lisa Thompson[919]; born 24 September 1965[919].
+ 409   ii.   Angela Jane Dickinson, born 29 December 1967.

255. Tammy Lynnette[8] **Pope** (Preston Carr[7], Amy Lee[6] Jackson, Elisha Moore[5], Hayburn[4], Hayburn[3], Unidentified[2], Unknown[1])[920,921] was born 12 June 1964 in Clinton, Sampson County, North Carolina[922,923,923]. She married **Charles Davis Smith**[924] 22 June 1982 in Clinton, North Carolina, son of Charles Smith and Jackie Jackson. He was born 03 April 1961 in Clinton, Sampson County, North Carolina[924].

Children of Tammy Pope and Charles Smith are:

+	410	i.	Charles Terry Smith, born 17 September 1983.
+	411	ii.	Amanda Dawn Smith, born 09 October 1984.

256. Robert Wayne[8] **Adams** (Astraudia Brown[7] Lockamy, Nina Metherbell[6] Jackson, Elisha Moore[5], Hayburn[4], Hayburn[3], Unidentified[2], Unknown[1])[925] was born 28 February 1950 in Dunn Hospital, North Carolina[926]. He married **Christie Leigh Shaw**[926] 01 June 1973[927], daughter of Clifford Shaw and Dorothy Pepin. She was born 26 July 1952 in Galena Park, Texas[928].

Children of Robert Adams and Christie Shaw are:

412	i.	Amy Charriene LaVal Adams[930], born 13 August 1974[930].
413	ii.	Angelyn Marie Stellaundine Adams[931], born 18 March 1977[932].
414	iii.	Robert Wayne Adams, Jr.[933], born Bet. 1977 - 1981.
415	iv.	Amber Christine Hennritta Adams[934], born 27 December 1979[934].

Generation No. 7

261. William Ellis[9] **Jackson** (William B.[8], Randall B.[7], Wiley B.[6], Wiley Calvin[5], Hayburn[4], Hayburn[3], Unidentified[2], Unknown[1])[935] was born 03 July 1957[935]. He married **Susan Carol Sumner**[936]. She was born 31 December 1956[937].

William Ellis Jackson and Susan Carol Sumner are divorced.

Children of William Jackson and Susan Sumner are:

+	416	i.	Erica Susan Jackson, born 12 March 1980 in Unknown.
+	417	ii.	Heather Joyce Jackson, born 17 April 1982.

264. Rodney Keith[9] **Honeycutt** (Claudia Priscilla[8] Jackson, Randall B.[7], Wiley B.[6], Wiley Calvin[5], Hayburn[4], Hayburn[3],

Unidentified[2], Unknown[1])[938] was born 30 April 1965 in Ft. Benning, Georgia[938]. He married **(1) Patricia Ann Wiley**[939] About 1984. She was born 18 June 1968[940]. He married **(2) Melissa Gurley**[941] 21 April 2007[941].

Rodney Keith Honeycutt and Patricia Ann Wiley are divorced

Child of Rodney Honeycutt and Patricia Wiley is:

418   i.   Samantha Lynn Honeycutt[942], born 25 December 1985 in Sampson County, North Carolina.

265. Randall Franklin[9] **Jackson** (J. W.[8], Randall B.[7], Wiley B.[6], Wiley Calvin[5], Hayburn[4], Hayburn[3], Unidentified[2], Unknown[1])[943] was born 19 July 1963[944]. He married **Anna Marie Unknown**[945]. She was born 23 March 1967[946].

Randall Jackson and Anna Marie Unknown are divorced.

Child of Randall Jackson and Anna Unknown is:

419   i.   Randall J. Jackson[947], born 20 April 1988 in Cumberland County, North Carolina[947].

266. Andrew[9] **Jackson** (J. W.[8], Randall B.[7], Wiley B.[6], Wiley Calvin[5], Hayburn[4], Hayburn[3], Unidentified[2], Unknown[1])[948] was born 21 August 1964[949]. He married **Donna Parker**[950]. She was born 27 June 1966[951].
Child of Andrew Jackson and Donna Parker is:

420   i.   Hope Jackson[952], born 22 September 1986[953].

277. Marie J.[9] **Jackson** (Bernice Franklin[8], Tommy Franklin[7], Wiley B.[6], Wiley Calvin[5], Hayburn[4], Hayburn[3], Unidentified[2], Unknown[1])[954]. She married **Joseph Henry Lee**[955,956].

Child of Marie Jackson and Joseph Lee is:

421   i. Raven Nicole Lee[956].

279. William Franklin[9] **Jackson** (William Robert[8], Tommy Franklin[7], Wiley B.[6], Wiley Calvin[5], Hayburn[4], Hayburn[3], Unidentified[2], Unknown[1])[956] was born 11 December 1957[956], and died 20 March 1999[956]. He married **Brenda Unknown.**

William Franklin Jackson was buried in Spell-Tyndall Grove Cemetery near Clinton, North Carolina

Children of William Jackson and Brenda Unknown are:

422   i. Christopher Allen Jackson[956].
423   ii. Billy Jackson[956].

           Billy's name may be "William".

424   iii. Tommy Calvin Jackson[956].

280. Barbara Ellen[9] **Jackson** (William Robert[8], Tommy Franklin[7], Wiley B.[6], Wiley Calvin[5], Hayburn[4], Hayburn[3], Unidentified[2], Unknown[1])[956] was born 17 May 1963. She married **Timmy Blackmon**[956].

Child of Barbara Jackson and Timmy Blackmon is:

425   i. Nicklos Blackmon[956].

281. Thomas Jerome[9] **Jackson** (Thomas A.[8], Tommy Franklin[7], Wiley B.[6], Wiley Calvin[5], Hayburn[4], Hayburn[3], Unidentified[2], Unknown[1])[957] was born 03 March 1970 in Sampson County, North Carolina[957]. He married **Elizabeth Anzelia Willsins**[958].

Children of Thomas Jackson and Elizabeth Willsins are:

426   i.   Nathan Thomas Jackson[958], born 24 August 1989 in Samson Memorial Hospital, Sampson County, North Carolina[959].

427   ii. Caelyn Jackson[960].

282. Stephanie Denice[9] Jackson (Thomas A.[8], Tommy Franklin[7], Wiley B.[6], Wiley Calvin[5], Hayburn[4], Hayburn[3], Unidentified[2], Unknown[1])[960] was born 07 January 1973[960]. She married **Wayne Neil Bass**[960] Unknown.

Children of Stephanie Jackson and Wayne Bass are:

428   i.   Michael Wayne Bass[960], born 30 March 1992 in Sampson Memorial Hospital, Sampson County , North Carolina[961].

429   ii. Christian Tyler Bass[962], born 11 November 1998 in Sampson Memorial Hospital, Sampson County , North Carolina[963].

       Christian Tyler Bass is a free bleeder. He has the Factor 8 missing from his blood.

283. Teresa Rose[9] Jackson (Thomas A.[8], Tommy Franklin[7], Wiley B.[6], Wiley Calvin[5], Hayburn[4], Hayburn[3], Unidentified[2], Unknown[1])[964] was born 11 October 1975[964]. She married **Johnny Edward Lucas II**[964].

Children of Teresa Jackson and Johnny Lucas are:

430   i.   Johnny Edward Lucas III[964], born 15 October 1991 in Sampson County Memorial Hospital, Clinton, North Carolina[965].

431   ii. Jason Scott Lucas[966], born 15 June 1993 in Sampson County Memorial Hospital, Clinton, North Carolina[967].

432   iii. Donald Lee Lucas[968], born 01 August 1994 in Sampson County Memorial Hospital, Clinton, North Carolina[969].

433   iv. Amanda Lynn Lucas[970], born 08 July 1996 in Fort Myers, FL[971].

287. Tina Michelle[9] Milligan (Wanda Faye[8] Jackson, William C.[7], Wiley B.[6], Wiley Calvin[5], Hayburn[4], Hayburn[3], Unidentified[2], Unknown[1])[972] was born Unknown. She married **Lee Lane**[972]. He was born Unknown.

Child of Tina Milligan and Lee Lane is:

434   i. Erica Lane[972], born Unknown.

291.   Lora Lynn[9] Bass (Eunice Mae[8] Owen, Mittie Lee[7] Lockamy, Flora Lee[6] Jackson, Wiley Calvin[5], Hayburn[4], Hayburn[3], Unidentified[2], Unknown[1])[973,974] was born 29 December 1965 in Clinton, Sampson County, North Carolina[975]. She married **(1) Allen Carroll Bass**[976] 11 May 1985 in Taylors Bridge Township, Sampson County, North Carolina[976], son of Cecil Bass and Elizabeth Ryals. He was born 03 August 1962 in Wake County, North Carolina[976]. She married **(2) Johnny Marshall**[977] About 1989.

Child of Lora Bass and Allen Bass is:

435   i. Allen Zachary Bass[978], born 18 March 1988 in Clinton, Sampson County, North Carolina[978].

Children of Lora Bass and Johnny Marshall are:

436   i. Meredith Leigh Marshall[979], born 28 June 1990[979].
437   ii. Kyle Marshall[979], born 18 January 2002[979].

294.   Rose Marie[9] McLaurin (Edna Lee[8] Lockamy, David Martin[7], Flora Lee[6] Jackson, Wiley Calvin[5], Hayburn[4], Hayburn[3], Unidentified[2], Unknown[1])[979] was born 10 March 1957[979]. She married **Joe Paul Edmondson**[979] 03 September 1977[979]. Rose Marie McLaurin and John Paul Edmondson are divorced.

Child of Rose McLaurin and Joe Edmondson is:

438   i. Joshua Paul Edmondson[979], born 10 July 1982[979].

295. Elizabeth Mae[9] **McLaurin** (Edna Lee[8] Lockamy, David Martin[7], Flora Lee[6] Jackson, Wiley Calvin[5], Hayburn[4], Hayburn[3], Unidentified[2], Unknown[1])[980] was born 09 January 1960[981]. She married **(1) Earnest Durwood Carter**[981] 29 October 1978[981]. She married **(2) John Wade**[981] 31 August 1986.

Elizabeth and Durwood divorced.

Child of Elizabeth McLaurin and Earnest Carter is:

439   i. Adam Ivey Carter[981], born 20 April 1979[981].

Children of Elizabeth McLaurin and John Wade are:

440   i. Evan Parrish Wade[981], born 03 December 1996[981].
441   ii. Heather Marie Wade.

296. David Merel[9] **McLaurin** (Edna Lee[8] Lockamy, David Martin[7], Flora Lee[6] Jackson, Wiley Calvin[5], Hayburn[4], Hayburn[3], Unidentified[2], Unknown[1])[981] was born 04 June 1967[981]. He married **Kimberly Jo Nobles**[981] 16 December 1995.

Child of David McLaurin and Kimberly Nobles is:

442   i. Connnor David McLaurin[981], born 18 September 2000[981].

299. Yvonne[9] **Lockamy** (Wiley Martin[8], David Martin[7], Flora Lee[6] Jackson, Wiley Calvin[5], Hayburn[4], Hayburn[3], Unidentified[2], Unknown[1])[981] was born 06 January 1964. She married **Art Marino**[981].

Children of Yvonne Lockamy and Art Marino are:

443   i. Montana McIntosh Marino[981], born 28 August 1983[981].
444   ii. Malayna Marino[981], born 26 June 1991[981].

300. Kimberley Valentina[9] Lockamy (Wiley Martin[8], David Martin[7], Flora Lee[6] Jackson, Wiley Calvin[5], Hayburn[4], Hayburn[3], Unidentified[2], Unknown[1])[981] was born 25 March 1969[981]. She married **William Rhoades**.

Children of Kimberley Lockamy and William Rhoades are:

445   i. Kiger Rhoades[981], born 03 December 2000[981].
446   ii. Karah Rhoades[981], born 17 March 2004[981].

302. Jessica Lockamy[9] Hackney (Alice Faye[8] Lockamy, David Martin[7], Flora Lee[6] Jackson, Wiley Calvin[5], Hayburn[4], Hayburn[3], Unidentified[2], Unknown[1])[981] was born 03 November 1968[981]. She married **Charles Richard Williams**[981] 20 September 1997.

Children of Jessica Hackney and Charles Williams are:

447   i. Bailey Allison Williams[981], born 29 August 1992[981].
448   ii. Jacob Dean Williams[981], born 06 February 1999[981].

306. Regina Gray[9] Williams (Fannie Lee[8] Lockamy, Beulah Jane[7], Flora Lee[6] Jackson, Wiley Calvin[5], Hayburn[4], Hayburn[3], Unidentified[2], Unknown[1])[981] was born 17 October 1969 in Sampson County, North Carolina[981]. She married **George Thomas Speight**[981]. He was born 03 September 1965[981].

Children of Regina Williams and George Speight are:

449   i. William Thomas Speight[981], born 29 January 2001[981].
450   ii. Anna Lee Speight, born 29 January 2001.

307. Barbara Gail[9] Bass (Doris Allese[8] McLamb, Lizzie Adeline[7] Lockamy, Flora Lee[6] Jackson, Wiley Calvin[5], Hayburn[4], Hayburn[3], Unidentified[2], Unknown[1])[982] was born 26 July 1950 in

Clinton, Sampson County, North Carolina[982]. She married **Stephen Elmore**.

Children of Barbara Bass and Stephen Elmore are:

451   i.   Amy Jennifer Elmore[983]. She married Jason Lee Roberson[983] 21 May 2000[983].

        More About Jason Roberson and Amy Elmore:
        Marriage: 21 May 2000[983]

452   ii. Stephen Eric Elmore[983].

308.   Steven Johnson[9] **Bass** (Doris Allese[8] McLamb, Lizzie Adeline[7] Lockamy, Flora Lee[6] Jackson, Wiley Calvin[5], Hayburn[4], Hayburn[3], Unidentified[2], Unknown[1])[984] was born 02 October 1955 in Clinton, Sampson County, North Carolina[985]. He married **Linda Gail Bass**[986] 02 May 1976 in Halls Township, Sampson County, North Carolina[987], daughter of Mack Bass and Elizabeth Thornton. She was born 07 September 1955 in Clinton, Sampson County, North Carolina[988].

Children of Steven Bass and Linda Bass are:

453   i.   Johnson Delcon Bass[990], born 28 December 1977 in Clinton, Sampson County, North Carolina[990].

454   ii. Phyllis Alene Bass[990], born 13 March 1979 in Clinton, Sampson County, North Carolina[990]; died 29 December 1980 in Clinton, Sampson County, North Carolina.

        Phyllis Alene Bass was buried in Mt. Gilead Baptist Church Cemetery, Sampson County, North Carolina

455   iii. William Edwin Bass[990], born 18 April 1981 in Clinton, Sampson County, North Carolina[990]. He married Elizabeth Ellen Henry[991] 04 June 2005[991].

456   iv. Amanda Gail Bass[992], born 14 May 1984 in Clinton, Sampson County, North Carolina[992].

457   v. Sharon Grace Bass[992], born 31 August 1988 in Clinton, Sampson County, North Carolina[992].

309. Edith Joan[9] **Bass** (Doris Allese[8] McLamb, Lizzie Adeline[7] Lockamy, Flora Lee[6] Jackson, Wiley Calvin[5], Hayburn[4], Hayburn[3], Unidentified[2], Unknown[1])[992] was born 14 March 1963 in Clinton, Sampson County, North Carolina[993]. She married **Anthony Edward Lane**[994] 25 September 1988 in Taylors Bridge Township, Sampson County, North Carolina[994]. He was born 18 June 1961 in Clinton, Sampson County, North Carolina[994].

Children of Edith Bass and Anthony Lane are:

458	i.	Brittaney Elizabeth Lane[995].
459	ii.	Ashley Brooke Lane[995].
460	iii.	Matthew Jordan Lane[995].

311. Jeffrey[9] **Ashworth** (Joyce Ann[8] Jackson, Andrew Davis[7], Ewell Sanford[6], Wiley Calvin[5], Hayburn[4], Hayburn[3], Unidentified[2], Unknown[1])[996]. He married **<Unnamed>**.

Child of Jeffrey Ashworth and <Unnamed> is:

461	i.	Caroline Ashworth[996].

321. Houston Lee[9] **Lockamy** (James Houston[8], James Lee[7], Jemima Jewel[6] Jackson, Wiley Calvin[5], Hayburn[4], Hayburn[3], Unidentified[2], Unknown[1])[997] was born 25 February 1944[997]. He married **(1) Judy Lewis**[997] Bef. 1981. He married **(2) Judy Gaye Springs King**[997] 18 January 1992 in Dillon, South Carolina. She was born 12 March 1946[997].

Houston Lockamy and Judy Lewis are divorced.

Child of Houston Lockamy and Judy Lewis is:

462	i.	James Lee Lockamy[997], born 10 October 1981[997].

323. Omie Kaye[9] **Lockamy** (James Houston[8], James Lee[7], Jemima Jewel[6] Jackson, Wiley Calvin[5], Hayburn[4], Hayburn[3], Unidentified[2], Unknown[1])[997] was born 09 February 1948[998]. She married **George Henry Cox**[999] 08 March 1969 in Dillon, South Carolina[1000]. He was born 08 April 1947[1001].

Children of Omie Lockamy and George Cox are:

	463	i.	Ronald Paul Cox[1003], born 27 December 1969[1003].
+	464	ii.	Cynthia Kaye Cox, born 26 September 1975.

324. Jimmy McThomas[9] **Lockamy** (James Houston[8], James Lee[7], Jemima Jewel[6] Jackson, Wiley Calvin[5], Hayburn[4], Hayburn[3], Unidentified[2], Unknown[1])[1004] was born 27 March 1950[1004]. He married **Gwendolyn Kay West**[1004,1005] 21 June 1970 in Holly Grove Presbyterian Church[1006]. She was born 15 January 1953[1006].

Gwendolyn Kay West's nickname is 'Gwen'.

Children of Jimmy Lockamy and Gwendolyn West are:

	465	i.	June Michelle Lockamy, born 31 May 1973.
	466	ii.	Amy Nichole Lockamy[1006], born 29 July 1976[1006].
	467	iii.	Jimmy McThomas Lockamy, Jr[1006], born 10 July 1979[1006].

325. Jackie Lou[9] **Lockamy** (James Houston[8], James Lee[7], Jemima Jewel[6] Jackson, Wiley Calvin[5], Hayburn[4], Hayburn[3], Unidentified[2], Unknown[1])[1006] was born 26 September 1953[1006]. She married **James Guilford Daughtry**[1007] 26 November 1972 in Dillon, South Carolina[1007]. He was born 14 November 1949[1007].

Children of Jackie Lockamy and James Daughtry are:

468	i.	James Clifford Daughtry[1007], born 04 July 1976[1008]. He married Shannon Lynn Williamson[1009] 17 September 2002[1009].

469   ii. Derek Allen Daughtry[1009], born 02 October 1983[1009]. He married Dawn Boone[1009].

326. Ronald Keith[9] **Hairr** (Floyd Lutrell[8], Lula Bee[7] Lockamy, Jemima Jewel[6] Jackson, Wiley Calvin[5], Hayburn[4], Hayburn[3], Unidentified[2], Unknown[1])[1010] was born 08 June 1959[1010]. He married **Julia Gautier**[1010].

Children of Ronald Hairr and Julia Gautier are:

470   i. Donna Hairr[1010].
471   ii. Stillborn Hairr.

327. Shelia Rose[9] **Hairr** (Floyd Lutrell[8], Lula Bee[7] Lockamy, Jemima Jewel[6] Jackson, Wiley Calvin[5], Hayburn[4], Hayburn[3], Unidentified[2], Unknown[1])[1011] was born 11 April 1965[1012]. She married **Tommy Jones**[1012] in Owens Grove Pentecostal FWB Church, Sampson County, North Carolina[1012].

Child of Shelia Hairr and Tommy Jones is:

472   i. Thomas Luke Jones[1012], born About 1992[1012].

328. Ronnie Best[9] **Jordan** (Willa Dean[8] Lockamy, Robert C.[7], Jemima Jewel[6] Jackson, Wiley Calvin[5], Hayburn[4], Hayburn[3], Unidentified[2], Unknown[1])[1013] was born 14 November 1952 in Sampson County , North Carolina[1014]. He married **Dixie Lou Owen** 07 April 1977 in Grove Park Baptist Church, Clinton, North Carolina[1015]. She was born 17 October 1956.

Children of Ronnie Jordan and Dixie Owen are:

473   i. Chadwick Best Jordan[1016], born 31 January 1978 in Sampson County , North Carolina[1016]; died 01 February 1978 in Sampson County , North Carolina[1017,1018].

Chadwick Best Jordan was buried in Grandview Memorial Gardens, Clinton, Sampson County, North Carolina[1019]

+ 474   ii.   Dana Owen Jordan, born 11 July 1979.

329. Linda Lee[9] **Jordan** (Willa Dean[8] Lockamy, Robert C.[7], Jemima Jewel[6] Jackson, Wiley Calvin[5], Hayburn[4], Hayburn[3], Unidentified[2], Unknown[1])[1020] was born 11 May 1949[1020]. She married Kenneth Honeycutt.

Linda Lee and Kenneth Honeycutt are divorced.

Children of Linda Lee Jordan and Kenneth Honeycutt are:

475   i.   Maurice Lee Honeycutt[1020], born 27 November 1965[1020]; died 05 August 1995[1020].

Maurice Lee Honeycutt was buried in Grandview Memorial Gardens, Clinton, Sampson County, North Carolina[1020]

476   ii.   Arthur Julian Honeycutt[1020], born 16 June 1967[1020]; died 31 May 2004[1021].

477   iii.   Stacy M. Honeycutt[1022], born 29 August 1969[1022].

330. William Glenn[9] **Jordan** (Willa Dean[8] Lockamy, Robert C.[7], Jemima Jewel[6] Jackson, Wiley Calvin[5], Hayburn[4], Hayburn[3], Unidentified[2], Unknown[1])[1022] was born 19 May 1964[1022]. He married **Jackie Desiree McKenzie**[1022] 30 May 1989 in Emanuel Baptist Church, Clinton, North Carolina[1022]. She was born 11 September 1964[1022].

Children of William Jordan and Jackie McKenzie are:

478   i.   Dylan Glenn Jordan[1022], born 19 June 1994[1022].

479   ii.   Garrett McKenzie Jordan[1022], born 12 March 1999[1022].

335. Carla Jean[9] **Lockamy** (Thomas Daniel[8], Robert C.[7], Jemima Jewel[6] Jackson, Wiley Calvin[5], Hayburn[4], Hayburn[3], Unidentified[2], Unknown[1])[1023] was born 29 March 1953 in Clinton, Sampson

County, North Carolina[1023]. She married **Monty Christopher Peterson**[1023] 26 May 1973 in Clinton, North Carolina[1023], son of Claxton Peterson and Irma Bass. He was born 03 October 1950 in Taylors Bridge Township, Sampson County, North Carolina[1023].

Monty Christopher Peterson is called 'Chris.'

Child of Carla Lockamy and Monty Peterson is:

> 480   i.   David Peterson[1023].

338.   Darrin Grey[9] **Kennedy** (Velva Jewell[8] Dixon, Martha Anna[7] Lockamy, Jemima Jewel[6] Jackson, Wiley Calvin[5], Hayburn[4], Hayburn[3], Unidentified[2], Unknown[1])[1024] was born 30 September 1969[1025]. He married **Donna Boone**[1026].

Children of Darrin Kennedy and Donna Boone are:

> 481   i.   Dalton Grey Kennedy[1026], born 25 July 1995[1027].
> 482   ii. Deanna Morgan Kennedy[1028], born 30 March 1997[1029].

343.   Joseph Richard[9] **Pleitt** (Nancy Eveline[8] Jackson, Oscar Davis[7], Haburn Rice[6], Wiley Calvin[5], Hayburn[4], Hayburn[3], Unidentified[2], Unknown[1])[1030] was born 05 December 1961 in Lutheran General Hospital, Park Ridge, Cook County, Illinois[1030]. He married **Denise Rose Dion**[1031] 09 August 1986 in Sacred Heart Catholic Church, Lombard, Du Page County, Illinois[1032], daughter of Edward Dion and Marcella Stoffel. She was born 19 April 1961 in Oak Lawn, Cook County, Illinois[1033].

Joseph Richard has a B.S. in Chemical Engineering from the University of Missouri, Columbia. He was in ROTC 1981-1982.

Confirmation name for Denise Rose Dion is 'Denise Rose Ann Dion.' Denise has an Associate Degree in Applied Science.

Children of Joseph Pleitt and Denise Dion are:

483   i. Jason Joseph Pleitt[1035], born 26 August 1987 in Lombard, Du Page County, Illinois[1035].

484   ii. Kristina Rose Pleitt[1036], born 06 February 1990 in Lombard, Du Page, Illinois[1036].

485   iii. Nicholas Richard Pleitt[1037], born 11 July 1995 in Lombard, Du Page, Illinois[1037]; died 19 July 1995 in Loyola University Medical Center, Maywood, Cook County, Illinois[1037].

Nicholas Richard Pleitt was buried on 21 July 1995 in Assumption Cemetery, Winfield, Du Page County, Illinois[1037]

486   iv. Nathan Alexander Pleitt[1038], born 03 September 1998 in Lombard, Du Page, Illinois[1038].

344.   **Anna Bernadette[9] Pleitt** (Nancy Eveline[8] Jackson, Oscar Davis[7], Haburn Rice[6], Wiley Calvin[5], Hayburn[4], Hayburn[3], Unidentified[2], Unknown[1])[1039,1040] was born 13 January 1965 in Holy Family Hospital, Cook County, Illinois[1041]. She married **William Peter Kootstra**[1042] 05 November 1992 in Island Lake, Lake County, Illinois[1043], son of Peiter Kootstra. He was born 26 June 1964 in Canada[1044].

Anna Bernadette Pleitt Kootstra graduated from Northeastern Illinois Univeristy, Chicago, Illinois, with a B.S. in Biology.

Children of Anna Pleitt and William Kootstra are:

487   i. Peter Willem Kootstra[1046], born 12 June 1993 in Good Shepherd Hospital, Barrington, Lake County, Illinois[1046].

488   ii. Haley Marie Kootstra[1047], born 10 May 1995 in Good Shepherd Hospital, Barrington, Lake County, Illinois[1047].

345. Charles Davis[9] Smith (Jackie Olene[8] Jackson, Oscar Davis[7], Haburn Rice[6], Wiley Calvin[5], Hayburn[4], Hayburn[3], Unidentified[2], Unknown[1])[1048] was born 03 April 1961 in Clinton, Sampson County, North Carolina[1048]. He married **Tammy Lynnette Pope**[1049,1050] 22 June 1982 in Clinton, North Carolina, daughter of Preston Pope and Helen Sinclair. She was born 12 June 1964 in Clinton, Sampson County, North Carolina[1051,1052,1052].

Children are listed above under (255) Tammy Lynnette Pope.

346. Michael Edward[9] **Smith** (Jackie Olene[8] Jackson, Oscar Davis[7], Haburn Rice[6], Wiley Calvin[5], Hayburn[4], Hayburn[3], Unidentified[2], Unknown[1])[1053,1054] was born 29 May 1962 in Bethel, Pitt County, North Carolina[1055,1056]. He married **Lecia Allen Boyd**[1057] 06 May 1983 in Dillon, South Carolina, daughter of William Boyd and Rachel Thornton. She was born 20 September 1966 in Sampson County, North Carolina[1057].

Michael Edward started about 1972 to have problems with mitral valve prolapse. His and Lecia's son, Jonah Phillip was born with Atrial Septal Defect and had surgery to correct it at about age two.

Jonah's doctors first told Lecia and Mike that they suspected Jonah's problem was inherited and when the doctors were told that Michael had problems as a child they explained that there has been an association between A.S.D. and Mitral Valve Prolapse and they believed there was a connection between Mike and Jonah's problem. At least two other descendants of Oscar Davis Jackson and Roberta Holland had or have similar heart problems; one died after surgery when only eight days old and one, age 70, with Mitral Valve Prolapse is still living in 2006. A cousin from the Jackson and Holland lines was born with a similar severe problems and had surgery at about age two.

Children of Michael Smith and Lecia Boyd are:

+ 489   i. Michael Allen Smith, born 26 January 1986 in Sampson County, North Carolina.
490   ii. Brittany Faith Smith[1057], born 17 March 1989 in Sampson County, North Carolina[1057].
491   iii. Jonah Phillip Smith[1057], born 28 September 1991 in Sampson County, North Carolina[1057].

Jonah Phillip Smith was born with Atrial Septal Defect. Surgery was performed to correct the problem and Jonah is in very good health today.

492   iv.   Rachel Courtney Smith[1057], born 04 April 1993 in Sampson County, North Carolina[1057].

493   v.   Destiny Hope Smith[1057], born 29 May 1995 in Sampson County, North Carolina[1057].

494   vi.   Gage Ransom Smith, born 07 June 2005 in Sampson County, North Carolina.

495   vii.   Jaden Reid Smith[1058], born 08 November 2006 in Sampson County , North Carolina[1058].

347. Jackie Gregory[9] **Smith** (Jackie Olene[8] Jackson, Oscar Davis[7], Haburn Rice[6], Wiley Calvin[5], Hayburn[4], Hayburn[3], Unidentified[2], Unknown[1])[1059] was born 22 April 1966 in Tarboro, North Carolina[1060,1061]. He married **Linda Ann McClenny**[1062] 28 July 1984 in Dillon, South Carolina[1062], daughter of Joseph McClenny and Carrie Unknown. She was born 13 March 1965 in Clinton, Sampson County, North Carolina[1062].

Children of Jackie Smith and Linda McClenny are:

+ 496   i.   Erica Nicole Smith, born 18 December 1985 in Clinton, Sampson County, North Carolina.

497   ii.   Heather Nicole Smith[1062], born 15 April 1992 in Clinton, Sampson County, North Carolina[1062].

498   iii.   Savannah Lynn Smith[1062], born 31 July 1998 in Clinton, Sampson County, North Carolina[1062].

350. Clyde Earl[9] **Gallagher** (Margaret Ann[8] Parker, Mattie Ruth[7] Jackson, Haburn Rice[6], Wiley Calvin[5], Hayburn[4], Hayburn[3], Unidentified[2], Unknown[1])[1063] was born 04 February 1962[1064]. He married **Lisa Johnson**[1065]. She was born 21 July 1965[1066].

Child of Clyde Gallagher and Lisa Johnson is:

499   i.   Emily Ann Gallagher[1067], born 27 August 1996[1068].

351. Melanie Joy[9] **Parker** (Miles Joel[8], Mattie Ruth[7] Jackson, Haburn Rice[6], Wiley Calvin[5], Hayburn[4], Hayburn[3], Unidentified[2],

Unknown[1])[1069] was born 10 September 1960 in Honeycutts Township, Sampson County, North Carolina[1069]. She married **(1) Joseph Devane Capps, Jr.**[1069], son of Joseph Capps and Sonja Williams. He was born 03 February 1960 in Clinton, Sampson County, North Carolina[1069]. She married **(2) Derold Cannady**[1070]. He was born About 1960[1071].

Child of Melanie Parker and Joseph Capps is:

 500 i. Jennifer Dawn Capps[1072], born 19 May 1981[1073].

Child of Melanie Parker and Derold Cannady is:

 501 i. Miles Cannady[1074], born About 1982.

 352. Melina Jill[9] **Parker** (Miles Joel[8], Mattie Ruth[7] Jackson, Haburn Rice[6], Wiley Calvin[5], Hayburn[4], Hayburn[3], Unidentified[2], Unknown[1])[1075] was born 26 December 1964 in Sampson County , North Carolina[1076]. She married **David Lynn Horner**[1077,1078]. He was born 05 December 1961 in Bluefield, West Virginia[1079].

Melina Jill has been diabetic since age 17.

Children of Melina Parker and David Horner are:

 502 i. Dustin Frank Horner[1079], born About 1987[1080].
 503 ii. Parker Horner[1081], born About 1992[1082].

 354. Anthony Ray[9] **Honeycutt** (Rena Florence[8] Parker, Mattie Ruth[7] Jackson, Haburn Rice[6], Wiley Calvin[5], Hayburn[4], Hayburn[3], Unidentified[2], Unknown[1])[1083] was born 23 March 1959[1084]. He married **Kimberly Ann Brickman**[1085]. She was born 20 May 1957[1086].

Child of Anthony Honeycutt and Kimberly Brickman is:

 504 i. Rachel Ann Honeycutt[1087], born 16 November 1991.

355.   Leonard Scott[9] King (Rena Florence[8] Parker, Mattie Ruth[7] Jackson, Haburn Rice[6], Wiley Calvin[5], Hayburn[4], Hayburn[3], Unidentified[2], Unknown[1])[1088] was born 06 March 1965[1088]. He married **Billie Jo Butler**[1089]. She was born 11 June 1967[1089].

Child of Leonard King and Billie Butler is:

505   i.   Dalton Scott King[1090], born 08 March 1995.

356.   Timmy Maxwell[9] King (Rena Florence[8] Parker, Mattie Ruth[7] Jackson, Haburn Rice[6], Wiley Calvin[5], Hayburn[4], Hayburn[3], Unidentified[2], Unknown[1])[1091] was born 26 January 1968[1091]. He married **Lesa Thigpin**[1092]. She was born 18 September 1965[1092].

Child of Timmy King and Lesa Thigpin is:

506   i.   Payson Trot King, born 22 December 2002.

357.   Breezy[9] Bradshaw (Rena Florence[8] Parker, Mattie Ruth[7] Jackson, Haburn Rice[6], Wiley Calvin[5], Hayburn[4], Hayburn[3], Unidentified[2], Unknown[1])[1093] was born 17 July 1977[1094].

Child of Breezy Bradshaw is:

507   i.   Takoda Sean-Maxwell Bradshaw[1094], born 07 February 2000[1095].

362. Terry Wayne[9] Long (William Craven[8], Mary Jane[7] Jackson, Haburn Rice[6], Wiley Calvin[5], Hayburn[4], Hayburn[3], Unidentified[2], Unknown[1])[1096,1097] was born 22 December 1959[1098]. He married **Lisa Sumner**[1099]. She was born 01 April 1961[1099].

Child of Terry Long and Lisa Sumner is:

508   i.   Courtney Ray Long[1100], born 01 April 1985[1101].

368. Sondra Jean[9] **Long** (Robert Earl[8], Mary Jane[7] Jackson, Haburn Rice[6], Wiley Calvin[5], Hayburn[4], Hayburn[3], Unidentified[2], Unknown[1])[1102] was born 07 December 1966 in Sampson County , North Carolina[1102]. She married **(1) Robert McFarland**[1102] Bef. 1985.   She married **(2) Louis Marlin LaRouche**[1103] 18 January 1997. He was born 28
July 1970[1103].

Children of Sondra Long and Robert McFarland are:

509	i.	Kevin Wayne McFarland[1104], born 08 August 1985[1104].
510	ii.	Ashley Jean McFarland[1104], born 27 October 1986[1104]; died 12 May 2003 in Sampson County, North Carolina[1105].

Child of Sondra Long and Louis LaRouche is:

511	i.	Karla M. Lockamy LaRouche[1106], born 21 June 1992[1106].

369. Charles Franklin[9] **Long** (Robert Earl[8], Mary Jane[7] Jackson, Haburn Rice[6], Wiley Calvin[5], Hayburn[4], Hayburn[3], Unidentified[2], Unknown[1])[1107] was born 08 September 1971 in Cumberland County, North Carolina[1107]. He married **Joy Hairr**[1108]. She was born 05 February 1971 in Sampson County , North Carolina[1109].

Child of Charles Long and Joy Hairr is:

512	i.	Joshua Earl Long[1110], born 06 October 1992 in Sampson County , North Carolina[1110].

370. James Elvin[9] **Jackson, Jr.** (James Elvin[8], Elvin Sikes[7], Haburn Rice[6], Wiley Calvin[5], Hayburn[4], Hayburn[3], Unidentified[2], Unknown[1])[1111] was born 21 January 1968 in Raleigh, North Carolina[1112]. He married **(1) Rebecca Rivers**[1113].   He married **(2) Sharon Jacquline Umstead**[1114] 28 July 1995 in Garner, North Carolina[1115], daughter of Alexander Umstead and Jacquline Thigpen. She was born 16 January 1968 in Raleigh, North Carolina[1116].

James Elvin Jackson, Jr. is called "Jimmy."

Sharon Jacquline Umstead has a B.S. from UNCW and is in Health Care.

Child of James Jackson and Rebecca Rivers is:

    513   i.   Joshua Arthur Jackson[1118], born 08 February 1994.

Children of James Jackson and Sharon Umstead are:

    514   i.   James Alexander Jackson[1119], born 24 September 1996[1120].
    515   ii.   Jenna Marie Jackson[1121], born 12 May 2000[1122].

371.   John Trent[9] Jackson (James Elvin[8], Elvin Sikes[7], Haburn Rice[6], Wiley Calvin[5], Hayburn[4], Hayburn[3], Unidentified[2], Unknown[1])[1123] was born 15 December 1974[1124]. He married **Michele Angelique Garceau** 27 July 1996 in Highland Baptist Church, Raleigh, North Carolina. She was born 26 June 1974[1125].

John Trent Jackson is divorced. Called "Johnny."

Child of John Jackson and Michele Garceau is:
    516   i.   JoAnn Nicole Jackson[1126], born 07 January 1999[1127].

372.   Joseph Wayne[9] Jackson (James Elvin[8], Elvin Sikes[7], Haburn Rice[6], Wiley Calvin[5], Hayburn[4], Hayburn[3], Unidentified[2], Unknown[1])[1128] was born 15 December 1974. He married **Misty Jo Allen**[1129]. She was born 12 July 1975[1130].

Joseph Wayne Jackson is called "Jody."

Child of Joseph Jackson and Misty Allen is:

517   i.   Joseph Allen Jackson[1131], born 15 February 2003[1132].

375.   Angela Rochelle[9] **Wallace** (Lorenda Kaye[8] Jackson, Elvin Sikes[7], Haburn Rice[6], Wiley Calvin[5], Hayburn[4], Hayburn[3], Unidentified[2], Unknown[1])[1133] was born 14 December 1970[1134]. She married **(1) Robert Ryan Massengill**[1135]. He was born 15 December 1969[1136]. She married **(2) John Lance Jackson**[1137]. He was born 11 December 1966.

Child of Angela Wallace and Robert Massengill is:

518   i.   Aaron Richard Massengill[1138], born 28 January 1994 in Smithfield, North Carolina[1139].

376.   Cheryl Elaine[9] **Tyndall** (Heidi Jane[8] Jackson, Elvin Sikes[7], Haburn Rice[6], Wiley Calvin[5], Hayburn[4], Hayburn[3], Unidentified[2], Unknown[1])[1140] was born 13 April 1968 in Clinton, Sampson County, North Carolina[1141]. She married **Thomas Worth Smith**[1142] 01 September 1990 in Salemburg, North Carolina[1143]. He was born 19 September 1967 in Statesville, North Carolina[1144].

Children of Cheryl Tyndall and Thomas Smith are:

519   i.   Hunter Worth Smith[1146], born 18 October 1993[1147].
520   ii.   Jennie Gayle Smith[1148], born 21 November 1996[1149].
521   iii.   Thomas Edwin Smith[1150], born 03 May 2002[1151].

387.   Stacy Lynn[9] **Simkhobitch** (Thelma Dean[8] Beasley, Addie May[7] Jackson, Osway W.[6], Elisha Moore[5], Hayburn[4], Hayburn[3], Unidentified[2], Unknown[1])[1152] was born 16 December 1970[1152]. She married **Scott Dolese**[1152].

Child of Stacy Simkhobitch and Scott Dolese is:

522   i.   Michael Dolese[1152].

394. Melanie[9] **Wise** (David Franklin[8], James Franklin[7], Alice Jane[6] Jackson, Elisha Moore[5], Hayburn[4], Hayburn[3], Unidentified[2], Unknown[1])[1153]. She married **Jerry Herring**[1154].

Children of Melanie Wise and Jerry Herring are:

523	i.	Benjamin Herring[1154].
524	ii.	Adam Herring[1154].

395. Wendy[9] **Wise** (David Franklin[8], James Franklin[7], Alice Jane[6] Jackson, Elisha Moore[5], Hayburn[4], Hayburn[3], Unidentified[2], Unknown[1])[1155]. She married **Vann Williford**[1156].

Child of Wendy Wise and Vann Williford is:

525	i.	Chandler Williford[1156].

396. Robert Keith[9] **Wise** (Robert Howell[8], James Franklin[7], Alice Jane[6] Jackson, Elisha Moore[5], Hayburn[4], Hayburn[3], Unidentified[2], Unknown[1])[1157] was born 22 November 1964 in Clinton, Sampson County, North Carolina[1157]. He married **Lisa Lowe**[1158].

Children of Robert Wise and Lisa Lowe are:

526	i.	Blake Wise[1158].
527	ii.	Matthew Wise[1158].

400. James Roland[9] **Sessoms** (Billy Roland[8], Celester[7] Wise, Alice Jane[6] Jackson, Elisha Moore[5], Hayburn[4], Hayburn[3], Unidentified[2], Unknown[1])[1159] was born 23 June 1965[1160]. He married **Tammy Hall**[1161].

Children of James Sessoms and Tammy Hall are:

528	i.	Ashley Sessoms[1162].
529	ii.	Meagan Sessoms[1162].

401.   Karen Celester[9] **Sessoms** (Billy Roland[8], Celester[7] Wise, Alice Jane[6] Jackson, Elisha Moore[5], Hayburn[4], Hayburn[3], Unidentified[2], Unknown[1])[1163] was born About 1968[1164]. She married **(1) Donnie Fleet Sessoms**[1165], son of Earl Sessoms and Sallie Sessoms. He was born 10 September 1952[1165]. She married **(2) Unknown Lucas**[1166].

Child of Karen Sessoms and Unknown Lucas is:

530   i. Billy Lucas[1166].

402.   Deana LeeAnn[9] **Sessoms** (Billy Roland[8], Celester[7] Wise, Alice Jane[6] Jackson, Elisha Moore[5], Hayburn[4], Hayburn[3], Unidentified[2], Unknown[1])[1166] was born About 1972[1167]. She married **Eddie Dryer**[1168].

Child of Deana Sessoms and Eddie Dryer is:

531   i. Danielle Dryer[1168].

403.   Kimberly Ann[9] **Sessoms** (Jackie Lester[8], Celester[7] Wise, Alice Jane[6] Jackson, Elisha Moore[5], Hayburn[4], Hayburn[3], Unidentified[2], Unknown[1]) was born 01 August 1967. She married **Timothy Farmer**.

Children of Kimberly Sessoms and Timothy Farmer are:

532   i. Dustin Farmer.
533   ii. Nicholus Farmer.

404.   Melonie Denice[9] **Sessoms** (Jackie Lester[8], Celester[7] Wise, Alice Jane[6] Jackson, Elisha Moore[5], Hayburn[4], Hayburn[3], Unidentified[2], Unknown[1])[1168] was born 03 August 1971[1168]. She married **Rodney Hall**[1168].

Children of Melonie Sessoms and Rodney Hall are:

534   i. Madelyn Hall[1168].
535   ii. Colin Hall[1168].

405. Kevin Earl[9]**Tanner** (Brenda[8] Sessoms, Celester[7] Wise, Alice Jane[6] Jackson, Elisha Moore[5], Hayburn[4], Hayburn[3], Unidentified[2], Unknown[1])[1169] was born 11 April 1972[1169]. He married **Cindy Hall**[1169].

Child of Kevin Tanner and Cindy Hall is:

536   i. Kacey Jane Tanner[1169], born 12 February 2001[1169].

409. Angela Jane[9] **Dickinson** (Margie Geraldene[8] Bass, Annie Kathleen[7] Wise, Alice Jane[6] Jackson, Elisha Moore[5], Hayburn[4], Hayburn[3], Unidentified[2], Unknown[1])[1170] was born 29 December 1967[1170]. She married **Michael Robert Singleton**[1170]. He was born 08 January 1968[1170].

Children of Angela Dickinson and Michael Singleton are:

537   i. Stuart Jarob Singleton[1170], born 09 September 1992[1170].
538   ii. Michaela Anne Singleton[1170], born 09 November 1994[1170].

410. Charles Terry[9] **Smith** (Charles Davis[9], Jackie Olene[8] Jackson, Oscar Davis[7], Haburn Rice[6], Wiley Calvin[5], Hayburn[4], Hayburn[3], Unidentified[2], Unknown[1])[1171] was born 17 September 1983[1171]. He married **Cherish Nicole Daw**[1172] 23 July 2005 in Turkey Pentecostal Free Will Baptist Church, Turkey, North Carolina. She was born 06 February 1986[1173].

Child of Charles Smith and Cherish Daw is:

539   i. Charles Dawson Smith[1174], born 21 March 2006[1175].

411. Amanda Dawn[9] **Smith** (Charles Davis[9], Jackie Olene[8] Jackson, Oscar Davis[7], Haburn Rice[6], Wiley Calvin[5], Hayburn[4],

Hayburn[3], Unidentified[2], Unknown[1])[1176] was born 09 October 1984[1176]. She married **Dennis Nelson Vann II**[1177], son of Dennis Vann and Brenda Unknown. He was born About 1984.

Children of Amanda Smith and Dennis Vann are:

540	i.	Madison Page Vann[1178], born 09 April 2004[1178].
541	ii.	Dennis Nelson Vann III[1178], born 07 November 2005[1178].

        Dennis weighed nine pounds when born.

Generation No. 8

416. Erica Susan[10] **Jackson** (William Ellis[9], William B.[8], Randall B.[7], Wiley B.[6], Wiley Calvin[5], Hayburn[4], Hayburn[3], Unidentified[2], Unknown[1])[1179] was born 12 March 1980 in Unknown[1179]. She married **Antonio Shane Batts**[1179] 15 April 1999 in Owens Grove Pentecostal FWB Church, Sampson County, North Carolina[1180]. He was born 14 March 1980 in Unknown[1181].

Child of Erica Jackson and Antonio Batts is:

542	i.	Dawson Shane Batts[1183], born 11 October 2001.

417. Heather Joyce[10] **Jackson** (William Ellis[9], William B.[8], Randall B.[7], Wiley B.[6], Wiley Calvin[5], Hayburn[4], Hayburn[3], Unidentified[2], Unknown[1])[1183] was born 17 April 1982[1184]. She married **Thomas Ray Avery**[1185] 23 March 2002 in Owens Grove Pentecostal FWB Church, Sampson County, North Carolina[1185]. He was born 12 November 1972[1186].

Children of Heather Jackson and Thomas Avery are:

543	i.	Colin Ray Avery[1188].
544	ii.	Tyler Avery[1188].

545   iii.   Lilly Avery[1188].

464.   Cynthia Kaye[10] **Cox** (Omie Kaye[9] Lockamy, James Houston[8], James Lee[7], Jemima Jewel[6] Jackson, Wiley Calvin[5], Hayburn[4], Hayburn[3], Unidentified[2], Unknown[1])[1189] was born 26 September 1975[1190]. She married **Todd**[1191].

Child of Cynthia Cox and Todd is:

546   i.   Erica Desiree Todd[1192], born 14 December 2001[1192].

465.   June Michelle[10] **Lockamy** (Jimmy McThomas[9], James Houston[8], James Lee[7], Jemima Jewel[6] Jackson, Wiley Calvin[5], Hayburn[4], Hayburn[3], Unidentified[2], Unknown[1])[1193] was born 31 May 1973[1193]. She married **Daniel Mark Holland**[1193]. He was born 27 July 1971[1193].

Children of June Lockamy and Daniel Holland are:

547   i.   Dustin Mark Holland[1193], born 17 March 1999[1193].
548   ii. Caitlyn Michelle Holland[1193], born 24 August 2002[1193].

474. Dana Owen[10] **Jordan** (Ronnie Best[9], Willa Dean[8] Lockamy, Robert C.[7], Jemima Jewel[6] Jackson, Wiley Calvin[5], Hayburn[4], Hayburn[3], Unidentified[2], Unknown[1])[1194] was born 11 July 1979[1194]. She married **Jeffrey Jones**[1194].

Child of Dana Jordan and Jeffrey Jones is:

549   i.   Jayna Madison Jones[1194], born 20 November 2002[1195].

489.   Michael Allen[10] **Smith** (Michael Edward[9], Jackie Olene[8] Jackson, Oscar Davis[7], Haburn Rice[6], Wiley Calvin[5], Hayburn[4], Hayburn[3], Unidentified[2], Unknown[1])[1196] was born 26 January 1986 in Sampson County, North Carolina[1196]. He married **Angel Avery**[1197].

Child of Michael Smith and Angel Avery is:

550   i.   Kimberly Breanna Smith[1197], born 31 January 2006[1197].

496.   Erica Nicole[10] **Smith** (Jackie Gregory[9], Jackie Olene[8] Jackson, Oscar Davis[7], Haburn Rice[6], Wiley Calvin[5], Hayburn[4], Hayburn[3], Unidentified[2], Unknown[1])[1198] was born 18 December 1985 in Clinton, Sampson County, North Carolina[1198].

Children of Erica Nicole Smith are:

551   i.   Austin Blake Smith[1199], born 27 June 2003 in Clinton, Sampson County, North Carolina[1200].
552   ii. Aaron Gregory Smith, born 16 September 2006 in Sampson County , North Carolina.

1. *County or State records.*

2. 1830 Federal Census, Sampson County, North Carolina, Roll M19-125, page 202. Image 397..

3. 1820 Federal Census for Sampson County, North Carolina, Roll M33-85, Image 223, page 304. Capt. Godwin's District..

4. Census Records for North Carolina.

5. *County or State records.*

6. Census Records for North Carolina.

7. Oscar M. Bizzell, Editor, *The Heritage of Sampson County, North Carolina, 1784-1984. Vol. 2. Oscar M. Bizzell, Editor. Associate Editor, Virginia Lohr Bizzell.*, 486, Profile # 776.

8. Sampson County Court Minutes at North Carolina Archives, CR087.301.9 - August Term 1842.

9. Oscar M. Bizzell, Editor, *The Heritage of Sampson County, North Carolina, 1784-1984. Vol. 2. Oscar M. Bizzell, Editor. Associate Editor, Virginia Lohr Bizzell.*, Page 486, Profile # 776.

10. Sampson County Court Minutes at North Carolina Archives, CR087.301.9 - August Term 1842.

11. Oscar M. Bizzell, Editor, *The Heritage of Sampson County, North Carolina, 1784-1984. Vol. 2. Oscar M. Bizzell, Editor. Associate Editor, Virginia Lohr Bizzell.*, Page 486, Profile # 776.

12. Sampson County Court Minutes at North Carolina Archives, CR087.301.9 - August Term 1842.

13. *Internet research at Ancestry.com,* "Electronic."

14. Sampson County Court Minutes at North Carolina Archives, CR087.301.9 - August Term 1842.

15. Virginis Lohr Bizzell, *1850 Sampson County, North Carolina Census,* (Transcribed for the Sampson County Historical Society).

16. Sampson County Court Minutes at North Carolina Archives, CR087.301.9 - August Term 1842.

17. Virginis Lohr Bizzell, *1850 Sampson County, North Carolina Census,* (Transcribed for the Sampson County Historical Society).

18. Sampson County Court Minutes at North Carolina Archives, CR087.301.9 - August Term 1842.

19. Virginis Lohr Bizzell, *1850 Sampson County, North Carolina Census,* (Transcribed for the Sampson County Historical Society).

20. Oscar M. Bizzell, Editor, *The Heritage of Sampson County, North Carolina, 1784-1984. Vol. 2. Oscar M. Bizzell, Editor. Associate Editor, Virginia Lohr Bizzell.*, Page 486, Profile # 776.

21. Elizabeth E. Ross, *Sampson County Will Abstracts 1784-1900*, page 111.

22. *1850, 1860 and 1870 Federal Censuses for Sampson County, North Carolina*, 1850 Federal Census.

23. Elizabeth E. Ross, *Sampson County Will Abstracts 1784-1900*, page 111.

24. *The Heritage of Sampson County, North Carolina, 1784-1984. Vol. 1. Oscar M. Bizzell, Editor*, page 242.

25. *1850, 1860 and 1870 Federal Censuses for Sampson County, North Carolina.*

26. Elizabeth E. Ross, *Sampson County Will Abstracts 1784-1900*, page 111.

27. Sampson County Court Minutes at North Carolina Archives, CR087.301.9 - August Term 1842.

28. *1850, 1860 and 1870 Federal Censuses for Sampson County, North Carolina.*

29. Virginia Lohr Bizzell, *1860 Federal Census for Sampson County, North Carolina,* (Transcribed for the Sampson County Historical Society).

30. Virginia Lohr Bizzell, *1870 Federal Census for Sampson County, North Carolina,* (Transcribed for the Sampson County Historical Society).

31. *Knowledge of Family..*

32. *Census records. One or more 1850 - 1930 posted on internet.*

33. *County or State records.*

34. Certificate of Death for Mary Jane Jackson. Copy in possession of Nancy J. Fenner

35. Bradley Lee West, *Nineteenth Century Vital Statistics Of Sampson County and Duplin County, North Carolina, Vol. 1*, 163.

36. *Certificate of Death for Mary Jane Jackson.*

37. *Census records. One or more 1850 - 1930 posted on internet.*

38. *Certificate of Death for Mary Jane Jackson.*

39. *Family knowledge of and writer's visit to cemetery.*

40. *Certificate of Death for Mary Jane Jackson.*

41. Bradley Lee West, *Nineteenth Century Vital Statistics Of Sampson County and Duplin County, North Carolina, Vol. 1*, 163.

42. *1930 Federal Census for Sampson County, North Carolina.*

43. Virginia Lohr Bizzell, *1870 Federal Census for Sampson County, North Carolina,* (Transcribed for the Sampson County Historical Society).

44. Family Descendants.

45. *Knowledge of Family..*

46. *1900 Federal Census, North Carolina.*

47. *County or State records.*

48. *1850, 1860 and 1870 Federal Censuses for Sampson County, North Carolina.*

49. *Internet research at Ancestry.com,* "Electronic."

50. *Marriage Index (Register) for Sampson County, North Carolina, USA.*

51. *Internet research at Ancestry.com,* "Electronic."

52. *Marriage Index (Register) for Sampson County, North Carolina, USA.*

53. Virginia Lohr Bizzell, *1870 Federal Census for Sampson County, North Carolina,* (Transcribed for the Sampson County Historical Society).

54. Oscar M. Bizzell, Editor, *The Heritage of Sampson County, North Carolina, 1784-1984. Vol. 2. Oscar M. Bizzell, Editor. Associate Editor, Virginia Lohr Bizzell.*, Page 486, Profile # 776.

55. *1850, 1860 and 1870 Federal Censuses for Sampson County, North Carolina.*

56. 1880 Federal Census, Ancestry.com, 1880 Federal Census for Honeycutts Township, Sampson County, North Carolina.

57. Vital Statistics, Sampson County, North Carolina.

58. *Certificate of Death for Hepsie Jackson, daughter of Sallie A. Hudson and Jonas Branch.*

59. *1900 Federal Census, North Carolina.*

60. Virginia Lohr Bizzell, *1870 Federal Census for Sampson County, North Carolina,* (Transcribed for the Sampson County Historical Society).

61. Vital Statistics, Sampson County, North Carolina.

62. *1900 Federal Census, North Carolina.*

63. *Cemetery Records.*

64. *1910 Federal Census for Honeycutts Township, Sampson County, North Carolina.*

65. *1900 Federal Census, North Carolina.*

66. *Knowledge of Family..*

67. 1880 Federal Census, Ancestry.com, 1880 Federal Census for Honeycutts Township, Sampson County, North Carolina.

68. *Cemetery records at Piney Green Baptist Church, Salemburg, Sampson County, North Carolina.*

69. *Knowledge of Family..*

70. *Cemetery records at Piney Green Baptist Church, Salemburg, Sampson County, North Carolina.*

71. Oscar M. Bizzell, Editor, *The Heritage of Sampson County, North Carolina, 1784-1984. Vol. 2. Oscar M. Bizzell, Editor. Associate Editor, Virginia Lohr Bizzell.*, Page 486, Profile 776.

72. *Cemetery records at Piney Green Baptist Church, Salemburg, Sampson County, North Carolina.*

73. Oscar M. Bizzell, Editor, *The Heritage of Sampson County, North Carolina, 1784-1984. Vol. 2. Oscar M. Bizzell, Editor. Associate Editor, Virginia Lohr Bizzell.*, Page 486, Profile 776.

74. *Cemetery records at Piney Green Baptist Church, Salemburg, Sampson County, North Carolina.*

75. Virginia Lohr Bizzell, *1870 Federal Census for Sampson County, North Carolina*, (Transcribed for the Sampson County Historical Society).

76. Virginia Lohr Bizzell, *1860 Federal Census for Sampson County, North Carolina*, (Transcribed for the Sampson County Historical Society).

77. *Internet research at Ancestry.com,* "Electronic."

78. 1880 Federal Census, Ancestry.com.

79. *Internet research at Ancestry.com,* "Electronic."

80. Virginia Lohr Bizzell, *1860 Federal Census for Sampson County, North Carolina*, (Transcribed for the Sampson County Historical Society).

81. 1880 Federal Census, Ancestry.com.

82. Virginia Lohr Bizzell, *1870 Federal Census for Sampson County, North Carolina*, (Transcribed for the Sampson County Historical Society).

83. Virginia Lohr Bizzell, *1860 Federal Census for Sampson County, North Carolina*, (Transcribed for the Sampson County Historical Society).

84. Bradley Lee West, Kenneth Dale Register, *Northern Sampson County, NC (North Carolina) Cemeteries, Vol. 3.*

85. Virginia Lohr Bizzell, *1860 Federal Census for Sampson County, North Carolina*, (Transcribed for the Sampson County Historical Society).

86. *Marriage Index (Register) for Sampson County, North Carolina, USA.*

87. Bradley Lee West, *Nineteenth Century Vital Statistics of Sampson County and Duplin County, North Carolina, (1871-1892) Vol. 2.*

88. Virginia Lohr Bizzell, *1860 Federal Census for Sampson County, North Carolina*, (Transcribed for the Sampson County Historical Society).

89. *Marriage Index (Register) for Sampson County, North Carolina, USA.*

90. Bradley Lee West, *Nineteenth Century Vital Statistics of Sampson County and Duplin County, North Carolina, (1871-1892) Vol. 2.*

91. John C. Rosser, Jr., *Coharie to Cape Fear, The Descendants of John Williams and Katharine Galbreth of Sampson and Cumberland Counties in North Carolina (1740-1990)*, (Walsworth Publishing Company, Marceline, Missouri 64658, April 1990. Only 100 copies printed. Copy in Deed office, Clinton, North Carolina).

92. Certificate of Death for Wiley B. Jackson, Book for 1947, Page 92 in Honeycutts Township, Sampson County, North Carolina. Copy of certificate in possession of Nancy J. Fenner.

93. *Certificate of Death for Wiley B. Jackson.*

94. *Marriage Index (Register) for Sampson County, North Carolina, USA,* Index for 1892-1899.

95. *1910 Federal Census for Honeycutts Township, Sampson County, North Carolina,* The 1910 census notes a middle name of 'Anna.'.

96. *Marriage Index (Register) for Sampson County, North Carolina, USA.*

97. County or State records. Certificate of Death from Cumberland County, North Carolina

98. County or State records. Certificate of Death from Cumberland County, North Carolina. Residence in Sampson County, North Carolina.

99. *Certificate of Death for Wiley B. Jackson.*

100. *Marriage Index (Register) for Sampson County, North Carolina, USA.*

101. Certificate of Death for Wiley Calvin Jackson, Wiley Calvin Jackson, born October 9, 1907 and died Janaury 30, 1995. Parents were Wiley B. Jackson and Mollie Lockamy.

102. Certificate of Death for Wiley Calvin Jackson.

103. Certificate of Death for Wiley Calvin Jackson, Page 216, Registration District No. 082-70.

104. *Certificate of Death for Mollie Parson Jackson,* Book 68, Page 178, Sampson County, North Carolina.

105. *Southern Sampson County, NC Cemeteries. Compiled by Bradley Lee West and Kenneth Dale Register,* Page 71.

106. *Certificate of Death for Mollie Parson Jackson,* Book 68, Page 178, Sampson County, North Carolina.

107. *Certificate of Death for Mollie Parson Jackson,* Book 68, Page 178.

108. *Southern Sampson County, NC Cemeteries. Compiled by Bradley Lee West and Kenneth Dale Register,* Page 71.

109. *Knowledge of Family..*

110. *1920 Federal Census.*

111. *Knowledge of Family.*

112. *Knowledge of Family..*

113. Annie Carolyn Tew and Fannie Lee Lockamy Williams, Footprints from Kitty Fork, Published in 2006. Sampson County, North Carolina.

114. *Certificate of Death for Eliza J. Jackson,* Page 135.

115. *Knowledge of Family..*

116. *Certificate of Death for Eliza J. Jackson.*

117. *Certificate of Death for Eliza J. Jackson,* Page 135 in Honeycutts Township for the 1935 year.

118. *Certificate of Death for Eliza J. Jackson.*

119. *Knowledge of Family..*

120. *Certificate of Death for Minnie Jackson,* Page 218, South Clinton Township.

121. *1900 Federal Census, North Carolina.*

122. *Certificate of Death for Minnie Jackson.*

123. Oscar M. Bizzell, Editor, *The Heritage of Sampson County, North Carolina, 1784-1984. Vol. 2. Oscar M. Bizzell, Editor. Associate Editor, Virginia Lohr Bizzell.,* Page 485.

124. *Personal knowledge of Family of Nancy J. Fenner.*

125. *Northern Sampson County, NC Cemeteries. Vol. 2. Compiled by Bradley Lee West, Kenneth Dale Register and Phyllis Jeanette West.,* Page 249.

126. Oscar M. Bizzell, Editor, *The Heritage of Sampson County, North Carolina, 1784-1984. Vol. 2. Oscar M. Bizzell, Editor. Associate Editor, Virginia Lohr Bizzell.,* Page 485, Lockamy

Family profiled by Robert Wayne Adams from Family Bible, census, wills, personal interviews and cemetery markers.

127. *Northern Sampson County, NC Cemeteries. Vol. 2. Compiled by Bradley Lee West, Kenneth Dale Register and Phyllis Jeanette West.*, Page 249.

128. *Northern Sampson County, NC Cemeteries. Vol. 2. Compiled by Bradley Lee West, Kenneth Dale Register and Phyllis Jeanette West.*, 249.

129. *Northern Sampson County, NC Cemeteries. Vol. 2. Compiled by Bradley Lee West, Kenneth Dale Register and Phyllis Jeanette West.*, Page 249.

130. Oscar M. Bizzell, Editor, *The Heritage of Sampson County, North Carolina, 1784-1984. Vol. 2. Oscar M. Bizzell, Editor. Associate Editor, Virginia Lohr Bizzell.*, Page 485, Lockamy Family profiled by Robert Wayne Adams from Family Bible, census, wills, personal interviews and cemetery markers.

131. Annie Carolyn Tew and Fannie Lee Lockamy Williams, Footprints from Kitty Fork, Published in 2006. Sampson County, North Carolina.

132. Oscar M. Bizzell, Editor, *The Heritage of Sampson County, North Carolina, 1784-1984. Vol. 2. Oscar M. Bizzell, Editor. Associate Editor, Virginia Lohr Bizzell.*, Page 485.

133. *Northern Sampson County, NC Cemeteries. Vol. 2. Compiled by Bradley Lee West, Kenneth Dale Register and Phyllis Jeanette West.*, Page 249, NC TEC4 CO B 724 MIL POL BN WWII.

134. *Northern Sampson County, NC Cemeteries. Vol. 2. Compiled by Bradley Lee West, Kenneth Dale Register and Phyllis Jeanette West.*, Page 2249.

135. *Northern Sampson County, NC Cemeteries. Vol. 2. Compiled by Bradley Lee West, Kenneth Dale Register and Phyllis Jeanette West.*, Page 249.

136. *Knowledge of Family.*.

137. *Marriage License for E. S. Jackson and Ada Ann Strickland dated September 16, 1914,* License # 263.

138. *1900 Federal Census, North Carolina.*

139. *Northern Sampson County, NC Cemeteries. Vol. 2. Compiled by Bradley Lee West, Kenneth Dale Register and Phyllis Jeanette West.*, Page 277.

140. *Family Bibles now in possession of Jackie Olene Smith.*

141. *Marriage License for E. S. Jackson and Ada Ann Strickland dated September 16, 1914,* License # 263.

142. *Northern Sampson County, NC Cemeteries. Vol. 2. Compiled by Bradley Lee West, Kenneth Dale Register and Phyllis Jeanette West.*, Page 277.

143. *1900 Federal Census, North Carolina.*

144. *Northern Sampson County, NC Cemeteries. Vol. 2. Compiled by Bradley Lee West, Kenneth Dale Register and Phyllis Jeanette West.*, Page 277.

145. *Marriage License for E. S. Jackson and Ada Ann Strickland dated September 16, 1914,* License # 263.

146. *Certificate of Birth for Cornelious Mathew Jackson*, 513. File No. 90, Corrected on April 5, 1966. Ada E. Tew was originally listed as his mother and was replaced by Ada Strickland. When it was corrected a P. H. Jackson was crossed out for the father and replaced by Ewell S. Jackson.

147. *Certificate of Birth for Cornelius Mathew Jackson.*

148. *Social Security Death Index.*

149. *Knowledge of Family.*.

150. *Certificate of Death for 'Stillborn'; parents Ewell S. Jackson and Ada Strickland.*

151. *Knowledge of Family.*

152. *Northern Sampson County, NC Cemeteries. Vol. 2. Compiled by Bradley Lee West, Kenneth Dale Register and Phyllis Jeanette West.*, Page 277.

153. *Northern Sampson County, NC Cemeteries. Vol. 2. Compiled by Bradley Lee West, Kenneth Dale Register and Phyllis Jeanette West.*, Page 241.

154. *Knowledge of Family.*, Bible of Haburn Rice Jackson now in possession of Jackie Olene Smith, states her full name as noted here. Gregory Bryan Dixon's research indicates that the full name was Jemima Jewel Jackson.

155. Descendants of James Thomas Lockamy and Jemima Jewel Jackson and members of their families.

156. *Northern Sampson County, NC Cemeteries. Vol. 2. Compiled by Bradley Lee West, Kenneth Dale Register and Phyllis Jeanette West.*, Page 241.

157. Descendants of James Thomas Lockamy and Jemima Jewel Jackson and members of their families.

158. *Northern Sampson County, NC Cemeteries. Vol. 2. Compiled by Bradley Lee West, Kenneth Dale Register and Phyllis Jeanette West.*, Page 241.

159. Descendants of James Thomas Lockamy and Jemima Jewel Jackson and members of their families.

160. *Northern Sampson County, NC Cemeteries. Vol. 2. Compiled by Bradley Lee West, Kenneth Dale Register and Phyllis Jeanette West.*, Page 241.

161. Descendants of James Thomas Lockamy and Jemima Jewel Jackson and members of their families.

162. *Northern Sampson County, NC Cemeteries. Vol. 2. Compiled by Bradley Lee West, Kenneth Dale Register and Phyllis Jeanette West.*, Page 241.

163. Descendants of James Thomas Lockamy and Jemima Jewel Jackson and members of their families.

164. *Northern Sampson County, NC Cemeteries. Vol. 2. Compiled by Bradley Lee West, Kenneth Dale Register and Phyllis Jeanette West.*, Page 241.

165. Descendants of James Thomas Lockamy and Jemima Jewel Jackson and members of their families.

166. *Northern Sampson County, NC Cemeteries. Vol. 2. Compiled by Bradley Lee West, Kenneth Dale Register and Phyllis Jeanette West.*, Page 241.

167. Descendants of James Thomas Lockamy and Jemima Jewel Jackson and members of their families.

168. *Northern Sampson County, NC Cemeteries. Vol. 2. Compiled by Bradley Lee West, Kenneth Dale Register and Phyllis Jeanette West.*, Page 241.

169. Descendants of James Thomas Lockamy and Jemima Jewel Jackson and members of their families.

170. *Northern Sampson County, NC Cemeteries. Vol. 2. Compiled by Bradley Lee West, Kenneth Dale Register and Phyllis Jeanette West.*, Page 241.

171. *Certificate of Death for Haburn Rice Jackson*, In possession of Nancy Jackson Fenner.

172. *Certificate of Death for Haburn Rice Jackson.*

173. *Certificate of Death for Molsey Eveline Jackson*, Page 192.

174. *1900-1919 Marriage Index (Register) for Sampson County, North Carolina, USA.*

175. *Family Bibles now in possession of Jackie Olene Smith.*

176. *Certificate of Death for Molsey Eveline Jackson.*

177. *Family Bibles now in possession of Jackie Olene Smith.*

178. *Certificate of Death for Joanna Naylor Jackson*, Page 160, Honeycutts Township, District 8200, Sampson County, North Carolina, USA.

179. *Marriage Index (Register) for Sampson County, North Carolina, USA.*

180. John C. Rosser, Jr., *The Descendants of Abraham Naylor and John Baggett of Sampson County, North Carolina*, (Draft of June 20, 1994), page 19.

181. *Cemetery Records.*

182. *Certificate of Death for Molsey Eveline Jackson.*

183. *1900-1919 Marriage Index (Register) for Sampson County, North Carolina, USA.*

184. John C. Rosser, Jr., *The Descendants of Abraham Naylor and John Baggett of Sampson County, North Carolina,* (Draft of June 20, 1994), page 19.

185. *Marriage Index (Register) for Sampson County, North Carolina, USA.*

186. *Certificate of Death for Mary Catherine Jackson,* Page 207. Registration District No. 82-60. Sampson County, North Carolina.

187. *Family Bibles now in possession of Jackie Olene Smith.*

188. *Certificate of Death for Mary Catherine Jackson.*

189. *Certificate of Death for James Trulove Jackson,* Certificate 20, Page 131 in book for 1941. Honeycutts Township, Sampson County, North Carolina.

190. *Certificate of Death for James Trulove Jackson.*

191. *Certificate of Death for Mary Catherine Jackson.*

192. *Certificate of Death for James Trulove Jackson.*

193. *Knowledge of Family..*

194. *Certificate of Birth for Joseph Paul Jackson,* Registration No. 14, Page 549-A. Honeycutts Township, Sampson County, North Carolina.

195. *Northern Sampson County, NC Cemeteries. Vol. 2. Compiled by Bradley Lee West, Kenneth Dale Register and Phyllis Jeanette West.,* Page 233.

196. Family Descendants.

197. Sue Cannady Barefoot, Jean Watson Moore, Nancy Cannady Manning and Joyce Cannady Lucas., *Cannady Family History Addendum, Ancestors and Descendants, 1665-2002,* page 136A(Vol.2).

198. *Northern Sampson County, NC Cemeteries. Vol. 2. Compiled by Bradley Lee West, Kenneth Dale Register and Phyllis Jeanette West.,* Page 233.

199. Certificate of Birth for Susanna Jackson, Page 448 under Honeycutts Township, Sampson County, North Carolina.

200. *Certificate of Birth for Susanna Jackson.*

201. Annie Carolyn Tew and Fannie Lee Lockamy Williams, Footprints from Kitty Fork, Published in 2006. Sampson County, North Carolina.

202. *Certificate of Death for Osway W. Jackson.*

203. *Interview with Lattie Pearl Jackson.*

204. Certificate of Death for Osway Jackson. Page 167, Honeycutts Township Vital Records.

205. *Certificate of Death for Osway Jackson.*

206. *Certificate of Death for Katie Lee Jackson,* Honeycutts Township. Vital records for Sampson County, North Carolina.

207. *Interview with Lattie Pearl Jackson.*

208. *Certificate of Death for Katie Lee Jackson.*

209. *Certificate of Death for Osway Jackson.*

210. *Certificate of Death for Katie Lee Jackson.*

211. *Certificate of Birth for Hosea Alomon Jackson,* 402, Certificate No. 75., Born in Honeycutts Township, Sampson County, North Carolina.

212. *Knowledge of Family.*

213. *Certificate of Birth for Hosea Alomon Jackson,* 402, Certificate # 75., Text notes he was the son of Osway Jackson and Cattie Lee Strickland.

214. *Northern Sampson County, NC Cemeteries. Vol. 2. Compiled by Bradley Lee West, Kenneth Dale Register and Phyllis Jeanette West.,* Page 233.

215. *Northern Sampson County, NC Cemeteries. Vol. 2. Compiled by Bradley Lee West, Kenneth Dale Register and Phyllis Jeanette West.*, 233, Hosea Almond Jackson born October 04, 1918; died August 18, 1941. Son of O. W. and Katie Lee Jackson.

216. *Northern Sampson County, NC Cemeteries. Vol. 2. Compiled by Bradley Lee West, Kenneth Dale Register and Phyllis Jeanette West.*, Page 233.

217. Sue Cannady Barefoot, Jean Watson Moore, Nancy Cannady Manning and Joyce Cannady Lucas., *Cannady Family History, Ancestors and Descendants 1665 - 2002, Vol. 1,* Pages 136A and B-6, Vol. 2, Data provided by Ron Hudson.

218. *Knowledge of Family.*.

219. Sue Cannady Barefoot, Jean Watson Moore, Nancy Cannady Manning and Joyce Cannady Lucas., *Cannady Family History, Ancestors and Descendants 1665 - 2002, Vol. 1,* Page 136A. Vol. 2.

220. *Social Security Death Index.*

221. Sue Cannady Barefoot, Jean Watson Moore, Nancy Cannady Manning and Joyce Cannady Lucas., *Cannady Family History, Ancestors and Descendants 1665 - 2002, Vol. 1,* Page 136A. Vol. 2.

222. *Social Security Death Index.*

223. *Knowledge of Family.*.

224. *Northern Sampson County, NC Cemeteries. Vol. 2. Compiled by Bradley Lee West, Kenneth Dale Register and Phyllis Jeanette West.*, Page 233.

225. Family Descendants.

226. *Northern Sampson County, NC Cemeteries. Vol. 2. Compiled by Bradley Lee West, Kenneth Dale Register and Phyllis Jeanette West.*, Page 233.

227. *Certificate of Death for Raymond D. Jackson*, Page 181, Born January 08, 1931 in Sampson County North Carolina. Died February 23, 1994 in Sampson County Memorial Hospital, Clinton, North Carolina.

228. *Certificate of Death for Raymond D. Jackson*, Page 181.

229. Certificate of Death for John Thomas Jackson, Page 181; Never married; son of Osway Jackson and Katie Strickland. .

230. *Certificate of Death for John Thomas Jackson.*

231. *Certificate of Death for Henry M. Jackson*, Page 122, Died at age one month. Cause unknown.

232. *Certificate of Death for Henry M. Jackson*, Page 122, Died at one month of age; cause unknown.

233. *Certificate of Death for Henry M. Jackson*, Page 122, Died at age one month of unknown cause.

234. *telephone interview with Astor Washington Jackson.*

235. *Certificate of Death for James Trulove Jackson*, Certificate 20, Page 131 in book for 1941. Honeycutts Township, Sampson County, North Carolina.

236. *Certificate of Death for James Trulove Jackson.*

237. Oscar M. Bizzell, Editor, *The Heritage of Sampson County, North Carolina, 1784-1984. Vol. 2. Oscar M. Bizzell, Editor. Associate Editor, Virginia Lohr Bizzell.*, page 487.

238. *Certificate of Death for Mary Catherine Jackson*, Page 207. Registration District No. 82-60. Sampson County, North Carolina.

239. *Family Bibles now in possession of Jackie Olene Smith.*

240. *Certificate of Death for Mary Catherine Jackson.*

241. *Certificate of Death for James Trulove Jackson.*

242. *Certificate of Death for Mary Catherine Jackson.*

243. Oscar M. Bizzell, Editor, *The Heritage of Sampson County, North Carolina, 1784-1984. Vol. 2. Oscar M. Bizzell, Editor. Associate Editor, Virginia Lohr Bizzell.*, Page 453, Profile 713.

244. *Social Security Death Index.*

245. Oscar M. Bizzell, Editor, *The Heritage of Sampson County, North Carolina, 1784-1984. Vol. 2. Oscar M. Bizzell, Editor. Associate Editor, Virginia Lohr Bizzell.*, Page 453, Profile # 713.

246. *Knowledge of Family..*

247. *Northern Sampson County, NC Cemeteries. Vol. 2. Compiled by Bradley Lee West, Kenneth Dale Register and Phyllis Jeanette West.*, Page 233.

248. Sue Cannady Barefoot, Jean Watson Moore, Nancy Cannady Manning and Joyce Cannady Lucas., *Cannady Family History, Ancestors and Descendants, 1665 - 2002, Vol. 2,* page 134E.

249. *Northern Sampson County, NC Cemeteries. Vol. 2. Compiled by Bradley Lee West, Kenneth Dale Register and Phyllis Jeanette West.*, Page 233.

250. *Knowledge of Family..*

251. *Northern Sampson County, NC Cemeteries. Vol. 2. Compiled by Bradley Lee West, Kenneth Dale Register and Phyllis Jeanette West.*, Page 233.

252. *Knowledge of Family..*

253. *Knowledge of Family.*

254. *Northern Sampson County, NC Cemeteries. Vol. 2. Compiled by Bradley Lee West, Kenneth Dale Register and Phyllis Jeanette West.*, Page 232.

255. *Knowledge of Family..*

256. *Knowledge of Family.*

257. Sue Cannady Barefoot, Jean Watson Moore, Nancy Cannady Manning and Joyce Cannady Lucas., *Cannady Family History, Ancestors and Descendants 1665 - 2002, Vol. 1,* Page 134A. Vol. 2.

258. Sue Cannady Barefoot, Jean Watson Moore, Nancy Cannady Manning and Joyce Cannady Lucas., *Cannady Family History, Ancestors and Descendants 1665 - 2002, Vol. 1,* Page 134A, Vol. 2.

259. Sue Cannady Barefoot, Jean Watson Moore, Nancy Cannady Manning and Joyce Cannady Lucas., *Cannady Family History, Ancestors and Descendants 1665 - 2002, Vol. 1,* Page 134B, Vol. 2.

260. *Knowledge of Family.*

261. *Northern Sampson County, NC Cemeteries. Vol. 2. Compiled by Bradley Lee West, Kenneth Dale Register and Phyllis Jeanette West.*, Page 234.

262. *Knowledge of Family.*

263. *Northern Sampson County, NC Cemeteries. Vol. 2. Compiled by Bradley Lee West, Kenneth Dale Register and Phyllis Jeanette West.*, Pager 234. Vol. 2.

264. *Northern Sampson County, NC Cemeteries. Vol. 2. Compiled by Bradley Lee West, Kenneth Dale Register and Phyllis Jeanette West.*, Page 234.

265. *Northern Sampson County, NC Cemeteries. Vol. 2. Compiled by Bradley Lee West, Kenneth Dale Register and Phyllis Jeanette West.*, Page 234, Vol. 2.

266. *Northern Sampson County, NC Cemeteries. Vol. 2. Compiled by Bradley Lee West, Kenneth Dale Register and Phyllis Jeanette West.*, Page 234.

267. *Knowledge of Family*, Preston Carr Pope and telephone interview with Alice Daniels.

268. *Knowledge of Family*, Preston Carr Pope and telephone interview with Alice Pope Daniels.

269. *Knowledge of Family*, Preston Carr Pope provided name.

270. *Knowledge of Family.*

271. *Northern Sampson County, NC Cemeteries. Vol. 2. Compiled by Bradley Lee West, Kenneth Dale Register and Phyllis Jeanette West.*, Page 234, Vol. 2.

272. *Northern Sampson County, NC Cemeteries. Vol. 2. Compiled by Bradley Lee West, Kenneth Dale Register and Phyllis Jeanette West.*, Page 234. Vol. 2.

273. *Northern Sampson County, NC Cemeteries. Vol. 2. Compiled by Bradley Lee West, Kenneth Dale Register and Phyllis Jeanette West.*, Page 234, Vol. 2.

274. *Knowledge of Family.*

275. *Northern Sampson County, NC Cemeteries. Vol. 2. Compiled by Bradley Lee West, Kenneth Dale Register and Phyllis Jeanette West.*, Page 234, Vol. 2.

276. Northern Sampson County, NC Cemeteries. Vol. 2. Compiled by Bradley Lee West, Kenneth Dale Register and Phyllis Jeanette West., Page 234, Vol. 2.

277. *Knowledge of Family.*

278. *Northern Sampson County, NC Cemeteries. Vol. 2. Compiled by Bradley Lee West, Kenneth Dale Register and Phyllis Jeanette West.*, page 234.

279. *Northern Sampson County, NC Cemeteries. Vol. 2. Compiled by Bradley Lee West, Kenneth Dale Register and Phyllis Jeanette West.*, Page 234.

280. *Northern Sampson County, NC Cemeteries. Vol. 2. Compiled by Bradley Lee West, Kenneth Dale Register and Phyllis Jeanette West.*, Page 234, Vol. 2..

281. *Northern Sampson County, NC Cemeteries. Vol. 2. Compiled by Bradley Lee West, Kenneth Dale Register and Phyllis Jeanette West.*, Page 234, Vol. 2.

282. *Northern Sampson County, NC Cemeteries. Vol. 2. Compiled by Bradley Lee West, Kenneth Dale Register and Phyllis Jeanette West.*, Page 234. Vol. 2.

283. *Northern Sampson County, NC Cemeteries. Vol. 2. Compiled by Bradley Lee West, Kenneth Dale Register and Phyllis Jeanette West.*, Page 234, Vol. 2.

284. *Northern Sampson County, NC Cemeteries. Vol. 2. Compiled by Bradley Lee West, Kenneth Dale Register and Phyllis Jeanette West.*, Page 234. Vol 2.

285. *Northern Sampson County, NC Cemeteries. Vol. 2. Compiled by Bradley Lee West, Kenneth Dale Register and Phyllis Jeanette West.*, Page 234, Vol. 2.

286. *Knowledge of Family..*

287. *Internet research at Ancestry.com*, "Electronic," Family trees posted on Ancestry.com Web Site.

288. *Internet research at Ancestry.com*, "Electronic."

289. *Census records. One or more 1850 - 1930 posted on internet.*

290. Sue Cannady Barefoot, Jean Watson Moore, Nancy Cannady Manning and Joyce Cannady Lucas., *Cannady Family History, Ancestors and Descendants 1665 - 2002, Vol. 1*, 136B. Vol. 2.

291. *Internet research at Ancestry.com*, "Electronic."

292. Sue Cannady Barefoot, Jean Watson Moore, Nancy Cannady Manning and Joyce Cannady Lucas., *Cannady Family History, Ancestors and Descendants 1665 - 2002, Vol. 1*, Page 136B. Vol. 2.

293. Oscar M. Bizzell, Editor, *The Heritage of Sampson County, North Carolina, 1784-1984. Vol. 2. Oscar M. Bizzell, Editor. Associate Editor, Virginia Lohr Bizzell.*, Pages 486 and 487, Profiles # 776 and 777.

294. *Cemetery Records.*

295. *Social Security Death Index.*

296. Oscar M. Bizzell, Editor, *The Heritage of Sampson County, North Carolina, 1784-1984. Vol. 2. Oscar M. Bizzell, Editor. Associate Editor, Virginia Lohr Bizzell.*, Page 487, Profile 777.

297. *The Heritage of Sampson County, North Carolina, 1784-1984. Vol. 1. Oscar M. Bizzell, Editor,* Pages 486 and 487, Profiles, 776 and 777.

298. Oscar M. Bizzell, Editor, *The Heritage of Sampson County, North Carolina, 1784-1984. Vol. 2. Oscar M. Bizzell, Editor. Associate Editor, Virginia Lohr Bizzell.*, Page 487, Profile 777.

299. *Northern Sampson County, NC Cemeteries. Vol. 2. Compiled by Bradley Lee West, Kenneth Dale Register and Phyllis Jeanette West.*, 234.

300. *Northern Sampson County, NC Cemeteries. Vol. 2. Compiled by Bradley Lee West, Kenneth Dale Register and Phyllis Jeanette West.*, Page 234.

301. *The Heritage of Sampson County, North Carolina, 1784-1984. Vol. 1. Oscar M. Bizzell, Editor*, Pages 486 and 487, Profiles, 776 and 777.

302. *The Heritage of Sampson County, North Carolina, 1784-1984. Vol. 1. Oscar M. Bizzell, Editor*, Pages 486 and 487, Profile # 776 submitted by Robert Wayne Adams.

303. *The Heritage of Sampson County, North Carolina, 1784-1984. Vol. 1. Oscar M. Bizzell, Editor*, Page 488, Profile # 779.

304. *The Heritage of Sampson County, North Carolina, 1784-1984. Vol. 1. Oscar M. Bizzell, Editor*, Pages 488 and 489, Profile # 779.

305. *Social Security Death Index.*

306. *The Heritage of Sampson County, North Carolina, 1784-1984. Vol. 1. Oscar M. Bizzell, Editor*, Pages 488 and 489, Profile 779.

307. *Internet research at Ancestry.com*, "Electronic."

308. *Certificate of Death for Randall B. Jackson from Sampson County, North Carolina*, Page 170 in book for 1965, Registration District No 82-00.

309. *Knowledge of Family..*

310. *Certificate of Death for Randall B. Jackson from Sampson County, North Carolina*, Page 170 in book for 1965, Registration District No. 82-00.

311. *Certificate of Death for Randall B. Jackson from Sampson County, North Carolina*, Page 170.

312. *Marriage Index (Register) for Sampson County, North Carolina, USA.*

313. *Northern Sampson County, NC Cemeteries. Vol. 2. Compiled by Bradley Lee West, Kenneth Dale Register and Phyllis Jeanette West.*, Page 242.

314. *Certificate of Death for Randall B. Jackson from Sampson County, North Carolina*, Page 170 in Book for 1965, Registration District No. 82-000.

315. *Northern Sampson County, NC Cemeteries. Vol. 2. Compiled by Bradley Lee West, Kenneth Dale Register and Phyllis Jeanette West.*, Page 242.

316. *Marriage Index (Register) for Sampson County, North Carolina, USA.*

317. *Claudia Priscilla Jackson Honeycutt Fields*, Family Knowledge and records.

318. *Claudia Priscilla Jackson Honeycutt Fields*, Family knowledge and records.

319. *Claudia Priscilla Jackson Honeycutt Fields*, Family knowledge.

320. *Northern Sampson County, NC Cemeteries. Vol. 2. Compiled by Bradley Lee West, Kenneth Dale Register and Phyllis Jeanette West.*, Page 26, Her tombstone by Warren Stancil Jackson notes her date of birth.

321. *Certificate of Death for Tommy Franklin Jackson.*

322. *Certificate of Death for Tommy Franklin Jackson*, Page 183. Registration District No. 82-70.

323. Telephone interview with Callie Estelle Jackson.

324. *Knowledge of Family.*

325. *Southern Sampson County, NC Cemeteries. Compiled by Bradley Lee West and Kenneth Dale Register*, Page 71.

326. *Certificate of Death for Tommy Franklin Jackson.*

327. *Southern Sampson County, NC Cemeteries. Compiled by Bradley Lee West and Kenneth Dale Register*, Page 71.

328. *Knowledge of Family*.

329. County or State records. Certificate of Death

330. County or State records. Certificate of Death.

331. County or State records. Certificate of Death.

332. *Knowledge of Family*..

333. *1910 Federal Census for Honeycutts Township, Sampson County, North Carolina*, This census records notes her name as 'Effie Jane', age 2. Wiley C. is also noted as age 2. Twins?

334. Bradley Lee West, Kenneth Dale Register, *Northern Sampson County, NC (North Carolina) Cemeteries, Vol. 3*.

335. *Knowledge of Family*..

336. Bradley Lee West, Kenneth Dale Register, *Northern Sampson County, NC (North Carolina) Cemeteries, Vol. 3*.

337. *1900 Federal Census, North Carolina*.

338. Bradley Lee West, Kenneth Dale Register, *Northern Sampson County, NC (North Carolina) Cemeteries, Vol. 3*.

339. Annie Carolyn Tew and Fannie Lee Lockamy Williams, Footprints from Kitty Fork, Published in 2006. Sampson County, North Carolina.

340. Bradley Lee West, Kenneth Dale Register, *Northern Sampson County, NC (North Carolina) Cemeteries, Vol. 3*.

341. *Interview with Lattie Pearl Jackson*.

342. *Northern Sampson County, NC Cemeteries. Vol. 2. Compiled by Bradley Lee West, Kenneth Dale Register and Phyllis Jeanette West.*, Page 250.

343. *Interview with Lattie Pearl Jackson*.

344. *Northern Sampson County, NC Cemeteries. Vol. 2. Compiled by Bradley Lee West, Kenneth Dale Register and Phyllis Jeanette West.*, Page 250.

345. *Interview with Lattie Pearl Jackson*.

346. *Knowledge of Family*..

347. *The Heritage of Sampson County, North Carolina, 1784-1984. Vol. 1. Oscar M. Bizzell, Editor*, Pages 538 and 539, Profile # 882.

348. *Northern Sampson County, NC Cemeteries. Vol. 2. Compiled by Bradley Lee West, Kenneth Dale Register and Phyllis Jeanette West.*, Page 242.

349. Oscar M. Bizzell, Editor, *The Heritage of Sampson County, North Carolina, 1784-1984. Vol. 2. Oscar M. Bizzell, Editor. Associate Editor, Virginia Lohr Bizzell*..

350. Annie Carolyn Tew and Fannie Lee Lockamy Williams, Footprints from Kitty Fork, Published in 2006. Sampson County, North Carolina.

351. *Northern Sampson County, NC Cemeteries. Vol. 2. Compiled by Bradley Lee West, Kenneth Dale Register and Phyllis Jeanette West.*, Page 242.

352. *The Heritage of Sampson County, North Carolina, 1784-1984. Vol. 1. Oscar M. Bizzell, Editor*, Pages 538 and 539, Profile # 882.

353. *Family, Descendant or Member of Extended Family*.

354. *The Heritage of Sampson County, North Carolina, 1784-1984. Vol. 1. Oscar M. Bizzell, Editor*, Page 352 and 353.

355. *The Heritage of Sampson County, North Carolina, 1784-1984. Vol. 1. Oscar M. Bizzell, Editor*, Pages 352 and 353, Profile # 527. Vol. 1.

356. *Family, Descendant or Member of Extended Family*.

357. *The Heritage of Sampson County, North Carolina, 1784-1984. Vol. 1. Oscar M. Bizzell, Editor*, Pages 352 and 353, Profile # 527. Vol. 1.

358. *The Heritage of Sampson County, North Carolina, 1784-1984. Vol. 1. Oscar M. Bizzell, Editor*, Pages 485 and 488, Profile #s 773 and 779.

359. *1910 Federal Census for Honeycutts Township, Sampson County, North Carolina.*

360. Annie Carolyn Tew and Fannie Lee Lockamy Williams, Footprints from Kitty Fork, Published in 2006. Sampson County, North Carolina.

361. *The Heritage of Sampson County, North Carolina, 1784-1984. Vol. 1. Oscar M. Bizzell, Editor*, Pages 488, Profile # 779.

362. Annie Carolyn Tew and Fannie Lee Lockamy Williams, Footprints from Kitty Fork, Published in 2006. Sampson County, North Carolina.

363. *The Heritage of Sampson County, North Carolina, 1784-1984. Vol. 1. Oscar M. Bizzell, Editor*, Pages 488 and 489, Profile 779.

364. *The Heritage of Sampson County, North Carolina, 1784-1984. Vol. 1. Oscar M. Bizzell, Editor*, Page 488, Profile # 779.

365. *The Heritage of Sampson County, North Carolina, 1784-1984. Vol. 1. Oscar M. Bizzell, Editor*, Pages 488 and 489, Profile # 779.

366. *Social Security Death Index.*

367. Annie Carolyn Tew and Fannie Lee Lockamy Williams, Footprints from Kitty Fork, Published in 2006. Sampson County, North Carolina.

368. Oscar M. Bizzell, Editor, *The Heritage of Sampson County, North Carolina, 1784-1984. Vol. 2. Oscar M. Bizzell, Editor. Associate Editor, Virginia Lohr Bizzell.*, Page 485, Lockamy Family profiled by Robert Wayne Adams from Family Bible, census records, wills, personal interviews and cemetery markers.

369. *Northern Sampson County, NC Cemeteries. Vol. 2. Compiled by Bradley Lee West, Kenneth Dale Register and Phyllis Jeanette West.*, Page 249.

370. Annie Carolyn Tew and Fannie Lee Lockamy Williams, Footprints from Kitty Fork, Published in 2006. Sampson County, North Carolina.

371. *Northern Sampson County, NC Cemeteries. Vol. 2. Compiled by Bradley Lee West, Kenneth Dale Register and Phyllis Jeanette West.*, Page 249.

372. Oscar M. Bizzell, Editor, *The Heritage of Sampson County, North Carolina, 1784-1984. Vol. 2. Oscar M. Bizzell, Editor. Associate Editor, Virginia Lohr Bizzell.*, Page 485.

373. Annie Carolyn Tew and Fannie Lee Lockamy Williams, Footprints from Kitty Fork, Published in 2006. Sampson County, North Carolina.

374. *Northern Sampson County, NC Cemeteries. Vol. 2. Compiled by Bradley Lee West, Kenneth Dale Register and Phyllis Jeanette West.*, Page 249.

375. Annie Carolyn Tew and Fannie Lee Lockamy Williams, Footprints from Kitty Fork, Published in 2006. Sampson County, North Carolina.

376. *Northern Sampson County, NC Cemeteries. Vol. 2. Compiled by Bradley Lee West, Kenneth Dale Register and Phyllis Jeanette West.*, Page 249.

377. Oscar M. Bizzell, Editor, *The Heritage of Sampson County, North Carolina, 1784-1984. Vol. 2. Oscar M. Bizzell, Editor. Associate Editor, Virginia Lohr Bizzell.*, Page 485.

378. *1910 Federal Census for Honeycutts Township, Sampson County, North Carolina.*

379. *Northern Sampson County, NC Cemeteries. Vol. 2. Compiled by Bradley Lee West, Kenneth Dale Register and Phyllis Jeanette West.*, Page 237.

380. Oscar M. Bizzell, Editor, *The Heritage of Sampson County, North Carolina, 1784-1984. Vol. 2. Oscar M. Bizzell, Editor. Associate Editor, Virginia Lohr Bizzell.*, Page 485.

381. Annie Carolyn Tew and Fannie Lee Lockamy Williams, Footprints from Kitty Fork, Published in 2006. Sampson County, North Carolina.

382. *Northern Sampson County, NC Cemeteries. Vol. 2. Compiled by Bradley Lee West, Kenneth Dale Register and Phyllis Jeanette West.*, Page 237.

383. Annie Carolyn Tew and Fannie Lee Lockamy Williams, Footprints from Kitty Fork, Published in 2006. Sampson County, North Carolina.

384. John C. Rosser, Jr., *The Descendants of Abraham Naylor and John Baggett of Sampson County, North Carolina*, (Draft of June 20, 1994), page 109.

385. Oscar M. Bizzell, Editor, *The Heritage of Sampson County, North Carolina, 1784–1984. Vol. 2. Oscar M. Bizzell, Editor. Associate Editor, Virginia Lohr Bizzell.*, Page 485, Lockamy Family profiled by Robert Wayne Adams from Family Bible, census, wills, personal interviews and cemeteries markers.

386. *1910 Federal Census for Honeycutts Township, Sampson County, North Carolina.*

387. *Northern Sampson County, NC Cemeteries. Vol. 2. Compiled by Bradley Lee West, Kenneth Dale Register and Phyllis Jeanette West..*

388. John C. Rosser, Jr., *The Descendants of Abraham Naylor and John Baggett of Sampson County, North Carolina*, (Draft of June 20, 1994), page 109.

389. *Northern Sampson County, NC Cemeteries. Vol. 2. Compiled by Bradley Lee West, Kenneth Dale Register and Phyllis Jeanette West..*

390. Annie Carolyn Tew and Fannie Lee Lockamy Williams, Footprints from Kitty Fork, Published in 2006. Sampson County, North Carolina.

391. *Knowledge of Family.*, Interview with Ruby Doris Jackson Lee and Perry Scott Jackson.

392. *Family knowledge and cemetery records from "Northern Sampson County, NC Cemeteries, Vol. 2".*, Page 277, The book by compiled by Bradley Lee West, Kenneth Dale Register and Phyllis Jeanette West.

393. *Certificate of Death for Andrew Davis Jackson*, Page 164.

394. *Knowledge of Family..*

395. *1920 Federal Census.*

396. *Northern Sampson County, NC Cemeteries. Vol. 2. Compiled by Bradley Lee West, Kenneth Dale Register and Phyllis Jeanette West.*, Page 277.

397. *1920 Federal Census.*

398. *Northern Sampson County, NC Cemeteries. Vol. 2. Compiled by Bradley Lee West, Kenneth Dale Register and Phyllis Jeanette West.*, Page 277.

399. Family knowledge and cemetery records from "Northern Sampson County, NC Cemeteries, Vol. 2". Book was compiled by Bradley Lee West, Kenneth Dale Register and Phyllis Jeanette West.

400. *Northern Sampson County, NC Cemeteries. Vol. 2. Compiled by Bradley Lee West, Kenneth Dale Register and Phyllis Jeanette West.*, Page 277.

401. *Interview with Ruby Doris Jackson Lee.*

402. *Knowledge of Family..*

403. Family knowledge and cemetery records from "Northern Sampson County, NC Cemeteries, Vol. 2". Book compiled by Bradley Lee West, Kenneth Dale Register and Phyllis Jeanette West.

404. *Interview with Ruby Doris Jackson Lee.*

405. *Interview with Ruby Doris Jackson Lee and Perry Scott Jackson.*

406. *Knowledge of Family..*

407. *Interview with Ruby Doris Jackson Lee and Perry Scott Jackson.*

408. *Knowledge of Family.*, May be living in Maryland, near her children.

409. *Northern Sampson County, NC Cemeteries. Vol. 2. Compiled by Bradley Lee West, Kenneth Dale Register and Phyllis Jeanette West.*, Page 277.

410. *Interview with Ruby Doris Jackson Lee and Perry Scott Jackson.*

411. Edited by Nancy Fisher Ewing and Robert McLemore Butler, *Cumberland County Cemetery Survey, Vol Two*, (Published by the Cumberland County, North Carolina Genealogical Society), Page 94, Published by Cumberland County Genealogical Society. Edited by Nancy Fisher Ewing and Robert McLemore Butler. February 12, 2001.

412. Edited by Nancy Fisher Ewing and Robert McLemore Butler, *Cumberland County Cemetery Survey, Vol Two*, (Published by the Cumberland County, North Carolina Genealogical Society), Page 94, Published by Cumberland County Genealogical Society Edited by Nancy Fisher Ewing and Robert McLemore Butler. February 12, 2001.

413. *Interview with Ruby Doris Jackson Lee and Perry Scott Jackson.*

414. Edited by Nancy Fisher Ewing and Robert McLemore Butler, *Cumberland County Cemetery Survey, Vol Three*, (August 2002 by Cumberland County Genealogical Society, North Carolina), Page 94, Published by Cumberland County Genealogical Society. Edited by Nancy Fisher and Robert McLemore Butler. February 12, 2001.

415. *Family, Descendant or Member of Extended Family.*

416. Edited by Nancy Fisher Ewing and Robert McLemore Butler, *Cumberland County Cemetery Survey, Vol Two*, (Published by the Cumberland County, North Carolina Genealogical Society).

417. *Family, Descendant or Member of Extended Family.*

418. John C. Rosser, Jr., *Coharie to Cape Fear, The Descendants of John Williams and Katharine Galbreth of Sampson and Cumberland Counties in North Carolina (1740-1990)*, (Walsworth Publishing Company, Marceline, Missouri 64658, April 1990. Only 100 copies printed. Copy in Deed office, Clinton, North Carolina).

419. Descendants of James Thomas Lockamy and Jemima Jewel Jackson and members of their families.

420. *Northern Sampson County, NC Cemeteries. Vol. 2. Compiled by Bradley Lee West, Kenneth Dale Register and Phyllis Jeanette West.*, Page 237.

421. Descendants of James Thomas Lockamy and Jemima Jewel Jackson and members of their families.

422. *Northern Sampson County, NC Cemeteries. Vol. 2. Compiled by Bradley Lee West, Kenneth Dale Register and Phyllis Jeanette West.*, Page 237.

423. Descendants of James Thomas Lockamy and Jemima Jewel Jackson and members of their families.

424. *Northern Sampson County, NC Cemeteries. Vol. 2. Compiled by Bradley Lee West, Kenneth Dale Register and Phyllis Jeanette West.*, Page 237.

425. Descendants of James Thomas Lockamy and Jemima Jewel Jackson and members of their families.

426. *Northern Sampson County, NC Cemeteries. Vol. 2. Compiled by Bradley Lee West, Kenneth Dale Register and Phyllis Jeanette West.*, Page 237.

427. Descendants of James Thomas Lockamy and Jemima Jewel Jackson and members of their families, Provided by Barbara Jean Jordan Hairr.

428. *Northern Sampson County, NC Cemeteries. Vol. 2. Compiled by Bradley Lee West, Kenneth Dale Register and Phyllis Jeanette West.*, Page 242.

429. *Northern Sampson County, NC Cemeteries. Vol. 2. Compiled by Bradley Lee West, Kenneth Dale Register and Phyllis Jeanette West.*, 242.

430. Descendants of James Thomas Lockamy and Jemima Jewel Jackson and members of their families, Data provided by Barbara Jean Jordan Hairr.

431. *Northern Sampson County, NC Cemeteries. Vol. 2. Compiled by Bradley Lee West, Kenneth Dale Register and Phyllis Jeanette West.*, Page 242.

432. *Northern Sampson County, NC Cemeteries. Vol. 2. Compiled by Bradley Lee West, Kenneth Dale Register and Phyllis Jeanette West.*, 242.

433. *Northern Sampson County, NC Cemeteries. Vol. 2. Compiled by Bradley Lee West, Kenneth Dale Register and Phyllis Jeanette West.*, Page 242.

434. Descendants of James Thomas Lockamy and Jemima Jewel Jackson and members of their families, Provided by Barbara Jean Jordan Hairr.

435. *1930 Federal Census for Sampson County, North Carolina.*

436. Descendants of James Thomas Lockamy and Jemima Jewel Jackson and members of their families, Provided by Barbara Jean Jordan Hairr.

437. Descendants of James Thomas Lockamy and Jemima Jewel Jackson and members of their families.

438. *Northern Sampson County, NC Cemeteries. Vol. 2. Compiled by Bradley Lee West, Kenneth Dale Register and Phyllis Jeanette West.*, Page 241.

439. Descendants of James Thomas Lockamy and Jemima Jewel Jackson and members of their families.

440. *Northern Sampson County, NC Cemeteries. Vol. 2. Compiled by Bradley Lee West, Kenneth Dale Register and Phyllis Jeanette West.*, Page 241.

441. Descendants of James Thomas Lockamy and Jemima Jewel Jackson and members of their families, Name provided by Barbara Jean Jordan Hairr.

442. *1910 Federal Census for Honeycutts Township, Sampson County, North Carolina*, Downloaded from Ancestry.com.

443. *Northern Sampson County, NC Cemeteries. Vol. 2. Compiled by Bradley Lee West, Kenneth Dale Register and Phyllis Jeanette West.*, Page 241.

444. Descendants of James Thomas Lockamy and Jemima Jewel Jackson and members of their families, Data provided by Barbara Jean Jordan Hairr.

445. *County or State records.*

446. *Northern Sampson County, NC Cemeteries. Vol. 2. Compiled by Bradley Lee West, Kenneth Dale Register and Phyllis Jeanette West.*, Page 241.

447. Descendants of James Thomas Lockamy and Jemima Jewel Jackson and members of their families, Name provided by Barbara Jean Jordan hairr.

448. Annie Carolyn Tew and Fannie Lee Lockamy Williams, Footprints from Kitty Fork, Published in 2006. Sampson County, North Carolina.

449. *Northern Sampson County, NC Cemeteries. Vol. 2. Compiled by Bradley Lee West, Kenneth Dale Register and Phyllis Jeanette West.*, Page 22.

450. Descendants of James Thomas Lockamy and Jemima Jewel Jackson and members of their families, Name provided by Barbara Jean Jordan Hairr.

451. *Northern Sampson County, NC Cemeteries. Vol. 2. Compiled by Bradley Lee West, Kenneth Dale Register and Phyllis Jeanette West.*, Page 22.

452. Descendants of James Thomas Lockamy and Jemima Jewel Jackson and members of their families, Name provided by Barbara Jean Jordan Hairr.

453. Descendants of James Thomas Lockamy and Jemima Jewel Jackson and members of their families, Date provided by Barbara Jean Jordan Hairr.

454. *Southern Sampson County, NC Cemeteries. Compiled by Bradley Lee West and Kenneth Dale Register.*, Page 277.

455. Descendants of James Thomas Lockamy and Jemima Jewel Jackson and members of their families, Date provided by Barbara Jean Jordan Hairr.

456. *Southern Sampson County, NC Cemeteries. Compiled by Bradley Lee West and Kenneth Dale Register.*, Page 277.

457. Descendants of James Thomas Lockamy and Jemima Jewel Jackson and members of their families, Name provided by Barbara Jean Jordan Hairr.

458. Descendants of James Thomas Lockamy and Jemima Jewel Jackson and members of their families, Date provided by Barbara Jean Jordan Hairr.

459. *Southern Sampson County, NC Cemeteries. Compiled by Bradley Lee West and Kenneth Dale Register.*, Page 277.

460. Descendants of James Thomas Lockamy and Jemima Jewel Jackson and members of their families, Date provided by Barbara Jean Jordan Hairr.

461. *Southern Sampson County, NC Cemeteries. Compiled by Bradley Lee West and Kenneth Dale Register.*, Page 277.

462. Copies of Bible records in possession Nancy J. Fenner.

463. *Delayed Certificate of Birth for Oscar Davis Jackson.*

464. *Personal knowledge of Nancy Eveline Jackson Fenner.*

465. Copies of Bible records in possession Nancy J. Fenner.

466. *Personal knowledge of Nancy Eveline Jackson Fenner.*

467. Certificate of Death for Roberta Holland Jackson. Copy in possession of Nancy Eveline Jackson Pleitt Fenner. Original in courthouse, Clinton, Sampson County, North Carolina

468. "Obituary."

469. *Personal knowledge of Nancy Eveline Jackson Fenner.*

470. Copies of Bible records in possession Nancy J. Fenner.

471. *Family Bible of Jackie Olene Smith..*

472. *Personal knowledge of Nancy Eveline Jackson Fenner and Jackie Olene Jackson Smith.*

473. Certificate of Birth for Elon Adel Jackson, Page 841 in Honeycutts Township, Sampson County, North Carolina. Certificate No. 39. Copy in possession of Nancy Eveline Jackson Fenner.

474. Certificate of Birth for Elon Adel Jackson.

475. *Knowledge of Family.*, Personal knowledge of his sister, Nancy Eveline Jackson Pleitt Fenner.

476. *Sudie Mae Pruitt Jackson.*

477. *Sudie Mae Pruitt.*

478. Personal knowledge of Nancy Eveline Jackson Fenner and copies of obituaries.

479. *Sudie Mae Pruitt.*

480. Certificate of Death for Willard Paul Jackson, Page 179 in book for 1967.

481. Telephone interview with Callie Estelle Jackson.

482. *Social Security Death Index.*

483. Certificate of Death for Willard Paul Jackson, Page 179 in book for 1967.

484. Telephone interview with Callie Estelle Jackson.

485. Family provided Data.

486. Telephone interview with Callie Estelle Jackson.

487. *Certificate of Birth (Delayed) for Mattie Ruth Jackson,* Page 55.

488. *Knowledge of Family..*

489. John C. Rosser, Jr., *The Descendants of Abraham Naylor and John Baggett of Sampson County, North Carolina,* (Draft of June 20, 1994), Page 20.

490. *Northern Sampson County, NC Cemeteries. Vol. 2. Compiled by Bradley Lee West, Kenneth Dale Register and Phyllis Jeanette West.*, Page 231.

491. John C. Rosser, Jr., *The Descendants of Abraham Naylor and John Baggett of Sampson County, North Carolina,* (Draft of June 20, 1994), Page 20.

492. *Northern Sampson County, NC Cemeteries. Vol. 2. Compiled by Bradley Lee West, Kenneth Dale Register and Phyllis Jeanette West.*, Page 231.

493. *Certificate of Death for Stephen Senter Holland, Jr..*

494. John C. Rosser, Jr., *The Descendants of Abraham Naylor and John Baggett of Sampson County, North Carolina,* (Draft of June 20, 1994), Page 20.

495. *Northern Sampson County, NC Cemeteries. Vol. 2. Compiled by Bradley Lee West, Kenneth Dale Register and Phyllis Jeanette West.*, Page 231.

496. *Knowledge of Family.*, Name provided by mother, Mattie Ruth Jackson Parker Holland.

497. *Northern Sampson County, NC Cemeteries. Vol. 2. Compiled by Bradley Lee West, Kenneth Dale Register and Phyllis Jeanette West.*, Page 231.

498. *Certificate of Birth for Mary Jane Jackson*, Page 477, Honeycutts Township, Sampson County, North Carolina. Registration No. 29..

499. *Certificate of Death for Mary Jane Jackson*, Page 477, Honeycutts Township, Sampson County, North Carolina. Registration No. 29..

500. *Northern Sampson County, NC Cemeteries. Vol. 2. Compiled by Bradley Lee West, Kenneth Dale Register and Phyllis Jeanette West.*, Page 278.

501. *Knowledge of Family..*

502. *Northern Sampson County, NC Cemeteries. Vol. 2. Compiled by Bradley Lee West, Kenneth Dale Register and Phyllis Jeanette West.*, Page 278.

503. *Certificate of Birth for Elvin Sikes Jackson*, Certificate 70 on page 397, Honeycutts Township, Sampson County, North Carolina..

504. *Certificate of Birth for Elvin Sikes Jackson*, Page 397 in Honeycutts Township, Sampson County, North Carolina. Certificate No. 70.

505. Knowledge of Family. Date provided by Virginia Lee Horne Jackson Strickland.

506. *Knowledge of Family..*

507. Knowledge of Family. Date and place provided by Virginia Lee Horne Jackson Strickland.

508. Knowledge of Family. Date provided by Virginia Lee Horne Jackson Strickland.

509. *Knowledge of Family..*

510. Knowledge of Family. Date and place provided by Virginia Lee Horne Jackson Strickland.

511. *Knowledge of Family..*

512. Knowledge of Family. Date provided by Cornelie Ann Jackson Fite and Virginia Lee Horne Jackson Strickland.

513. Knowledge of Family. Full name provided by Cornelia Ann Jackson Fite.

514. Knowledge of Family. Date and place provided by Cornielia Ann Jackson Fite.

515. Knowledge of Family. Date provided by Cornelia Ann Jackson Fite.

516. Knowledge of Family. Date and place provided by Cornielia Ann Jackson Fite.

517. *Knowledge of Family..*

518. *Northern Sampson County, NC Cemeteries. Vol. 2. Compiled by Bradley Lee West, Kenneth Dale Register and Phyllis Jeanette West.*, Page 19.

519. Sue Cannady Barefoot, Jean Watson Moore, Nancy Cannady Manning and Joyce Cannady Lucas., *Cannady Family History, Ancestors and Descendants 1665 - 2002, Vol. 1*, Page 135.

520. John C. Rosser, Jr., *The Descendants of Abraham Naylor and John Baggett of Sampson County, North Carolina*, (Draft of June 20, 1994), page 273.

521. *Northern Sampson County, NC Cemeteries. Vol. 2. Compiled by Bradley Lee West, Kenneth Dale Register and Phyllis Jeanette West.*, 19.

522. John C. Rosser, Jr., *The Descendants of Abraham Naylor and John Baggett of Sampson County, North Carolina*, (Draft of June 20, 1994), page 273.

523. *Northern Sampson County, NC Cemeteries. Vol. 2. Compiled by Bradley Lee West, Kenneth Dale Register and Phyllis Jeanette West.*, Page 19.

524. *Northern Sampson County, NC Cemeteries. Vol. 2. Compiled by Bradley Lee West, Kenneth Dale Register and Phyllis Jeanette West.*, Page 233.

525. Sue Cannady Barefoot, Jean Watson Moore, Nancy Cannady Manning and Joyce Cannady Lucas., *Cannady Family History, Ancestors and Descendants 1665 - 2002, Vol. 1*, Page 135B. Vol. 2.

166

526. *Northern Sampson County, NC Cemeteries. Vol. 2. Compiled by Bradley Lee West, Kenneth Dale Register and Phyllis Jeanette West.*, Page 233.

527. Sue Cannady Barefoot, Jean Watson Moore, Nancy Cannady Manning and Joyce Cannady Lucas., *Cannady Family History, Ancestors and Descendants 1665 - 2002, Vol. 1*, Page 135B. Vol. 2.

528. *Northern Sampson County, NC Cemeteries. Vol. 2. Compiled by Bradley Lee West, Kenneth Dale Register and Phyllis Jeanette West.*, Page 233.

529. John C. Rosser, Jr., *The Descendants of Abraham Naylor and John Baggett of Sampson County, North Carolina*, (Draft of June 20, 1994), page 326.

530. Sue Cannady Barefoot, Jean Watson Moore, Nancy Cannady Manning and Joyce Cannady Lucas., *Cannady Family History, Ancestors and Descendants 1665 - 2002, Vol. 1*, Page 135.

531. John C. Rosser, Jr., *The Descendants of Abraham Naylor and John Baggett of Sampson County, North Carolina*, (Draft of June 20, 1994), page 273.

532. Sue Cannady Barefoot, Jean Watson Moore, Nancy Cannady Manning and Joyce Cannady Lucas., *Cannady Family History, Ancestors and Descendants 1665 - 2002, Vol. 1*, Page 135. Vol. 1.

533. *Knowledge of Family*.

534. John C. Rosser, Jr., *The Descendants of Abraham Naylor and John Baggett of Sampson County, North Carolina*, (Draft of June 20, 1994), pags 117, 273.

535. Family Descendants.

536. *Certificate of Birth for Addie May Jackson*, 549. Certificate No. 14.

537. *Certificate of Birth for Addie May Jackson*, Page 549. Certificate No. 14.

538. *Addie May Beasley*, Telephone interview on July 25, 2003.

539. Telephone interview with Callie Estelle Jackson.

540. *Southern Sampson County, NC Cemeteries. Compiled by Bradley Lee West and Kenneth Dale Register.*, Page 71.

541. Telephone interview with Callie Estelle Jackson.

542. *Social Security Death Index*.

543. Telephone interview with Callie Estelle Jackson.

544. *Interview with Lattie Pearl Jackson*.

545. *Northern Sampson County, NC Cemeteries. Vol. 2. Compiled by Bradley Lee West, Kenneth Dale Register and Phyllis Jeanette West.*, Page 250.

546. Member of Family.

547. *Telephone interview with Lincoln MacDonald Jackson.*.

548. *Telephone interview with Lincoln MacDonald Jackson.*, I called Lincoln MacDonald (Mack) Jackson around June 2003.

549. Telephone interview with Lincoln MacDonald Jackson, around June 2003, I called Lincoln MacDonald (Mack) Jackson.

550. Telephone interview with Lincoln MacDonald Jackson. I called Lincoln MacDonald (Mack) Jackson around June 2003.

551. Family Descendants.

552. Sue Cannady Barefoot, Cannady and Related Families.

553. Sue Cannady Barefoot, Jean Watson Moore, Nancy Cannady Manning and Joyce Cannady Lucas., *Cannady Family History, Ancestors and Descendants, 1665 - 2002, Vol. 2*, page 136A.

554. Sue Cannady Barefoot, Cannady and Related Families.

555. Sue Cannady Barefoot, Jean Watson Moore, Nancy Cannady Manning and Joyce Cannady Lucas., *Cannady Family History, Ancestors and Descendants, 1665 - 2002, Vol. 2*, page 136A.

556. Sue Cannady Barefoot, Jean Watson Moore, Nancy Cannady Manning and Joyce Cannady Lucas., *Cannady Family History, Ancestors and Descendants 1665 - 2002, Vol. 1,* Page 136A, Vol. 2.

557. *Social Security Death Index.*

558. Sue Cannady Barefoot, Jean Watson Moore, Nancy Cannady Manning and Joyce Cannady Lucas., *Cannady Family History, Ancestors and Descendants 1665 - 2002, Vol. 1,* Page 136A, Vol. 2.

559. *Knowledge of Family.*

560. Sue Cannady Barefoot, Jean Watson Moore, Nancy Cannady Manning and Joyce Cannady Lucas., *Cannady Family History, Ancestors and Descendants 1665 - 2002, Vol. 1,* Page 134.

561. Oscar M. Bizzell, Editor, *The Heritage of Sampson County, North Carolina, 1784-1984. Vol. 2. Oscar M. Bizzell, Editor. Associate Editor, Virginia Lohr Bizzell.*, page 594.

562. Sue Cannady Barefoot, Jean Watson Moore, Nancy Cannady Manning and Joyce Cannady Lucas., *Cannady Family History, Ancestors and Descendants 1665 - 2002, Vol. 1,* Page 134.

563. Oscar M. Bizzell, Editor, *The Heritage of Sampson County, North Carolina, 1784-1984. Vol. 2. Oscar M. Bizzell, Editor. Associate Editor, Virginia Lohr Bizzell.*, page 594.

564. Sue Cannady Barefoot, Jean Watson Moore, Nancy Cannady Manning and Joyce Cannady Lucas., *Cannady Family History, Ancestors and Descendants 1665 - 2002, Vol. 1,* Page 134.

565. Oscar M. Bizzell, Editor, *The Heritage of Sampson County, North Carolina, 1784-1984. Vol. 2. Oscar M. Bizzell, Editor. Associate Editor, Virginia Lohr Bizzell.*, page 594.

566. Sue Cannady Barefoot, Jean Watson Moore, Nancy Cannady Manning and Joyce Cannady Lucas., *Cannady Family History, Ancestors and Descendants 1665 - 2002, Vol. 1,* Page 134.

567. Oscar M. Bizzell, Editor, *The Heritage of Sampson County, North Carolina, 1784-1984. Vol. 2. Oscar M. Bizzell, Editor. Associate Editor, Virginia Lohr Bizzell.*, page 594.

568. Sue Cannady Barefoot, Jean Watson Moore, Nancy Cannady Manning and Joyce Cannady Lucas., *Cannady Family History, Ancestors and Descendants 1665 - 2002, Vol. 1,* Page 135A (Vol. 2.).

569. *Knowledge of Family,* Telephone interviews with several members of family.

570. *Knowledge of Family,* Telehone interviews with several members of family.

571. Sue Cannady Barefoot, Jean Watson Moore, Nancy Cannady Manning and Joyce Cannady Lucas., *Cannady Family History, Ancestors and Descendants 1665 - 2002, Vol. 1,* Page 135A. Vol. 2.

572. John C. Rosser, Jr., *Coharie to Cape Fear, The Descendants of John Williams and Katharine Galbreth of Sampson and Cumberland Counties in North Carolina (1740-1990),* (Walsworth Publishing Company, Marceline, Missouri 64658, April 1990. Only 100 copies printed. Copy in Deed office, Clinton, North Carolina), page 988, Vol. 2.

573. Sue Cannady Barefoot, Jean Watson Moore, Nancy Cannady Manning and Joyce Cannady Lucas., *Cannady Family History, Ancestors and Descendants 1665 - 2002, Vol. 1,* Page 135A. Vol. 2.

574. Sue Cannady Barefoot, Jean Watson Moore, Nancy Cannady Manning and Joyce Cannady Lucas., *Cannady Family History, Ancestors and Descendants 1665 - 2002, Vol. 1,* Page 135. Vol. 1.

575. Sue Cannady Barefoot, Jean Watson Moore, Nancy Cannady Manning and Joyce Cannady Lucas., *Cannady Family History, Ancestors and Descendants 1665 - 2002, Vol. 1,* Page 135A. Vol. 2.

576. Sue Cannady Barefoot, Jean Watson Moore, Nancy Cannady Manning and Joyce Cannady Lucas., *Cannady Family History, Ancestors and Descendants 1665 - 2002, Vol. 1*, Page 134E. Vol. 2.

577. Sue Cannady Barefoot, Jean Watson Moore, Nancy Cannady Manning and Joyce Cannady Lucas., *Cannady Family History, Ancestors and Descendants 1665 - 2002, Vol. 1*, Page 134E, Vol. 2.

578. Sue Cannady Barefoot, Jean Watson Moore, Nancy Cannady Manning and Joyce Cannady Lucas., *Cannady Family History, Ancestors and Descendants 1665 - 2002, Vol. 1*, Page 134E. Vol. 2.

579. John C. Rosser, Jr., *Coharie to Cape Fear, The Descendants of John Williams and Katharine Galbreth of Sampson and Cumberland Counties in North Carolina (1740-1990)*, (Walsworth Publishing Company, Marceline, Missouri 64658, April 1990. Only 100 copies printed. Copy in Deed office, Clinton, North Carolina).

580. Sue Cannady Barefoot, Jean Watson Moore, Nancy Cannady Manning and Joyce Cannady Lucas., *Cannady Family History, Ancestors and Descendants 1665 - 2002, Vol. 1*, Page 134E, Vol. 2.

581. Sue Cannady Barefoot, Jean Watson Moore, Nancy Cannady Manning and Joyce Cannady Lucas., *Cannady Family History, Ancestors and Descendants 1665 - 2002, Vol. 1*, page 134E, Vol. 2.

582. Sue Cannady Barefoot, Jean Watson Moore, Nancy Cannady Manning and Joyce Cannady Lucas., *Cannady Family History, Ancestors and Descendants 1665 - 2002, Vol. 1*, Page 134E, Vol. 2.

583. John C. Rosser, Jr., *Coharie to Cape Fear, The Descendants of John Williams and Katharine Galbreth of Sampson and Cumberland Counties in North Carolina (1740-1990)*, (Walsworth Publishing Company, Marceline, Missouri 64658, April 1990. Only 100 copies printed. Copy in Deed office, Clinton, North Carolina).

584. Sue Cannady Barefoot, Jean Watson Moore, Nancy Cannady Manning and Joyce Cannady Lucas., *Cannady Family History, Ancestors and Descendants 1665 - 2002, Vol. 1*, Page 134B, Vol. 2.

585. *Internet research at Ancestry.com*, "Electronic."

586. *1930 Federal Census for Sampson County, North Carolina.*

587. Annie Carolyn Tew and Fannie Lee Lockamy Williams, Footprints from Kitty Fork, Published in 2006. Sampson County, North Carolina.

588. Sue Cannady Barefoot, Jean Watson Moore, Nancy Cannady Manning and Joyce Cannady Lucas., *Cannady Family History, Ancestors and Descendants 1665 - 2002, Vol. 1*, Page 134B, Vol. 2.

589. John C. Rosser, Jr., *The Descendants of Abraham Naylor and John Baggett of Sampson County, North Carolina*, (Draft of June 20, 1994), Page 134.

590. *1930 Federal Census for Sampson County, North Carolina.*

591. Annie Carolyn Tew and Fannie Lee Lockamy Williams, Footprints from Kitty Fork, Published in 2006. Sampson County, North Carolina.

592. *Northern Sampson County, NC Cemeteries. Vol. 2. Compiled by Bradley Lee West, Kenneth Dale Register and Phyllis Jeanette West.*, Page 26, Vol. 2.

593. *Northern Sampson County, NC Cemeteries. Vol. 2. Compiled by Bradley Lee West, Kenneth Dale Register and Phyllis Jeanette West.*, Page 239.

594. *Northern Sampson County, NC Cemeteries. Vol. 2. Compiled by Bradley Lee West, Kenneth Dale Register and Phyllis Jeanette West.*, page 230.

595. *Northern Sampson County, NC Cemeteries. Vol. 2. Compiled by Bradley Lee West, Kenneth Dale Register and Phyllis Jeanette West.*, Page 239.

596. *Northern Sampson County, NC Cemeteries. Vol. 2. Compiled by Bradley Lee West, Kenneth Dale Register and Phyllis Jeanette West.*, Page 365.

597. John C. Rosser, Jr., *Coharie to Cape Fear, The Descendants of John Williams and Katharine Galbreth of Sampson and Cumberland Counties in North Carolina (1740-1990)*, (Walsworth Publishing Company, Marceline, Missouri 64658, April 1990. Only 100 copies printed. Copy in Deed office, Clinton, North Carolina).

598. *Northern Sampson County, NC Cemeteries. Vol. 2. Compiled by Bradley Lee West, Kenneth Dale Register and Phyllis Jeanette West.*, Page 365.

599. Sue Cannady Barefoot, Jean Watson Moore, Nancy Cannady Manning and Joyce Cannady Lucas., *Cannady Family History, Ancestors and Descendants 1665 - 2002, Vol. 1*, Page 134C, Vol. 2.

600. *Northern Sampson County, NC Cemeteries. Vol. 2. Compiled by Bradley Lee West, Kenneth Dale Register and Phyllis Jeanette West.*.

601. Sue Cannady Barefoot, Jean Watson Moore, Nancy Cannady Manning and Joyce Cannady Lucas., *Cannady Family History, Ancestors and Descendants 1665 - 2002, Vol. 1*, Page 134C, Vol. 2.

602. Sue Cannady Barefoot, Jean Watson Moore, Nancy Cannady Manning and Joyce Cannady Lucas., *Cannady Family History, Ancestors and Descendants 1665 - 2002, Vol. 1*, Page 134, Vol. 2.

603. Sue Cannady Barefoot, Jean Watson Moore, Nancy Cannady Manning and Joyce Cannady Lucas., *Cannady Family History, Ancestors and Descendants 1665 - 2002, Vol. 1*, Page 134C, Vol. 2.

604. Sue Cannady Barefoot, Jean Watson Moore, Nancy Cannady Manning and Joyce Cannady Lucas., *Cannady Family History, Ancestors and Descendants 1665 - 2002, Vol. 1*, Page 134E, Vol. 2.

605. Preston Carr Pope provided data.

606. John C. Rosser, Jr., *The Descendants of Abraham Naylor and John Baggett of Sampson County, North Carolina*, (Draft of June 20, 1994), pages 297, 298.

607. Preston Carr Pope provided data.

608. John C. Rosser, Jr., *The Descendants of Abraham Naylor and John Baggett of Sampson County, North Carolina*, (Draft of June 20, 1994), page 297.

609. Preston Carr Pope provided data.

610. *The Heritage of Sampson County, North Carolina, 1784-1984. Vol. 1. Oscar M. Bizzell, Editor*, Page 280, Profile 402.

611. *Northern Sampson County, NC Cemeteries. Vol. 2. Compiled by Bradley Lee West, Kenneth Dale Register and Phyllis Jeanette West.*, Page 235.

612. Oscar M. Bizzell, Editor, *The Heritage of Sampson County, North Carolina, 1784-1984. Vol. 2. Oscar M. Bizzell, Editor. Associate Editor, Virginia Lohr Bizzell.*, Page 279, Profile 401.

613. *The Heritage of Sampson County, North Carolina, 1784-1984. Vol. 1. Oscar M. Bizzell, Editor*, Page 280, Profile # 402.

614. *Southern Sampson County, NC Cemeteries. Compiled by Bradley Lee West and Kenneth Dale Register.*, Page 235.

615. *The Heritage of Sampson County, North Carolina, 1784-1984. Vol. 1. Oscar M. Bizzell, Editor*, Page 279, Profile # 401.

616. *Northern Sampson County, NC Cemeteries. Vol. 2. Compiled by Bradley Lee West, Kenneth Dale Register and Phyllis Jeanette West.*, Page 235.

617. *The Heritage of Sampson County, North Carolina, 1784-1984. Vol. 1. Oscar M. Bizzell, Editor*, Page 280, Profile # 402.

618. *The Heritage of Sampson County, North Carolina, 1784-1984. Vol. 1. Oscar M. Bizzell, Editor*, Pages 281 and 282, Profile 404.

619. Sue Cannady Barefoot, Jean Watson Moore, Nancy Cannady Manning and Joyce Cannady Lucas., *Cannady Family History, Ancestors and Descendants, 1665 - 2002, Vol. 2*, page 134A.

620. *The Heritage of Sampson County, North Carolina, 1784-1984. Vol. 1. Oscar M. Bizzell, Editor*, Pages 281 and 282, Profile 404.

621. *Internet research at Ancestry.com*, "Electronic."

622. Family Descendants, Data provided by member of family in a telephone interview or letter.

623. *Certificate of Death for William B. Jackson*, Page 217 in book for 1995.

624. Family Descendants, Telephone interview with Joyce Ellis Jackson.

625. *Claudia Priscilla Jackson Honeycutt Fields*, Family Knowledge and records.

626. *Claudia Priscilla Jackson Honeycutt Fields*.

627. *Claudia Priscilla Jackson Honeycutt Fields*, Family knowledge and records.

628. *Claudia Priscilla Jackson Honeycutt Fields*.

629. *Claudia Priscilla Jackson Honeycutt Fields*, Family knowledge and records.

630. *Knowledge of Family*, Claudia Priscilla Jackson Honeycutt Nickolson Fields provided data.

631. *Claudia Priscilla Jackson Honeycutt Fields*.

632. Family provided Data.

633. *Claudia Priscilla Jackson Honeycutt Fields*.

634. *Claudia Priscilla Jackson Honeycutt Fields*, Family knowledge and records.

635. *Claudia Priscilla Jackson Honeycutt Fields*.

636. *Claudia Priscilla Jackson Honeycutt Fields*, Family knowledge and records.

637. *Claudia Priscilla Jackson Honeycutt Fields*.

638. *Claudia Priscilla Jackson Honeycutt Fields*, Family knowledge and records.

639. *Claudia Priscilla Jackson Honeycutt Fields*, Family knowledge.

640. *Claudia Priscilla Jackson Honeycutt Fields*.

641. *Claudia Priscilla Jackson Honeycutt Fields*, Data provided to Priscilla by Diane Davis Jackson.

642. *Claudia Priscilla Jackson Honeycutt Fields*, Diane Davis Jackson provided date to Priscilla.

643. *Claudia Priscilla Jackson Honeycutt Fields*, Date provided to Priscilla by Diane Davis Jackson.

644. *Claudia Priscilla Jackson Honeycutt Fields*, Diane Davis Jackson provided date to Priscilla.

645. *Claudia Priscilla Jackson Honeycutt Fields*, Family Knowledge.

646. *Claudia Priscilla Jackson Honeycutt Fields*, Telephone interviews with Priscilla and written data provided by her.

647. *Claudia Priscilla Jackson Honeycutt Fields*, Telephone interviews and correspondence.

648. Telephone interview with Callie Estelle Jackson.

649. Annie Carolyn Tew and Fannie Lee Lockamy Williams, Footprints from Kitty Fork, Published in 2006. Sampson County, North Carolina.

650. Telephone interview with Callie Estelle Jackson.

651. *Social Security Death Index*.

652. Certificate of Death for Willard Paul Jackson, Page 179 in book for 1967.

653. Telephone interview with Callie Estelle Jackson.

654. *Southern Sampson County, NC Cemeteries. Compiled by Bradley Lee West and Kenneth Dale Register.*, Page 71.

655. Certificate of Death for Willard Paul Jackson, Page 179 in book for 1967.

656. Telephone interview with Callie Estelle Jackson.

657. *Northern Sampson County, NC Cemeteries. Vol. 2. Compiled by Bradley Lee West, Kenneth Dale Register and Phyllis Jeanette West.*, Page 250.

658. *Northern Sampson County, NC Cemeteries. Vol. 2. Compiled by Bradley Lee West, Kenneth Dale Register and Phyllis Jeanette West.*, page 250.

659. Telephone interview with Callie Estelle Jackson.

660. Annie Carolyn Tew and Fannie Lee Lockamy Williams, Footprints from Kitty Fork, Published in 2006. Sampson County, North Carolina.

661. Telephone interview with Callie Estelle Jackson.

662. Annie Carolyn Tew and Fannie Lee Lockamy Williams, Footprints from Kitty Fork, Published in 2006. Sampson County, North Carolina.

663. Telephone interview with Callie Estelle Jackson.

664. *Telephone interview with Bernice Franklin Jackson.*

665. *Northern Sampson County, NC Cemeteries. Vol. 2. Compiled by Bradley Lee West, Kenneth Dale Register and Phyllis Jeanette West.*, Page 76.

666. *Telephone interview with Bernice Franklin Jackson.*

667. *Claudia Priscilla Jackson Honeycutt Fields*, Obituary in "The Sampson Independent" Newspaper.

668. Telephone interview with Callie Estelle Jackson.

669. *Telephone interview with Bernice Franklin Jackson.*

670. *Claudia Priscilla Jackson Honeycutt Fields*, Obituary from "The Sampson Independent" Newspaper.

671. Telephone interview with Callie Estelle Jackson.

672. *Northern Sampson County, NC Cemeteries. Vol. 2. Compiled by Bradley Lee West, Kenneth Dale Register and Phyllis Jeanette West.*, Page 76.

673. *Northern Sampson County, NC Cemeteries. Vol. 2. Compiled by Bradley Lee West, Kenneth Dale Register and Phyllis Jeanette West.*.

674. *Northern Sampson County, NC Cemeteries. Vol. 2. Compiled by Bradley Lee West, Kenneth Dale Register and Phyllis Jeanette West.*, Page 76.

675. *Claudia Priscilla Jackson Honeycutt Fields*, Name from obituary in Sampson Independent Newspaper.

676. *Claudia Priscilla Jackson Honeycutt Fields*, Obituary of Linda's father.

677. Telephone interview with Callie Estelle Jackson.

678. Annie Carolyn Tew and Fannie Lee Lockamy Williams, Footprints from Kitty Fork, Published in 2006. Sampson County, North Carolina.

679. *Dwanda Rose Tyndall Jackson*, Written data provided.

680. John C. Rosser, Jr., *Coharie to Cape Fear, The Descendants of John Williams and Katharine Galbreth of Sampson and Cumberland Counties in North Carolina (1740-1990)*, (Walsworth Publishing Company, Marceline, Missouri 64658, April 1990. Only 100 copies printed. Copy in Deed office, Clinton, North Carolina).

681. Bradley Lee West, Kenneth Dale Register, *Northern Sampson County, NC (North Carolina) Cemeteries, Vol. 3.*

682. John C. Rosser, Jr., *Coharie to Cape Fear, The Descendants of John Williams and Katharine Galbreth of Sampson and Cumberland Counties in North Carolina (1740-1990)*, (Walsworth Publishing Company, Marceline, Missouri 64658, April 1990. Only 100 copies printed. Copy in Deed office, Clinton, North Carolina).

683. Bradley Lee West, Kenneth Dale Register, *Northern Sampson County, NC (North Carolina) Cemeteries, Vol. 3.*

684. *Interview with Lattie Pearl Jackson.*

685. Member of Family.

686. John C. Rosser, Jr., *The Descendants of Abraham Naylor and John Baggett of Sampson County, North Carolina,* (Draft of June 20, 1994), page 110.

687. Annie Carolyn Tew and Fannie Lee Lockamy Williams, Footprints from Kitty Fork, Published in 2006. Sampson County, North Carolina.

688. John C. Rosser, Jr., *The Descendants of Abraham Naylor and John Baggett of Sampson County, North Carolina,* (Draft of June 20, 1994), page 110.

689. Annie Carolyn Tew and Fannie Lee Lockamy Williams, Footprints from Kitty Fork, Published in 2006. Sampson County, North Carolina.

690. *Knowledge of Family..*

691. Annie Carolyn Tew and Fannie Lee Lockamy Williams, Footprints from Kitty Fork, Published in 2006. Sampson County, North Carolina.

692. *Family Bible.*

693. Annie Carolyn Tew and Fannie Lee Lockamy Williams, Footprints from Kitty Fork, Published in 2006. Sampson County, North Carolina.

694. *Family Bible.*

695. Annie Carolyn Tew and Fannie Lee Lockamy Williams, Footprints from Kitty Fork, Published in 2006. Sampson County, North Carolina.

696. *Knowledge of Family..*

697. Annie Carolyn Tew and Fannie Lee Lockamy Williams, Footprints from Kitty Fork, Published in 2006. Sampson County, North Carolina.

698. *Knowledge of Family..*

699. Annie Carolyn Tew and Fannie Lee Lockamy Williams, Footprints from Kitty Fork, Published in 2006. Sampson County, North Carolina.

700. John C. Rosser, Jr., *The Descendants of Abraham Naylor and John Baggett of Sampson County, North Carolina,* (Draft of June 20, 1994), page 109.

701. John C. Rosser, Jr., *The Descendants of Abraham Naylor and John Baggett of Sampson County, North Carolina,* (Draft of June 20, 1994), page 110.

702. John C. Rosser, Jr., *The Descendants of Abraham Naylor and John Baggett of Sampson County, North Carolina,* (Draft of June 20, 1994), page 109.

703. *Knowledge of Family.*, Interview with Ruby Doris Jackson Lee and Perry Scott Jackson.

704. *Knowledge of Family..*

705. *Knowledge of Family.*, Interview with Ruby Doris Jackson Lee and Perry Scott Jackson.

706. *Knowledge of Family.*

707. Annie Carolyn Tew and Fannie Lee Lockamy Williams, Footprints from Kitty Fork, Published in 2006. Sampson County, North Carolina.

708. *Interview with Ruby Doris Jackson Lee and Perry Scott Jackson.*

709. Annie Carolyn Tew and Fannie Lee Lockamy Williams, Footprints from Kitty Fork, Published in 2006. Sampson County, North Carolina.

710. *Interview with Ruby Doris Jackson Lee and Perry Scott Jackson.*

711. Annie Carolyn Tew and Fannie Lee Lockamy Williams, Footprints from Kitty Fork, Published in 2006. Sampson County, North Carolina.

712. *Interview with Ruby Doris Jackson Lee and Perry Scott Jackson.*

713. *Interview with Perry Scott Jackson and Kim Jernigan.*

714. Annie Carolyn Tew and Fannie Lee Lockamy Williams, Footprints from Kitty Fork, Published in 2006. Sampson County, North Carolina.

715. *Interview with Ruby Doris Jackson Lee and Perry Scott Jackson.*

716. *Interview with Perry Scott Jackson and Kim Jernigan.*

717. *Interview with Ruby Doris Jackson Lee and Perry Scott Jackson.*

718. *Interview with Perry Scott Jackson and Kim Jernigan.*

719. *Interview with Ruby Doris Jackson Lee and Perry Scott Jackson.*

720. Annie Carolyn Tew and Fannie Lee Lockamy Williams, Footprints from Kitty Fork, Published in 2006. Sampson County, North Carolina.

721. *Interview with Ruby Doris Jackson Lee and Perry Scott Jackson.*

722. *Northern Sampson County, NC Cemeteries. Vol. 2. Compiled by Bradley Lee West, Kenneth Dale Register and Phyllis Jeanette West.*, Page 63.

723. *Interview with Ruby Doris Jackson Lee and Perry Scott Jackson.*

724. Annie Carolyn Tew and Fannie Lee Lockamy Williams, Footprints from Kitty Fork, Published in 2006. Sampson County, North Carolina.

725. Descendants of James Thomas Lockamy and Jemima Jewel Jackson and members of their families.

726. *Northern Sampson County, NC Cemeteries. Vol. 2. Compiled by Bradley Lee West, Kenneth Dale Register and Phyllis Jeanette West.*, Page 55.

727. Descendants of James Thomas Lockamy and Jemima Jewel Jackson and members of their families.

728. *Northern Sampson County, NC Cemeteries. Vol. 2. Compiled by Bradley Lee West, Kenneth Dale Register and Phyllis Jeanette West.*, Page 55.

729. Descendants of James Thomas Lockamy and Jemima Jewel Jackson and members of their families.

730. *1930 Federal Census for Sampson County, North Carolina.*

731. Descendants of James Thomas Lockamy and Jemima Jewel Jackson and members of their families.

732. Annie Carolyn Tew and Fannie Lee Lockamy Williams, Footprints from Kitty Fork, Published in 2006. Sampson County, North Carolina.

733. *Northern Sampson County, NC Cemeteries. Vol. 2. Compiled by Bradley Lee West, Kenneth Dale Register and Phyllis Jeanette West.*, Page 55.

734. *1930 Federal Census for Sampson County, North Carolina.*

735. Sue Cannady Barefoot, Cannady and Related Families.

736. Descendants of James Thomas Lockamy and Jemima Jewel Jackson and members of their families.

737. Descendants of James Thomas Lockamy and Jemima Jewel Jackson and members of their families, Provided by Jackie Olene Jackson Smith and Barbara Jean Jordan Hairr.

738. *1930 Federal Census for Sampson County, North Carolina.*

739. Descendants of James Thomas Lockamy and Jemima Jewel Jackson and members of their families, Provided by Barbara Jean Jordan Hairr.

740. *Knowledge of Family.*

741. Descendants of James Thomas Lockamy and Jemima Jewel Jackson and members of their families, Willa Dean Lockamy Jordan provided data.

742. Descendants of James Thomas Lockamy and Jemima Jewel Jackson and members of their families, Willa Dean Lockamy provided data.

743. Descendants of James Thomas Lockamy and Jemima Jewel Jackson and members of their families, Data provided by Willa Dean Lockamy Jordan.

744. *Northern Sampson County, NC Cemeteries. Vol. 2. Compiled by Bradley Lee West, Kenneth Dale Register and Phyllis Jeanette West.*, Page 53.

745. Descendants of James Thomas Lockamy and Jemima Jewel Jackson and members of their families, Data provided by Willa Dean Lockamy Jordan.

746. *Knowledge of Family*, provided by Thomas Daniel Lockamy.

747. *Knowledge of Family*, Provided by Thomas Daniel Lockamy.

748. *Knowledge of Family*, Name provided by Thomas Daniel Lockamy.

749. Descendants of James Thomas Lockamy and Jemima Jewel Jackson and members of their families, Thomas Daniel (Sam) Lockamy provided the name.

750. Annie Carolyn Tew and Fannie Lee Lockamy Williams, Footprints from Kitty Fork, Published in 2006. Sampson County, North Carolina.

751. *Knowledge of Family*, Name provided by Thomas Daniel Lockamy.

752. Descendants of James Thomas Lockamy and Jemima Jewel Jackson and members of their families, Thomas Daniel (Sam) Lockamy provided the name.

753. *Knowledge of Family*, Name provided by Thomas Daniel Lockamy.

754. Descendants of James Thomas Lockamy and Jemima Jewel Jackson and members of their families, Thomas Daniel (Sam) Lockamy provided the name.

755. *Knowledge of Family*, Name provided by Thomas Daniel Lockamy.

756. Descendants of James Thomas Lockamy and Jemima Jewel Jackson and members of their families, Thomas Daniel (Sam) Lockamy provided the name.

757. Descendants of James Thomas Lockamy and Jemima Jewel Jackson and members of their families, Provided by Barbara Jean Jordan Dixon.

758. Descendants of James Thomas Lockamy and Jemima Jewel Jackson and members of their families, Provided by Nan McChrae Wright Dixon.

759. *Knowledge of Family.*, Name provided by Barbara Jean Jordan Hairr.

760. *Knowledge of Family.*, Date provided by Velva Jewel Dixon Smith.

761. *Knowledge of Family.*, Name provided by Velva Jewel Dixon Smith.

762. *Knowledge of Family.*, Date provided by Velva Jewel Dixon Smith.

763. *Knowledge of Family.*, Name provided by Velva Jewel Dixon Smith, her mother.

764. *Knowledge of Family.*, Date provided by her mother, Velva Jewel Dixon Smith.

765. *Knowledge of Family.*, Name provided by his mother, Velva Jewel Dixon Smith.

766. *Knowledge of Family.*, Date provided by his mother, Velva Jewel Dixon Smith.

767. *Certificate of Birth for Nancy Eveline Jackson*, 365, Honeycutts Township. Certificate No. 24. Reistration District No. 82-04. Fourth Ward.

768. *Certificate of Birth for Nancy Eveline Jackson.*

769. *Certificate of Marriage for Richard Joseph Pleitt and Nancy E. Jackson*, Richad J. Pleitt and Nancy E. Jackson were lawfully married on the 18th day of September 1954 according to the Rite of the Roman Catholic Church and in conformity with the laws of the State Of Illinois in the presence of Earl R. McClaughry and Rose Seiler, Witnesses.

770. Certificate of Birth for Richard Joseph Pleitt, Registration No. 47010. Primary Dist. No. 3104. Cook County, IL.

771. Certificate of Death for Richard Joseph Pleitt, File No. 3527. Milwaukee, Wisconsin

772. *Certificate of Death for Richard Joseph Pleitt.*

773. *Certificate of Marriage for Richard Joseph Pleitt and Nancy E. Jackson*, Richad J. Pleitt and Nancy E. Jackson were lawfully married on the 18th day of September 1954 according to the Rite of the Roman Catholic Church and in conformity with the laws of the State Of Illinois in the presence of Earl R. McClaughry and Rose Seiler, Witnesses.

774. Personal knowledge of Mother of Margaret Roberta Pleitt, Personal knowledge of Mother of Margaret Roberta Pleitt.

775. *Personal knowledge of Mother of Margaret Roberta Pleitt.*

776. *Knowledge of Family.*

777. *Personal knowledge of Mother of Margaret Roberta Pleitt.*

778. Keith Allen Clark.

779. *Personal knowledge of Mother of Margaret Roberta Pleitt.*

780. *Records of Resurrection Cemetery, Justice, Illinois.*

781. *Personal knowledge of Mother of Baby Girl Pleitt.*

782. *Records of Resurrection Cemetery, Justice, Illinois.*

783. *Personal knowledge of Mother of Baby Girl Pleitt.*

784. *Records of Resurrection Cemetery, Justice, Illinois.*

785. Bible records of Jackie Olene Smith.

786. *Personal knowledge of Jackie Olene Jackson Smith.*

787. Bible records of Jackie Olene Smith.

788. *Personal knowledge of Jackie Olene Jackson Smith.*

789. *Knowledge of Family.*, Name provided by mother, Mattie Ruth Parker Jackson Holland.

790. *Knowledge of Family.*, Date provided by her mother, Mattie Ruth Jackson Parker Holland.

791. *Social Security Death Index.*

792. *Knowledge of Family..*

793. *Knowledge of Family.*, Name provided by mother, Mattie Ruth Jackson Parker Holland.

794. *Knowledge of Family.*, Date provided by mother, Mattie Ruth Jackson Parker Holland.

795. *Knowledge of Family..*

796. Sue Cannady Barefoot, Cannady and Related Families.

797. John C. Rosser, Jr., *The Descendants of Abraham Naylor and John Baggett of Sampson County, North Carolina*, (Draft of June 20, 1994), Page 20, Mr. John C. Rosser, Jr.'s source was certificate of birth.

798. *Knowledge of Family.*, Date provided by his mother, Mattie Ruth Jackson Parker Holland.

799. *Knowledge of Family..*

800. John C. Rosser, Jr., *The Descendants of Abraham Naylor and John Baggett of Sampson County, North Carolina*, (Draft of June 20, 1994), page 48.

801. John C. Rosser, Jr., *The Descendants of Abraham Naylor and John Baggett of Sampson County, North Carolina*, (Draft of June 20, 1994), Page 20, Mr. Rosser, Jr confirmed by a vital record.

802. John C. Rosser, Jr., *The Descendants of Abraham Naylor and John Baggett of Sampson County, North Carolina*, (Draft of June 20, 1994), Page 20, Mr. Rosser, Jr. confirmed by a vital record.

803. John C. Rosser, Jr., *The Descendants of Abraham Naylor and John Baggett of Sampson County, North Carolina*, (Draft of June 20, 1994), Page 20, Mr. Rosser, Jr., confirmed by a vital record.

804. *Northern Sampson County, NC Cemeteries. Vol. 2. Compiled by Bradley Lee West, Kenneth Dale Register and Phyllis Jeanette West.*, Pager 230.

805. John C. Rosser, Jr., *The Descendants of Abraham Naylor and John Baggett of Sampson County, North Carolina*, (Draft of June 20, 1994), Page 20, Mr. Rosser, Jr., confirmed by a vital record.

806. *Knowledge of Family..*

807. *Knowledge of Family.*

808. V. Mayo Bundy, *Meet Our Ancestors, Culbreth, Autry, Maxwell-Bundy, Winslow, Henley and Allied Families (Second Edition)*, (Media, Inc., Greensboro, North Carolina, 1978), page 118.

809. *Knowledge of Family*, Mother provided date.

810. Bradley Lee West, Kenneth Dale Register, *Northern Sampson County, NC (North Carolina) Cemeteries, Vol. 3.*

811. Family provided Data.

812. Sue Cannady Barefoot, Jean Watson Moore, Nancy Cannady Manning and Joyce Cannady Lucas., *Cannady Family History, Ancestors and Descendants 1665 - 2002, Vol. 1*, page 133E (Vol. 2).

813. V. Mayo Bundy, *Meet Our Ancestors, Culbreth, Autry, Maxwell-Bundy, Winslow, Henley and Allied Families (Second Edition)*, (Media, Inc., Greensboro, North Carolina, 1978), page 118.

814. *Knowledge of Family.*

815. Sue Cannady Barefoot, Jean Watson Moore, Nancy Cannady Manning and Joyce Cannady Lucas., *Cannady Family History, Ancestors and Descendants 1665 - 2002, Vol. 1*, page 133E (Vol. 2).

816. *Knowledge of Family..*

817. John C. Rosser, Jr., *The Descendants of Abraham Naylor and John Baggett of Sampson County, North Carolina*, (Draft of June 20, 1994), Page 20, Mr. Rosser, Jr., verified by a vital record.

818. John C. Rosser, Jr., *The Descendants of Abraham Naylor and John Baggett of Sampson County, North Carolina*, (Draft of June 20, 1994), Page 20.

819. John C. Rosser, Jr., *The Descendants of Abraham Naylor and John Baggett of Sampson County, North Carolina*, (Draft of June 20, 1994), Page 20, Mr. Rosser, Jr., verified by records in Cumberland County, North Carolina.

820. John C. Rosser, Jr., *The Descendants of Abraham Naylor and John Baggett of Sampson County, North Carolina*, (Draft of June 20, 1994), Page 20, Mr. Rosser, Jr., verified by a vital record.

821. John C. Rosser, Jr., *The Descendants of Abraham Naylor and John Baggett of Sampson County, North Carolina*, (Draft of June 20, 1994), Page 29, Mr. Rosser, Jr., verified by a vital record.

822. John C. Rosser, Jr., *The Descendants of Abraham Naylor and John Baggett of Sampson County, North Carolina*, (Draft of June 20, 1994), Page 20, Mr. Rosser, Jr., verified by a vital record.

823. *Knowledge of Family..*

824. *Knowledge of Family.*, William Craven Long provided date.

825. Sue Cannady Barefoot, Jean Watson Moore, Nancy Cannady Manning and Joyce Cannady Lucas., *Cannady Family History, Ancestors and Descendants 1665 - 2002, Vol. 1*, page 133G (Vol. 2).

826. *Knowledge of Family.*, Mary Jane Jackson Long provided name.

827. *Knowledge of Family.*, Mary Jane Jackson Long provided full name.

828. Sue Cannady Barefoot, Jean Watson Moore, Nancy Cannady Manning and Joyce Cannady Lucas., *Cannady Family History, Ancestors and Descendants 1665 - 2002, Vol. 1*, page 133G (Vol. 2).

829. *Knowledge of Family.*, William Craven Long and Mary Jane Long provided full name.

830. *Knowledge of Family..*

831. *Knowledge of Family.*, Date provided by William Craven Long.

832. *Knowledge of Family..*

833. *Knowledge of Family.*, Name provided by Mary Jane Jackson Long.

834. *Knowledge of Family..*

835. *Knowledge of Family.*, Provided by Mary Jane Jackson Long.

836. *Knowledge of Family..*

837. *Knowledge of Family.*, Provided by Mary Jane Jackson Long.

838. *Knowledge of Family.*, William Craven Long and Mary Jane Jackson Long provided full name.

839. *Knowledge of Family.*, Date provided by William Craven Long.

840. *Knowledge of Family.*, Name provided by Mary Jane Jackson Long.

841. *Knowledge of Family.*, William Craven Long and Mary Jane Jackson Long provided full name.

842. *Knowledge of Family.*, Sondra Jean Long LaRouche and William Craven Long provided date.

843. *Knowledge of Family.*, Date provided by William Craven Long.

844. *Knowledge of Family.*, Sondra Jean Long McFarland LaRouche provided name.

845. *Knowledge of Family.*, Sondra Jean Long LaRouche provided date.

846. Knowledge of Family. Full name provided by Virginia Lee Horne Jackson Strickland.

847. Knowledge of Family. Date provided by Virginia Lee Horne Jackson Strickland.

848. Knowledge of Family. Name provided by Judy Katherine Barnes Jackson.

849. Family provided Data.

850. Knowledge of Family. Lorenda Kaye Jackson Wallace Hayes Carr provided information.

851. *Knowledge of Family.*.

852. Knowledge of Family. Lorenda Kaye Jackson Wallace Hayes Carr provided information.

853. Sue Cannady Barefoot, Jean Watson Moore, Nancy Cannady Manning and Joyce Cannady Lucas., Cannady Family History. Date was provided to the writers of "Cannady Family History" book.

854. Family provided Data.

855. Knowledge of Family. Date and location of marriage provided by Lorenda Kaye Jackson Hayes Carr.

856. Family provided Data.

857. Knowledge of Family. Date and location of marriage provided by Lorenda Kaye Jackson Hayes Carr.

858. Knowledge of Family. His mother provided full name.

859. Knowledge of Family. His mother provided date.

860. Knowledge of Family. His mother provided information.

861. Knowledge of Family. Mother, Lorenda Kaye Jackson Wallace Hayes Carr provided data.

862. *Knowledge of Family.*.

863. Knowledge of Family. Date provided by Heidi Jane Jackson and Virginia Lee Horne Jackson Strickland.

864. Knowledge of Family. Full name provided by Heidi Jane Jackson Tyndall Jackson.

865. John C. Rosser, Jr., *The Descendants of Abraham Naylor and John Baggett of Sampson County, North Carolina*, (Draft of June 20, 1994), page 122.

866. Knowledge of Family. Date and location provided by Heidi Jane Jackson Tyndall Jackson.

867. Family Descendants, Terry Lynn Jackson provided data.

868. Family Descendants, Terry Lynn provided name.

869. Sue Cannady Barefoot, Jean Watson Moore, Nancy Cannady Manning and Joyce Cannady Lucas., *Cannady Family History, Ancestors and Descendants 1665 - 2002, Vol. 1*, page 133J (Vol. 2), Family member provided data to writers of this book.

870. Family Descendants.

871. Sue Cannady Barefoot, Cannady and Related Families.

872. Sue Cannady Barefoot, Jean Watson Moore, Nancy Cannady Manning and Joyce Cannady Lucas., *Cannady Family History, Ancestors and Descendants 1665 - 2002, Vol. 1,* page 133J (Vol. 2), Family member provided data to writers of this book.

873. Knowledge of Family. Full name provided by Virginia Lee Horne Jackson Strickland.

874. *Knowledge of Family.*

875. Sue Cannady Barefoot, Jean Watson Moore, Nancy Cannady Manning and Joyce Cannady Lucas., *Cannady Family History, Ancestors and Descendants 1665 - 2002, Vol. 1,* page 133J (Vol. 2), Family member provided data to writers of this book.

876. Sue Cannady Barefoot, Jean Watson Moore, Nancy Cannady Manning and Joyce Cannady Lucas., *Cannady Family History, Ancestors and Descendants 1665 - 2002, Vol. 1.*

877. Sue Cannady Barefoot, Jean Watson Moore, Nancy Cannady Manning and Joyce Cannady Lucas., *Cannady Family History, Ancestors and Descendants 1665 - 2002, Vol. 1,* Full name provided by family member to writers of this book.

878. Sue Cannady Barefoot, Jean Watson Moore, Nancy Cannady Manning and Joyce Cannady Lucas., *Cannady Family History, Ancestors and Descendants 1665 - 2002, Vol. 1,* Date was provided for Cannady Family History book.

879. Sue Cannady Barefoot, Jean Watson Moore, Nancy Cannady Manning and Joyce Cannady Lucas., *Cannady Family History, Ancestors and Descendants 1665 - 2002, Vol. 1,* Full name was provided to the writers of the Cannady Family History book.

880. Sue Cannady Barefoot, Jean Watson Moore, Nancy Cannady Manning and Joyce Cannady Lucas., *Cannady Family History, Ancestors and Descendants 1665 - 2002, Vol. 1,* Date was provided for the writers of the Cannady Family History book.

881. *Addie May Beasley,* Telephone interview with Addie May Beasley on July 25, 2003.

882. *Addie May Beasley,* Telephone interview on July 25, 2003.

883. *Addie May Beasley,* Telephone interview with Addie May Beasley on July 25, 2003.

884. Sue Cannady Barefoot, Jean Watson Moore, Nancy Cannady Manning and Joyce Cannady Lucas., *Cannady Family History, Ancestors and Descendants 1665 - 2002, Vol. 1,* Page 135A. Vol. 2.

885. John C. Rosser, Jr., *Coharie to Cape Fear, The Descendants of John Williams and Katharine Galbreth of Sampson and Cumberland Counties in North Carolina (1740-1990),* (Walsworth Publishing Company, Marceline, Missouri 64658, April 1990. Only 100 copies printed. Copy in Deed office, Clinton, North Carolina), page 988, Vol. 2.

886. Sue Cannady Barefoot, Jean Watson Moore, Nancy Cannady Manning and Joyce Cannady Lucas., *Cannady Family History, Ancestors and Descendants 1665 - 2002, Vol. 1,* Page 135A. Vol. 2.

887. John C. Rosser, Jr., *Coharie to Cape Fear, The Descendants of John Williams and Katharine Galbreth of Sampson and Cumberland Counties in North Carolina (1740-1990),* (Walsworth Publishing Company, Marceline, Missouri 64658, April 1990. Only 100 copies printed. Copy in Deed office, Clinton, North Carolina), page 988, Vol. 2.

888. Sue Cannady Barefoot, Jean Watson Moore, Nancy Cannady Manning and Joyce Cannady Lucas., *Cannady Family History, Ancestors and Descendants 1665 - 2002, Vol. 1,* Page 135A. Vol. 2.

889. Sue Cannady Barefoot, Jean Watson Moore, Nancy Cannady Manning and Joyce Cannady Lucas., *Cannady Family History, Ancestors and Descendants 1665 - 2002, Vol. 1,* Page 135A. Vol 2.

890. Sue Cannady Barefoot, Jean Watson Moore, Nancy Cannady Manning and Joyce Cannady Lucas., *Cannady Family History, Ancestors and Descendants 1665 - 2002, Vol. 1,* Page 135A. Vol. 2.

891. Sue Cannady Barefoot, Cannady and Related Families.

892. Sue Cannady Barefoot, Jean Watson Moore, Nancy Cannady Manning and Joyce Cannady Lucas., *Cannady Family History, Ancestors and Descendants 1665 - 2002, Vol. 1*, Page 135A. Vol. 2.

893. Sue Cannady Barefoot, Jean Watson Moore, Nancy Cannady Manning and Joyce Cannady Lucas., *Cannady Family History, Ancestors and Descendants 1665 - 2002, Vol. 1*, Page 135A. Vol.2.

894. Sue Cannady Barefoot, Jean Watson Moore, Nancy Cannady Manning and Joyce Cannady Lucas., *Cannady Family History, Ancestors and Descendants 1665 - 2002, Vol. 1*, Page 135A. Vol. 2.

895. Sue Cannady Barefoot, Jean Watson Moore, Nancy Cannady Manning and Joyce Cannady Lucas., *Cannady Family History, Ancestors and Descendants 1665 - 2002, Vol. 1*, Page 135A, Vol. 2.

896. Sue Cannady Barefoot, Jean Watson Moore, Nancy Cannady Manning and Joyce Cannady Lucas., *Cannady Family History, Ancestors and Descendants 1665 - 2002, Vol. 1*, Page 134C, Vol. 2.

897. John C. Rosser, Jr., *The Descendants of Abraham Naylor and John Baggett of Sampson County, North Carolina*, (Draft of June 20, 1994), Page 134.

898. John C. Rosser, Jr., *The Descendants of Abraham Naylor and John Baggett of Sampson County, North Carolina*, (Draft of June 20, 1994), Pages 133, 134.

899. John C. Rosser, Jr., *The Descendants of Abraham Naylor and John Baggett of Sampson County, North Carolina*, (Draft of June 20, 1994), Page 134.

900. Annie Carolyn Tew and Fannie Lee Lockamy Williams, Footprints from Kitty Fork, Published in 2006. Sampson County, North Carolina.

901. Sue Cannady Barefoot, Jean Watson Moore, Nancy Cannady Manning and Joyce Cannady Lucas., *Cannady Family History, Ancestors and Descendants 1665 - 2002, Vol. 1*, Page 134C, Vol. 2.

902. Bradley Lee West, Kenneth Dale Register, *Northern Sampson County, NC (North Carolina) Cemeteries, Vol. 3*.

903. Sue Cannady Barefoot, Jean Watson Moore, Nancy Cannady Manning and Joyce Cannady Lucas., *Cannady Family History, Ancestors and Descendants 1665 - 2002, Vol. 1*, Page 134C, Vol. 2.

904. Bradley Lee West, Kenneth Dale Register, *Northern Sampson County, NC (North Carolina) Cemeteries, Vol. 3*.

905. Jerome D. Tew, researcher and author, *Tew Family Descendants*, (Data also posted on web sites and in historical newsletters), page 298.

906. Sue Cannady Barefoot, Jean Watson Moore, Nancy Cannady Manning and Joyce Cannady Lucas., *Cannady Family History, Ancestors and Descendants 1665 - 2002, Vol. 1*, Page 134C, Vol. 2.

907. Bradley Lee West, Kenneth Dale Register, *Northern Sampson County, NC (North Carolina) Cemeteries, Vol. 3*.

908. Jerome D. Tew, researcher and author, *Tew Family Descendants*, (Data also posted on web sites and in historical newsletters), page 298.

909. Sue Cannady Barefoot, Jean Watson Moore, Nancy Cannady Manning and Joyce Cannady Lucas., *Cannady Family History, Ancestors and Descendants 1665 - 2002, Vol. 1*, Page 134C, Vol. 2.

910. Bradley Lee West, Kenneth Dale Register, *Northern Sampson County, NC (North Carolina) Cemeteries, Vol. 3*.

911. Sue Cannady Barefoot, Jean Watson Moore, Nancy Cannady Manning and Joyce Cannady Lucas., *Cannady Family History, Ancestors and Descendants 1665 - 2002, Vol. 1*, Page 134C, Vol. 2.

912. Sue Cannady Barefoot, Jean Watson Moore, Nancy Cannady Manning and Joyce Cannady Lucas., *Cannady Family History, Ancestors and Descendants 1665 - 2002, Vol. 1*, Page 134C. Vol. 2.

913. Sue Cannady Barefoot, Jean Watson Moore, Nancy Cannady Manning and Joyce Cannady Lucas., *Cannady Family History, Ancestors and Descendants 1665 - 2002, Vol. 1*, Page 134C, Vol. 2.

914. John C. Rosser, Jr., *Coharie to Cape Fear, The Descendants of John Williams and Katharine Galbreth of Sampson and Cumberland Counties in North Carolina (1740-1990)*, (Walsworth Publishing Company, Marceline, Missouri 64658, April 1990. Only 100 copies printed. Copy in Deed office, Clinton, North Carolina).

915. Sue Cannady Barefoot, Jean Watson Moore, Nancy Cannady Manning and Joyce Cannady Lucas., *Cannady Family History, Ancestors and Descendants 1665 - 2002, Vol. 1*, Page 134D. Vol. 2.

916. John C. Rosser, Jr., *Coharie to Cape Fear, The Descendants of John Williams and Katharine Galbreth of Sampson and Cumberland Counties in North Carolina (1740-1990)*, (Walsworth Publishing Company, Marceline, Missouri 64658, April 1990. Only 100 copies printed. Copy in Deed office, Clinton, North Carolina).

917. Sue Cannady Barefoot, Jean Watson Moore, Nancy Cannady Manning and Joyce Cannady Lucas., *Cannady Family History, Ancestors and Descendants 1665 - 2002, Vol. 1*, Page 134D. Vol. 2.

918. Sue Cannady Barefoot, Jean Watson Moore, Nancy Cannady Manning and Joyce Cannady Lucas., *Cannady Family History, Ancestors and Descendants 1665 - 2002, Vol. 1*, Page 134E. Vol. 2.

919. Sue Cannady Barefoot, Jean Watson Moore, Nancy Cannady Manning and Joyce Cannady Lucas., *Cannady Family History, Ancestors and Descendants 1665 - 2002, Vol. 1*, Page 134C, Vol. 2.

920. Preston Carr Pope provided data.

921. Tammy Lynnette Pope Smith provided data.

922. Preston Carr Pope provided data.

923. Tammy Lynnette Pope Smith provided data.

924. Bible records of Jackie Olene Smith.

925. *The Heritage of Sampson County, North Carolina, 1784-1984. Vol. 1. Oscar M. Bizzell, Editor*, Pages 280 and 181, Profiles 402 and 403.

926. *The Heritage of Sampson County, North Carolina, 1784-1984. Vol. 1. Oscar M. Bizzell, Editor*, Pages 280 and 281, Profile 403.

927. *The Heritage of Sampson County, North Carolina, 1784-1984. Vol. 1. Oscar M. Bizzell, Editor*, Pages 180 and 281, Profile 403.

928. *The Heritage of Sampson County, North Carolina, 1784-1984. Vol. 1. Oscar M. Bizzell, Editor*, Pages 280 and 281, Profile 403.

929. *The Heritage of Sampson County, North Carolina, 1784-1984. Vol. 1. Oscar M. Bizzell, Editor*, Pages 180 and 281, Profile 403.

930. *The Heritage of Sampson County, North Carolina, 1784-1984. Vol. 1. Oscar M. Bizzell, Editor*, Pages 280 and 281, Profile 403.

931. *The Heritage of Sampson County, North Carolina, 1784-1984. Vol. 1. Oscar M. Bizzell, Editor*, Pages 280 and 281, Profile # 403.

932. *The Heritage of Sampson County, North Carolina, 1784-1984. Vol. 1. Oscar M. Bizzell, Editor*, Pages 280 and 281, Profile 403.

933. Sue Cannady Barefoot, Jean Watson Moore, Nancy Cannady Manning and Joyce Cannady Lucas., *Cannady Family History, Ancestors and Descendants 1665 - 2002, Vol. 1*, Page 134A, Vol. 2.

934. *The Heritage of Sampson County, North Carolina, 1784-1984. Vol. 1. Oscar M. Bizzell, Editor*, Pages 280 and 281, Profile 403.

935. Family Descendants, Telephone interview with his mother.

936. Descendants of James Thomas Lockamy and Jemima Jewel Jackson and members of their families, Name provided by Joyce Ellis Jackson.

937. Family Descendants, Telephone with Joyce Ellis Jackson.

938. *Claudia Priscilla Jackson Honeycutt Fields*, Family knowledge and records.

939. *Claudia Priscilla Jackson Honeycutt Fields*, Family knowledge and records   .

940. Family provided Data.

941. *Claudia Priscilla Jackson Honeycutt Fields*.

942. *Claudia Priscilla Jackson Honeycutt Fields*, Family knowledge and records.

943. *Claudia Priscilla Jackson Honeycutt Fields*, Family Knowledge.

944. *Claudia Priscilla Jackson Honeycutt Fields*.

945. *Claudia Priscilla Jackson Honeycutt Fields*, Diane Davis Jackson provided name to Priscilla.

946. *Claudia Priscilla Jackson Honeycutt Fields*, Diane Davis Jackson provided date to Priscilla.

947. *Claudia Priscilla Jackson Honeycutt Fields*, Diane Davis Jackson provided data to Priscilla.

948. *Claudia Priscilla Jackson Honeycutt Fields*, Family Knowledge.

949. *Claudia Priscilla Jackson Honeycutt Fields*.

950. *Claudia Priscilla Jackson Honeycutt Fields*, Linda Diane Davis Johnson Jackson provided data to Priscilla.

951. *Claudia Priscilla Jackson Honeycutt Fields*, Diane Davis Provided date to Priscilla.

952. *Claudia Priscilla Jackson Honeycutt Fields*, Diane Davis Jackson provided name to Priscilla.

953. *Claudia Priscilla Jackson Honeycutt Fields*, Diane Davis Jackson provided data to Priscilla.

954. *Claudia Priscilla Jackson Honeycutt Fields*, Name from obituary in The Sampson Independent Newspaper.

955. *Claudia Priscilla Jackson Honeycutt Fields*, Obituary of Linda's father.

956. Annie Carolyn Tew and Fannie Lee Lockamy Williams, Footprints from Kitty Fork, Published in 2006. Sampson County, North Carolina.

957. *Dwanda Rose Tyndall Jackson*, Written data provided.

958. *Dwanda Rose Tyndall Jackson*, provided written data.

959. *Dwanda Rose Tyndall Jackson*, Dwanda provided data.

960. *Dwanda Rose Tyndall Jackson*, provided written data.

961. *Dwanda Rose Tyndall Jackson*, Information provided by Dwanda.

962. *Dwanda Rose Tyndall Jackson*, provided written data.

963. *Dwanda Rose Tyndall Jackson*, Dwanda provided information.

964. *Dwanda Rose Tyndall Jackson*, provided written data.

965. *Dwanda Rose Tyndall Jackson*, Dwanda provided data.

966. *Dwanda Rose Tyndall Jackson*, provided written data.

967. *Dwanda Rose Tyndall Jackson*, Dwanda provided data.

968. *Dwanda Rose Tyndall Jackson*, provided written data.

969. *Dwanda Rose Tyndall Jackson*, Dwanda provided data.

970. *Dwanda Rose Tyndall Jackson*, provided written data.

971. *Dwanda Rose Tyndall Jackson*, Dwanda provided data.

972. *Interview with Lattie Pearl Jackson.*

973. *The Heritage of Sampson County, North Carolina, 1784-1984. Vol. 1. Oscar M. Bizzell, Editor*, Pages 538 and 539, Vol. 2, Profile # 882 submitted by Clarice Cannady Owens.

974. John C. Rosser, Jr., *The Descendants of Abraham Naylor and John Baggett of Sampson County, North Carolina*, (Draft of June 20, 1994), page 110.

975. *The Heritage of Sampson County, North Carolina, 1784-1984. Vol. 1. Oscar M. Bizzell, Editor*, Pages 538 and 539, Vol. 2, Profile # 882 submitted by Clarice Cannady Owens.

976. John C. Rosser, Jr., *The Descendants of Abraham Naylor and John Baggett of Sampson County, North Carolina*, (Draft of June 20, 1994), page 110.

977. Annie Carolyn Tew and Fannie Lee Lockamy Williams, Footprints from Kitty Fork, Published in 2006. Sampson County, North Carolina.

978. John C. Rosser, Jr., *The Descendants of Abraham Naylor and John Baggett of Sampson County, North Carolina*, (Draft of June 20, 1994), page 110.

979. Annie Carolyn Tew and Fannie Lee Lockamy Williams, Footprints from Kitty Fork, Published in 2006. Sampson County, North Carolina.

980. The Harmony Hall Restoration Committee, Bladen County, North Carolina, *Harmony Hall Cookbook*, (P. O. Box 297, White Oak, North Carolina 28399).

981. Annie Carolyn Tew and Fannie Lee Lockamy Williams, Footprints from Kitty Fork, Published in 2006. Sampson County, North Carolina.

982. John C. Rosser, Jr., *The Descendants of Abraham Naylor and John Baggett of Sampson County, North Carolina*, (Draft of June 20, 1994), page 109.

983. Annie Carolyn Tew and Fannie Lee Lockamy Williams, Footprints from Kitty Fork, Published in 2006. Sampson County, North Carolina.

984. John C. Rosser, Jr., *The Descendants of Abraham Naylor and John Baggett of Sampson County, North Carolina*, (Draft of June 20, 1994), page 109 and 110.

985. John C. Rosser, Jr., *The Descendants of Abraham Naylor and John Baggett of Sampson County, North Carolina*, (Draft of June 20, 1994), page 109.

986. John C. Rosser, Jr., *The Descendants of Abraham Naylor and John Baggett of Sampson County, North Carolina*, (Draft of June 20, 1994), page 109, 110.

987. John C. Rosser, Jr., *The Descendants of Abraham Naylor and John Baggett of Sampson County, North Carolina*, (Draft of June 20, 1994), page 109.

988. John C. Rosser, Jr., *The Descendants of Abraham Naylor and John Baggett of Sampson County, North Carolina*, (Draft of June 20, 1994), page 110.

989. John C. Rosser, Jr., *The Descendants of Abraham Naylor and John Baggett of Sampson County, North Carolina*, (Draft of June 20, 1994), page 109.

990. John C. Rosser, Jr., *The Descendants of Abraham Naylor and John Baggett of Sampson County, North Carolina*, (Draft of June 20, 1994), page 110.

991. Annie Carolyn Tew and Fannie Lee Lockamy Williams, Footprints from Kitty Fork, Published in 2006. Sampson County, North Carolina.

992. John C. Rosser, Jr., *The Descendants of Abraham Naylor and John Baggett of Sampson County, North Carolina*, (Draft of June 20, 1994), page 110.

993. John C. Rosser, Jr., *The Descendants of Abraham Naylor and John Baggett of Sampson County, North Carolina*, (Draft of June 20, 1994), page 109.

994. John C. Rosser, Jr., *The Descendants of Abraham Naylor and John Baggett of Sampson County, North Carolina*, (Draft of June 20, 1994), page 110.

995. Annie Carolyn Tew and Fannie Lee Lockamy Williams, Footprints from Kitty Fork, Published in 2006. Sampson County, North Carolina.

996. *Knowledge of Family.*, Interview with Ruby Doris Jackson Lee and Perry Scott Jackson.

997. Descendants of James Thomas Lockamy and Jemima Jewel Jackson and members of their families.

998. Descendants of James Thomas Lockamy and Jemima Jewel Jackson and members of their families, Provided by Omie Kaye Lockamy Cox in telephone interview.

999. Descendants of James Thomas Lockamy and Jemima Jewel Jackson and members of their families.

1000. Descendants of James Thomas Lockamy and Jemima Jewel Jackson and members of their families, Telephone interview with Omie Kaye Lockamy Cox.

1001. Descendants of James Thomas Lockamy and Jemima Jewel Jackson and members of their families, Provided by Omie Kaye Lockamy Cox in telephone interview.

1002. Descendants of James Thomas Lockamy and Jemima Jewel Jackson and members of their families, Telephone interview with Omie Kaye Lockamy Cox.

1003. Descendants of James Thomas Lockamy and Jemima Jewel Jackson and members of their families, Provided by Omie Kaye Lockamy Cox in telephone interview.

1004. Descendants of James Thomas Lockamy and Jemima Jewel Jackson and members of their families.

1005. *Telephone interview with Gwendolyn Kay West.*

1006. Descendants of James Thomas Lockamy and Jemima Jewel Jackson and members of their families.

1007. Descendants of James Thomas Lockamy and Jemima Jewel Jackson and members of their families, Telephone interview with Jackie Lou Lockamy Daughtry.

1008. Descendants of James Thomas Lockamy and Jemima Jewel Jackson and members of their families, Teleview with Jackie Lou Lockamy Daughtry.

1009. Descendants of James Thomas Lockamy and Jemima Jewel Jackson and members of their families, Telephone interview with Jackie Lou Lockamy Daughtry.

1010. Descendants of James Thomas Lockamy and Jemima Jewel Jackson and members of their families, Provided by Barbara Jean Jordan Hairr.

1011. Descendants of James Thomas Lockamy and Jemima Jewel Jackson and members of their families, Proviled by Barbara Jean Jordan Hairr.

1012. Descendants of James Thomas Lockamy and Jemima Jewel Jackson and members of their families, Provided by Barbara Jean Jordan Hairr.

1013. Descendants of James Thomas Lockamy and Jemima Jewel Jackson and members of their families, Data provided by Willia Dean Lockamy Jordan.

1014. Descendants of James Thomas Lockamy and Jemima Jewel Jackson and members of their families, Data provided by William Dean Lockamy Jordan.

1015. Descendants of James Thomas Lockamy and Jemima Jewel Jackson and members of their families, Data provided by Willa Dean lockamy Jordan.

1016. Descendants of James Thomas Lockamy and Jemima Jewel Jackson and members of their families, Data provided by Willa Dean Lockamy Jordan.

1017. *Northern Sampson County, NC Cemeteries. Vol. 2. Compiled by Bradley Lee West, Kenneth Dale Register and Phyllis Jeanette West.*, Page 48.

1018. Descendants of James Thomas Lockamy and Jemima Jewel Jackson and members of their families, Data provided by Willa Dean Lockamy Jordan.

1019. *Northern Sampson County, NC Cemeteries. Vol. 2. Compiled by Bradley Lee West, Kenneth Dale Register and Phyllis Jeanette West.*, Page 48.

1020. Descendants of James Thomas Lockamy and Jemima Jewel Jackson and members of their families, Data provided by Willa Dean Lockamy Jordan.

1021. Annie Carolyn Tew and Fannie Lee Lockamy Williams, Footprints from Kitty Fork, Published in 2006. Sampson County, North Carolina.

1022. Descendants of James Thomas Lockamy and Jemima Jewel Jackson and members of their families, Data provided by Willa Dean Lockamy Jordan.

1023. John C. Rosser, Jr., *The Descendants of Abraham Naylor and John Baggett of Sampson County, North Carolina,* (Draft of June 20, 1994), page 109.

1024. *Knowledge of Family.,* Name provided by his mother, Velva Jewel Dixon Smith.

1025. *Knowledge of Family.,* Date provided by his mother, Velva Jewel Dixon Smith.

1026. *Knowledge of Family.,* Name provided by Velva Jewel Dixon Smith.

1027. *Knowledge of Family.,* Date provided by Velva Jewel Dixon Smith.

1028. *Knowledge of Family.,* Name provided by Velva Jewel Dixon Smith.

1029. *Knowledge of Family.,* Date provided by Velva Jewel Dixon Smith.

1030. Personal knowledge of Mother of Joseph Richard Pleitt.

1031. Personal knowledge of Denise Rose Dion.

1032. Personal knowledge of family members.

1033. Personal knowledge of Denise Rose Dion.

1034. Personal knowledge of family members.

1035. Mother of Jason Joseph Pleitt.

1036. *Mother of Kristina Rose Pleitt.*

1037. Personal knowledge of parents of Nicholas Richard Pleitt.

1038. Personal knowledge of parents of Nathan Alexander Pleitt.

1039. *Personal knowledge of Mother of Anna Bernadette Pleitt.*

1040. *Certificate of Baptism for Anna Bernadette Pleitt,* Anna Bernadette Pleitt child of Richard Pleitt and Nancy Jackson was born in Chicago, Illinois on the 13th day of January 1965 was baptised on the 31st day of January 1965 according to the Rite of the Roman Catholic Church by The Rev. James Colleran. Sponsors being Jerome Back and Dianne Back as appears from the Baptismal Register of this Church. Dated March 2, 1965. The Rev. L. Delire, Pastor. 'Bac' was spelled incorrectly.

1041. *Certificate of Baptism for Anna Bernadette Pleitt.*

1042. *Mother of Peter Willem Kootstra.*

1043. *Personal knowledge of Mother of Anna Bernadette Pleitt.*

1044. Anna Kootstra, wife of William Peter Kootstra.

1045. *Personal knowledge of Mother of Anna Bernadette Pleitt.*

1046. *Mother of Peter Willem Kootstra.*

1047. *Mother of Haley Marie Kootstra.*

1048. Bible records of Jackie Olene Smith.

1049. Preston Carr Pope provided data.

1050. Tammy Lynnette Pope Smith provided data.

1051. Preston Carr Pope provided data.

1052. Tammy Lynnette Pope Smith provided data.

1053. Mother of Michael Edward Smith.

1054. *Bible records of Jackie Olene Jackson Smith.*

1055. Mother of Michael Edward Smith.

1056. *Bible records of Jackie Olene Jackson Smith.*

1057. Lecia Allen Boyd Jackson provided information.

1058. Family provided Data.

1059. Bible records of Jackie Olene Smith.

1060. *Jackie Olene Smith, Mother.*

1061. *Bible records of Jackie Olene Jackson Smith.*

1062. *Personal knowledge of Jackie Olene Jackson Smith.*

1063. Sue Cannady Barefoot, Jean Watson Moore, Nancy Cannady Manning and Joyce Cannady Lucas., *Cannady Family History, Ancestors and Descendants 1665 - 2002, Vol. 1,* 133D(Vol. 2), Data provided by member of extended family.

1064. Sue Cannady Barefoot, Jean Watson Moore, Nancy Cannady Manning and Joyce Cannady Lucas., *Cannady Family History, Ancestors and Descendants 1665 - 2002, Vol. 1*, page 133D (Vol. 2).

1065. Sue Cannady Barefoot, Jean Watson Moore, Nancy Cannady Manning and Joyce Cannady Lucas., *Cannady Family History, Ancestors and Descendants 1665 - 2002, Vol. 1*, page 133E(Vol. 2).

1066. Sue Cannady Barefoot, Cannady and Related Families.

1067. Sue Cannady Barefoot, Jean Watson Moore, Nancy Cannady Manning and Joyce Cannady Lucas., *Cannady Family History, Ancestors and Descendants 1665 - 2002, Vol. 1*, pages 133E(Vol. 2)., Data provided by member of extended family.

1068. Sue Cannady Barefoot, Cannady and Related Families.

1069. John C. Rosser, Jr., *The Descendants of Abraham Naylor and John Baggett of Sampson County, North Carolina*, (Draft of June 20, 1994), Page 20.

1070. *Knowledge of Family*..

1071. Sue Cannady Barefoot, Cannady and Related Families.

1072. John C. Rosser, Jr., *The Descendants of Abraham Naylor and John Baggett of Sampson County, North Carolina*, (Draft of June 20, 1994), Page 20, Mr. Rosser, Jr., confirmed by a vital record.

1073. John C. Rosser, Jr., *The Descendants of Abraham Naylor and John Baggett of Sampson County, North Carolina*, (Draft of June 20, 1994), Page 20, Mr. Rosser, Jr. confirmed by a vital record.

1074. *Knowledge of Family*..

1075. John C. Rosser, Jr., *The Descendants of Abraham Naylor and John Baggett of Sampson County, North Carolina*, (Draft of June 20, 1994), Page 20, Mr. Rosser, Jr., confirmed by a vital record.

1076. John C. Rosser, Jr., *The Descendants of Abraham Naylor and John Baggett of Sampson County, North Carolina*, (Draft of June 20, 1994), 20, Mr. Rosser, Jr., confirmed by a vital record.

1077. *Knowledge of Family*..

1078. John C. Rosser, Jr., *The Descendants of Abraham Naylor and John Baggett of Sampson County, North Carolina*, (Draft of June 20, 1994), Page 20.

1079. *Knowledge of Family*..

1080. Sue Cannady Barefoot, Cannady and Related Families.

1081. *Knowledge of Family*..

1082. Sue Cannady Barefoot, Cannady and Related Families.

1083. Sue Cannady Barefoot, Jean Watson Moore, Nancy Cannady Manning and Joyce Cannady Lucas., *Cannady Family History, Ancestors and Descendants 1665 - 2002, Vol. 1*, page 133E(Vol.2), data provided by a member of family.

1084. Sue Cannady Barefoot, Cannady and Related Families.

1085. Sue Cannady Barefoot, Jean Watson Moore, Nancy Cannady Manning and Joyce Cannady Lucas., *Cannady Family History, Ancestors and Descendants 1665 - 2002, Vol. 1*, page 133E (Vol. 2), data provided by a family member.

1086. Sue Cannady Barefoot, Cannady and Related Families.

1087. Sue Cannady Barefoot, Jean Watson Moore, Nancy Cannady Manning and Joyce Cannady Lucas., *Cannady Family History, Ancestors and Descendants 1665 - 2002, Vol. 1*, page 133E(Vol. 2), data provided by a family member.

1088. *Knowledge of Family*.

1089. Sue Cannady Barefoot, Jean Watson Moore, Nancy Cannady Manning and Joyce Cannady Lucas., *Cannady Family History, Ancestors and Descendants 1665 - 2002, Vol. 1*, page 133E(Vol. 2).

1090. Sue Cannady Barefoot, Jean Watson Moore, Nancy Cannady Manning and Joyce Cannady Lucas., *Cannady Family History, Ancestors and Descendants 1665 - 2002, Vol. 1*, page 133E (Vol. 2).
1091. *Knowledge of Family.*
1092. Sue Cannady Barefoot, Cannady and Related Families.
1093. *Knowledge of Family.*
1094. Sue Cannady Barefoot, Jean Watson Moore, Nancy Cannady Manning and Joyce Cannady Lucas., *Cannady Family History, Ancestors and Descendants 1665 - 2002, Vol. 1*, page 133E (Vol. 2).
1095. Sue Cannady Barefoot, Jean Watson Moore, Nancy Cannady Manning and Joyce Cannady Lucas., *Cannady Family History, Ancestors and Descendants 1665 - 2002, Vol. 1*, page 133E (Vol.2).
1096. *Knowledge of Family.*, Mary Jane Jackson Long provided name.
1097. Sue Cannady Barefoot, Jean Watson Moore, Nancy Cannady Manning and Joyce Cannady Lucas., *Cannady Family History, Ancestors and Descendants 1665 - 2002, Vol. 1*, page 133G (Vol. 2), Family member provided data for this book.
1098. Sue Cannady Barefoot, Jean Watson Moore, Nancy Cannady Manning and Joyce Cannady Lucas., *Cannady Family History, Ancestors and Descendants 1665 - 2002, Vol. 1*, page 133G (Vol. 2).
1099. Sue Cannady Barefoot, Cannady and Related Families.
1100. Sue Cannady Barefoot, Jean Watson Moore, Nancy Cannady Manning and Joyce Cannady Lucas., *Cannady Family History, Ancestors and Descendants 1665 - 2002, Vol. 1*, page 133G (Vol. 2), Full name provided for this book by family member.
1101. Sue Cannady Barefoot, Jean Watson Moore, Nancy Cannady Manning and Joyce Cannady Lucas., *Cannady Family History, Ancestors and Descendants 1665 - 2002, Vol. 1*, page 133G (Vol. 2), Date of birth provided for this book by unknown family member.
1102. *Sondra Jean Long LaRouche.*
1103. *Knowledge of Family.*, Sondra Jean Long LaRouche.
1104. *Sondra Jean Long LaRouche.*
1105. *Family, Descendant or Member of Extended Family.*
1106. *Sondra Jean Long LaRouche.*
1107. *Knowledge of Family.*, Sondra Jean Long LaRouche.
1108. *Sondra Jean Long LaRouche.*
1109. Family provided Data.
1110. *Sondra Jean Long LaRouche.*
1111. Knowledge of Family. Full name provided by his mother, Judy Katherine Barnes Jackson
1112. Knowledge of Family. Date and location provided by his mother, Judy Katherine Barnes Jackson.
1113. Sue Cannady Barefoot, Jean Watson Moore, Nancy Cannady Manning and Joyce Cannady Lucas., *Cannady Family History, Ancestors and Descendants 1665 - 2002, Vol. 1*, page 133H (Vol. 2, Name provided by a member of family for this book.
1114. Knowledge of Family. Name provided by Judy Katherine Barnes Jackson.
1115. *Knowledge of Family*, Date and location provided by Judy Katherine Barnes Jackson.
1116. Knowledge of Family. Date and location provided by Judy Katherine Barnes Jackson.
1117. *Knowledge of Family*, Date and location provided by Judy Katherine Barnes Jackson.

1118. Sue Cannady Barefoot, Jean Watson Moore, Nancy Cannady Manning and Joyce Cannady Lucas., *Cannady Family History, Ancestors and Descendants 1665 - 2002, Vol. 1*, page 133H (Vol. 2), data provided by a member of the family for this book.

1119. Knowledge of Family. Provided to the writers of "Cannady Family History" book.

1120. Sue Cannady Barefoot, Jean Watson Moore, Nancy Cannady Manning and Joyce Cannady Lucas., Cannady Family History. Date was provided to the writers of "Cannady Family History" book.

1121. Sue Cannady Barefoot, Jean Watson Moore, Nancy Cannady Manning and Joyce Cannady Lucas., *Cannady Family History, Ancestors and Descendants 1665 - 2002, Vol. 1*, Name was provided to the writers of "Cannady Family History" book.

1122. Sue Cannady Barefoot, Jean Watson Moore, Nancy Cannady Manning and Joyce Cannady Lucas., Cannady Family History. Date was provided to the writers of "Cannady Family History" book.

1123. Knowledge of Family. Full name provided by Judy Katherine Barnes Jackson.

1124. Knowledge of Family. Date was provided by Judy Katherine Barnes Jackson.

1125. Sue Cannady Barefoot, Jean Watson Moore, Nancy Cannady Manning and Joyce Cannady Lucas., Cannady Family History. Date was provided to the writers of "Cannady Family History" book.

1126. Sue Cannady Barefoot, Jean Watson Moore, Nancy Cannady Manning and Joyce Cannady Lucas., Cannady Family History. Name was provided to the writers of "Cannady Family History" book.

1127. Sue Cannady Barefoot, Jean Watson Moore, Nancy Cannady Manning and Joyce Cannady Lucas., Cannady Family History. Date was providers to the writers of "Cannady Family History" book.

1128. *Knowledge of Family*, Full name provided by Judy Katherine Barnes Jackson.

1129. Knowledge of Family. Name provided by Judy Katherine Barnes Jackson.

1130. Sue Cannady Barefoot, Jean Watson Moore, Nancy Cannady Manning and Joyce Cannady Lucas., Cannady Family History. Date was provided to the writers of "Cannady Family History" book.

1131. Sue Cannady Barefoot, Jean Watson Moore, Nancy Cannady Manning and Joyce Cannady Lucas., Cannady Family History. Name was provided to the writers of "Cannady Family History" book.

1132. Sue Cannady Barefoot, Jean Watson Moore, Nancy Cannady Manning and Joyce Cannady Lucas., Cannady Family History. Date was provided to the writers of "Cannady Family History" book.

1133. Knowledge of Family. Name was provided to Nancy Jackson Pleitt Fenner by Lorenda Kaye Jackson Wallace Hayes Carr.

1134. Sue Cannady Barefoot, Jean Watson Moore, Nancy Cannady Manning and Joyce Cannady Lucas., Cannady Family History. Date of birth was provided to the writers of "Cannady Family History" book.

1135. Sue Cannady Barefoot, Jean Watson Moore, Nancy Cannady Manning and Joyce Cannady Lucas., Cannady Family History. Full name provided to the writers of "Cannady Family History" book.

1136. Sue Cannady Barefoot, Jean Watson Moore, Nancy Cannady Manning and Joyce Cannady Lucas., Cannady Family History. Date was provided to the writers of "Cannady Family History" book.

1137. Knowledge of Family. Full name provided by Lorenda Kaye Jackson Hayes Carr.

1138. Knowledge of Family. Name provided by Lorenda Kaye Jackson Wallace Hayes Carr.

1139. *Knowledge of Family*, Date and Location of birth provided by Lorenda Jackson Hayes Carr.

1140. Knowledge of Family. Full name provided by Heidi Jane Jackson Tyndall Jackson.

1141. Knowledge of Family. Date and location provided by Heidi Jane Jackson Tyndall Jackson.

1142. Knowledge of Family. Full name provided by Heidi Jane Jackson Tyndall Jackson.

1143. Knowledge of Family. Date and location provided by Heidi Jane Jackson Tyndall Evans Jackson.

1144. Knowledge of Family. Date and location provided by Heidi Jane Jackson Tyndall Jackson.

1145. Knowledge of Family. Date and location provided by Heidi Jane Jackson Tyndall Evans Jackson.

1146. Knowledge of Family. Full name provided by Heidi Jane Jackson.

1147. Knowledge of Family. Date provided by Heidi Jane Jackson Tyndall Jackson.

1148. Knowledge of Family. Full name provided by Heidi Jane Jackson Tyndall Jackson.

1149. Knowledge of Family. Date provided by Heidi Jane Jackson Tyndall Jackson.

1150. Knowledge of Family. Full name provided by Heidi Jane Jackson Tyndall Jackson.

1151. Knowledge of Family. Date provided by Heidi Jane Jackson Tyndall Jackson.

1152. *Addie May Beasley*, Telephone interview with Addie May Beasley on July 25, 2003.

1153. Sue Cannady Barefoot, Jean Watson Moore, Nancy Cannady Manning and Joyce Cannady Lucas., *Cannady Family History, Ancestors and Descendants 1665 - 2002, Vol. 1*, Page 134C, Vol. 2.

1154. Annie Carolyn Tew and Fannie Lee Lockamy Williams, Footprints from Kitty Fork, Published in 2006. Sampson County, North Carolina.

1155. Sue Cannady Barefoot, Jean Watson Moore, Nancy Cannady Manning and Joyce Cannady Lucas., *Cannady Family History, Ancestors and Descendants 1665 - 2002, Vol. 1*, Page 134C, Vol. 2.

1156. Annie Carolyn Tew and Fannie Lee Lockamy Williams, Footprints from Kitty Fork, Published in 2006. Sampson County, North Carolina.

1157. John C. Rosser, Jr., *The Descendants of Abraham Naylor and John Baggett of Sampson County, North Carolina*, (Draft of June 20, 1994), Page 134.

1158. Annie Carolyn Tew and Fannie Lee Lockamy Williams, Footprints from Kitty Fork, Published in 2006. Sampson County, North Carolina.

1159. Sue Cannady Barefoot, Jean Watson Moore, Nancy Cannady Manning and Joyce Cannady Lucas., *Cannady Family History, Ancestors and Descendants 1665 - 2002, Vol. 1*, Page 134C, Vol. 2.

1160. John C. Rosser, Jr., *Coharie to Cape Fear, The Descendants of John Williams and Katharine Galbreth of Sampson and Cumberland Counties in North Carolina (1740-1990)*, (Walsworth Publishing Company, Marceline, Missouri 64658, April 1990. Only 100 copies printed. Copy in Deed office, Clinton, North Carolina).

1161. Sue Cannady Barefoot, Jean Watson Moore, Nancy Cannady Manning and Joyce Cannady Lucas., *Cannady Family History, Ancestors and Descendants 1665 - 2002, Vol. 1*, Page 134C, Vol. 2.

1162. Sue Cannady Barefoot, Jean Watson Moore, Nancy Cannady Manning and Joyce Cannady Lucas., *Cannady Family History, Ancestors and Descendants 1665 - 2002, Vol. 1*, Page 134D, Vol. 2.

1163. Sue Cannady Barefoot, Jean Watson Moore, Nancy Cannady Manning and Joyce Cannady Lucas., *Cannady Family History, Ancestors and Descendants, 1665 - 2002, Vol. 2*, page 134D.

1164. Sue Cannady Barefoot, Cannady and Related Families.

1165. John C. Rosser, Jr., *Coharie to Cape Fear, The Descendants of John Williams and Katharine Galbreth of Sampson and Cumberland Counties in North Carolina (1740-1990)*, (Walsworth Publishing Company, Marceline, Missouri 64658, April 1990. Only 100 copies printed. Copy in Deed office, Clinton, North Carolina).

1166. Sue Cannady Barefoot, Jean Watson Moore, Nancy Cannady Manning and Joyce Cannady Lucas., *Cannady Family History, Ancestors and Descendants, 1665 - 2002, Vol. 2*, page 134D.

1167. Sue Cannady Barefoot, Cannady and Related Families.

1168. Sue Cannady Barefoot, Jean Watson Moore, Nancy Cannady Manning and Joyce Cannady Lucas., *Cannady Family History, Ancestors and Descendants, 1665 - 2002, Vol. 2*, page 134D.

1169. Sue Cannady Barefoot, Jean Watson Moore, Nancy Cannady Manning and Joyce Cannady Lucas., *Cannady Family History, Ancestors and Descendants 1665 - 2002, Vol. 1*, Page 134D. Vol. 2.

1170. Sue Cannady Barefoot, Jean Watson Moore, Nancy Cannady Manning and Joyce Cannady Lucas., *Cannady Family History, Ancestors and Descendants 1665 - 2002, Vol. 1*, Page 134C, Vol. 2.

1171. Tammy Lynnette Pope Smith provided data.

1172. *Knowledge of Family.*.

1173. Family provided Data.

1174. *Knowledge of Family.*

1175. *Knowledge of Family.*.

1176. Tammy Lynnette Pope Smith provided data.

1177. *Knowledge of Family.*

1178. Family provided Data.

1179. Family Descendants, Telephone interview with Joyce Ellis Jackson.

1180. Family Descendants, Telephone Interview with Joyce Ellis Jackson.

1181. Family Descendants, Telephone with Joyce Ellis Jackson.

1182. Family Descendants, Telephone Interview with Joyce Ellis Jackson.

1183. Family Descendants, Telephone interview with Joyce Ellis Jackson.

1184. Family provided Data.

1185. Family Descendants, Telephone interview with Joyce Ellis Jackson.

1186. Family provided Data.

1187. Family Descendants, Telephone interview with Joyce Ellis Jackson.

1188. Annie Carolyn Tew and Fannie Lee Lockamy Williams, Footprints from Kitty Fork, Published in 2006. Sampson County, North Carolina.

1189. Descendants of James Thomas Lockamy and Jemima Jewel Jackson and members of their families, Provided by Omie Kaye Lockamy Cox in telephone interview.

1190. Descendants of James Thomas Lockamy and Jemima Jewel Jackson and members of their families, Telephone interview with Omie Kaye Lockamy Cox.

1191. Descendants of James Thomas Lockamy and Jemima Jewel Jackson and members of their families.

1192. Descendants of James Thomas Lockamy and Jemima Jewel Jackson and members of their families, Telephone interview with Omie Kaye Lockamy Cox.

1193. Descendants of James Thomas Lockamy and Jemima Jewel Jackson and members of their families.

1194. Descendants of James Thomas Lockamy and Jemima Jewel Jackson and members of their families, Data provided by Willa Dean Lockamy Jordan.

1195. Descendants of James Thomas Lockamy and Jemima Jewel Jackson and members of their families, Date provided by Willa Dean Lockamy Jordan.

1196. Lecia Allen Boyd Jackson provided information.
1197. *Knowledge of Family.*.
1198. *Personal knowledge of Jackie Olene Jackson Smith.*
1199. *Knowledge of Family.*, Jackie Olene Jackson Smith provided name.
1200. *Knowledge of Family.*, Jackie Olene Jackson Smith provided date.

Index

Jackson, Henry 37
Jackson, Henry M. 54, 156
Jackson, Hilda Grey 68
Jackson, Hosea Almond 52, 156
Jackson, Hosea Moore 36, 55
Jackson, J. W. 61, 91
Jackson, Jackie Olene 77, 165, 174,
    176, 185, 191
Jackson, James ix, 9, 54, 84, 115, 141
Jackson, James Andrew 69
Jackson, James Elvin, Jr. 80, 115, 141
Jackson, James Elvin, Sr 80, 115, 141
Jackson, James Leslie 55, 84
Jackson, James Trulove 36, 51, 155,
    156
Jackson, Jemima Jewel 29, 46, 154,
    163, 164, 174, 175, 182, 183,
    184, 190
Jackson, Joel 8, 11, 33
Jackson, John 8, 9, 13, 142
Jackson, Johnny Mac 68
Jackson, John Thomas 156
Jackson, John Trent 115, 141
Jackson, Joseph E. 15, 18, 19, 20, 31,
    32, 76
Jackson, Joseph Paul 26, 155
Jackson, Joseph Wayne 115, 142
Jackson, Kimberly 85, 119
Jackson, Larry Davis 68
Jackson, Lattie Pearl 53, 155, 160, 167,
    172, 182
Jackson, Leon Calvin 53, 82, 93
Jackson, Lewis 7
Jackson, Lincoln MacDonald 54, 167
Jackson, Linda Eileen 81
Jackson, Lorenda Kaye 80, 116, 178,
    188
Jackson, Lowden 4
Jackson, Lucille 56, 85
Jackson, Lula Mae 36
Jackson, Marie 124
Jackson, Marie J. 94
Jackson, Mary A. 20, 30
Jackson, Mary C. 25, 26, 30
Jackson, Mary Catherine 30, 51, 55,

155, 156
Jackson, Mary Jane 50, 150, 166, 177,
    178, 187
Jackson, Mattie Ruth 23, 26, 28, 50,
    77, 93, 165, 176
Jackson, Millard Cicero 28
Jackson, Minnie 40, 152
Jackson, Mollie Louise 54, 83
Jackson, Nancy iii, 7, 13, 19, 109, 110,
    154, 185, 188
Jackson, Nancy Eveline 19, 76, 105,
    165, 175
Jackson, Nathan 5, 6, 18
Jackson, Nina Metherbell 36, 59
Jackson, Noah Washington 36, 55
Jackson, Oscar 48, 76, 108
Jackson, Oscar Davis 26, 33, 50, 73,
    75, 136, 165
Jackson, Osway W. 36, 155
Jackson, Pamela Mae 85
Jackson, Pearl Austin 36, 58
Jackson, Perry Scott 45, 68, 162, 163,
    173, 174, 183
Jackson, Rachel 7, 13
Jackson, Raiford 11
Jackson, Randall B. 38, 60, 159
Jackson, Randall Franklin, 92
Jackson, Randall T. 29
Jackson, Ray 78
Jackson, Raymond D. 156
Jackson, Reddick 13, 14, 16
Jackson, Richard 7
Jackson, Robert Alan 85
Jackson, Robert Ashley 81
Jackson, Robyn Lisa 85
Jackson, Ruby Doris 45, 162, 163,
    173, 174, 183
Jackson, Sallie J. 35
Jackson, Samuel 45
Jackson, Spicey 37
Jackson, Stephanie Denice 95
Jackson, Susan 13, 21, 123
Jackson, Susannah 26
Jackson, Tempie 97, 99
Jackson, Teresa Rose 95

www.ingramcontent.com/pod-product-compliance
Lightning Source LLC
Chambersburg PA
CBHW061402280526
45784CB00001B/335